STRESS AND COPING
IN INFANCY
AND CHILDHOOD

STRESS AND COPING

A series of volumes sponsored by the University of Miami

Stress and Coping, T.M. Field, P.M. McCabe, and N. Schneiderman, Editors
Stress and Coping Across Development, T.M. Field, P.M. McCabe, and N. Schneiderman, Editors
Stress, Coping and Disease, P.M. McCabe, N. Schneiderman, T. M. Field, and J. S. Skyler, Editors
Stress and Coping in Infancy and Childhood, T.M. Field, P.M. McCabe, and N. Schneiderman, Editors

STRESS AND COPING IN INFANCY AND CHILDHOOD

Edited by

TIFFANY M. FIELD
PHILIP M. McCABE
NEIL SCHNEIDERMAN
University of Miami School of Medicine

LEA LAWRENCE ERLBAUM ASSOCIATES, PUBLISHERS
1992   Hillsdale, New Jersey   Hove and London

Lawrence Erlbaum Associates, Inc., Publishers
365 Broadway
Hillsdale, New Jersey 07642

Library of Congress Cataloging-in-Publication Data

Stress and coping in infancy and childhood / edited by Tiffany M.
 Field, Philip M. McCabe, Neil Schneiderman.
     p. cm.
   Consists primarily of papers presented at the 6th Annual
University of Miami Symposia on Stress and Coping held in 1988, as
well as several papers presented at the 5th Symposia in 1987.
   Includes bibliographical references and index.
   ISBN 0-8058-0944-9
     1. Stress in children—Congresses.   2. Chronically ill children—
Mental health—Congresses.   I. University of Miami Symposia on
Stress and Coping (6th : 1988)   II. University of Miami Symposia on
Stress and Coping (5th : 1987)   III. Field, Tiffany.   IV. McCabe,
Philip M.   V. Schneiderman, Neil.
   [DNLM: 1. Adaptation, Psychological—in infancy & childhood—
congresses.   2. Chronic Disease—in infancy & childhood—
congresses.   3. Chronic Disease—psychology—congresses.   4. Parent-
Child Relations—congresses.   5. Psychophysiology—in infancy &
childhood—congresses.   WS 350 S9145 1988]
RJ507.S77S87   1991
155.9'042'083—dc20
DNLM/DLC
for Library of Congress   91-25167
                                                                      CIP

Printed in the United States of America
10 9 8 7 6 5 4 3 2 1

Contents

Preface

This is the fourth volume based on the annual University of Miami symposia on stress and coping. These symposia focus on state-of-the-art research relating to developmental, physical, and mental health aspects of stress and coping. The first volume provided a general discussion of the concept of stress; an overview of psychophysiologic processes involved in stress and coping; and data relating behavioral stress to the immune response, sleep disorders, depression, and cardiovascular disease. The second volume focused on some representative stresses and coping mechanisms that occur during different stages of development including infancy, childhood, and adulthood. It included chapters on maternal deprivation stress during infancy; coronary-prone behavior in children; coping behaviors during medical stress, and diabetes management in childhood; and adulthood concerns including cancer stress, behavioral influences on the immune system, cardiovascular disease in depressed patients, and various forms of depression therapy. The second volume was a natural lead into the third volume, which was entitled *Stress, Coping, and Disease*. The third volume focused on the role of biopsychosocial factors in four of the most common health problems: cardiovascular disease, diabetes, cancer, and the AIDS epidemic.

This, the fourth volume, focuses on developmental stressors and clinical stressors during infancy and childhood. Developmental stressors are those that arise during normal development such as early separation stress, stranger anxiety, novelty stress, and personal distress in fear situations. The section on clinical stressors focuses on clinical conditions that are relatively common in infancy and early childhood. These include the stress of being born prematurely and undergoing invasive procedures, the stress of respiratory disease and the related anxiety parents experience surrounding apnea monitoring and near death experiences, and the stress of being a pediatric oncology patient as well as being a parent of one of these children. The section also discusses how various therapies such as relaxation therapy and massage can alleviate the stress associated with psychiatric conditions in childhood and adolescence, including depression and adjustment disorder.

In the first section on developmental stressors, Megan Gunnar compares maternal separation and activation of the adreno-cortical response in human infants with that of the primate species. She first presents data showing that the behavioral and hormonal responses to stress often do not mirror each other. For example, in the Old World rhesus monkey, the hormonal (adreno-cortical) response lasts less than 24 hours, while behavior agitation continues. In the New World squirrel monkeys, the opposite pattern occurs. Gunnar then relates data on repeated discharge examinations for newborns and swim classes for young infants, illustrating an attenuation of the physiological (cortisol) response to stress with repeated exposure. Several examples are given from her own work and the literature on the human infant's remarkable ability to physiologically cope with the stress of separation and novelty. Her chapter highlights the following three phenomena: (a) Differences might be expected in response systems because of differences in separation paradigms. (b) Differences can be expected across species and across cultures. For example, infants, unlike monkeys, spend much of their time separated from the primary caregiver, at least in Western cultures. (c) The human infant has a remarkable ability to acclimate or adapt to repeated separations as manifested by their attenuated responses to stress.

In the second chapter, data presented by Jacob Gewirtz and Martha Peláez-Nogueras suggest that infant separation distress is encouraged by mothers when they contingently respond to the stress. Gewirtz and Peláez-Nogueras illustrate with a rather impressive data set how the infant learns later in the first year to protest separations because their mothers encourage the very behavior that is stressful to all concerned (e.g., direct actions to block their departure, fretting and crying). In a series of laboratory paradigms, the authors demonstrate how infants who have not yet learned to protest can be taught to do so by their mothers' reactions to their behaviors. They then also illustrate how the separation protest can be minimized or eliminated by the mothers' use of noncontingent rather than contingent maternal responses to the protest (differential responding to behaviors other than protest). Too often, the infant's role in separation problems has been the primary focus without understanding the parent's role in this process. Mothers who are contingently responsive to their babies' smiles or vocalizations or who talk to their infants at play (instead of responding to their distress behaviors) tend to produce infants who do not show protest behavior. Importantly, understanding this process provides the basis for understanding not only early infant stress associated with separations but also how it can be applied to family, day care, and school settings where these separations occur.

In chapter 3 by Donovan and Leavitt, further attention is paid to the stress of the crying infant. For the parent, the greatest stressor during infancy is probably infant crying. Donovan and Leavitt propose and support a very interesting model that differing perceptions of control relate to effective versus ineffective coping styles in response to the demands of child care. Specifically, they found that high illusory control mothers, characterized by a depression-prone attributional style, are adversely affected by being paired with a difficult infant. "Depression-prone attributional style" (a term coined by Martin Seligman and his colleagues) refers to ascribing bad things to factors within oneself and good things to factors such as chance. This, they claim, is a maladaptive coping strategy that adversely affects infant developmental outcome, namely security of infant–mother attachment.

Brian Healy (chapter 4) reviews literature on sympathetic and parasympathetic system responses to stress. The thrust of his research is the relation between physiological response patterns and the development of individual differences in temperament as they relate to stress. Using twin studies in the search for heritability of autonomic reactivity, Healy points out that heart rate appears to be a genetic response but heart rate variability and vagal tone are significantly affected by environmental stresses. He points out that the effects of stress on parasympathetic activity or on the parasympathetic–sympathetic nervous system interaction have received very little attention. A specific stressor may cause an increase in heart rate and blood pressure, yet as Healy suggests, this response may be viewed not only as an indication of sympathetic activation but also as a parasympathetic inhibition. The purpose of his chapter is to provide data on the significance of vagal tone (parasympathetic activity) as it relates to behavioral responses to stress and to explore individual differences using a twin paradigm in the behavioral/physiological response to stress. Following a very comfortable session of viewing "Sesame Street," the behavior of each twin was observed during the presentation of a novel toy (a mechanical robot that moved on its own accord and presented itself as a potential stressor to the infants). Interestingly, the infants who were most attentive and reactive had higher vagal tone. Individual differences in vagal tone may reflect the infant's ability to attend to a new environmental event and to cope with mildly stressful situations. Those children who were more reluctant to approach the robot were rated by the mothers as being more difficult in temperament, more negative in mood, and more distractible. Those children with lower vagal tone were those who approached the toy immediately upon its presentation. These data are extremely interesting inasmuch as they are inconsistent with data reported by several others.

Nathan Fox (chapter 5) carries on this discussion with a review of the research he has conducted over the past decade on individual differences in temperament, responses to stress, and underlying EEG patterns. Being one of the first investigators to examine separation responses repeatedly over the first year, he has been able to show that there are consistent individual differences in infants' responses to separation with some always displaying distress and others only sporadically showing distress. Underlying this individual difference in behavior is a clear difference in EEG arousal. The infants predisposed to distress show greater relative right frontal arousal and those who do not cry exhibit left frontal arousal. Finally, Fox reviews data from other laboratories suggesting that children with greater left frontal arousal may also have strategies necessary to modulate negative arousal. That is, both sustained attention and distractibility, as well as verbal strategies, are left hemisphere competencies. Thus, as Fox concludes, language facility may help children cope with stress and novelty.

In a related chapter on slightly older children, Nancy Eisenberg (chapter 6) discusses the differences between sympathy, empathy, and personal distress as various forms of coping with others' distress. She provides examples of how children engage in emotion-focused versus problem-focused coping and, like adults, monitoring occurs in controllable situations and blunting occurs in uncontrollable situations. Children who are relatively reactive may be forced to develop effective coping strategies. Children with high levels of personal distress are not particularly helpful when they can escape from an anxiety-producing situation. Eisenberg also presents data suggesting that mothers' empathic dispositions are related to their children's empathic and prosocial behavior, suggesting a heritability aspect of this behavior.

The final chapter in this section, by Brooks-Gunn (chapter 7), reviews material and presents data suggesting that stress during the transition to adolescence is multidimensional. Although depression, aggressive affect, and eating problems increase during this period, large interindividual variation is noted, and these problems appear to derive more from social events than hormonal changes. Increases in estradiol levels, for example, accounted for less variance in depressive symptoms than negative life events. This was also true for aggressive behavior, although hormones did play a larger role in the aggressive behavior than in the depressive symptomatology. As Brooks-Gunn suggests, the interaction between negative events and hormonal change is further complicated by the timing and sequencing and the circumstances in which they occur, suggesting the need for new multidimensional models for describing the stresses associated with adolescent development.

Part II on clinical stressors begins with a chapter by Connie Morrow and Tiffany Field (chapter 8) on the stressful effects of invasive procedures and the nonstressful effects of noninvasive procedures on oxygen tension in preterm neonates treated in a neonatal intensive care unit. In their review of the literature, the authors note that medical procedures that involve handling have consistently been documented to cause declines in TcPO2 (oxygen tension). Consequently, a minimal touch policy for preterm infants has become standard protocol in many hospitals across the nation. Unfortunately, although the minimal handling protocols derive from research on medical and nursing procedures, the policy has been generalized to the social context. Unlike the full-term infant who receives considerable social stimulation and parental contact, the preterm infant's interactions occur primarily during necessary invasive medical or nursing procedures. Parental touching and holding is discouraged while the infant is in intensive care even though the effects of social stimulation have not been investigated. Morrow and Field reported data documenting the expected decreases in oxygen tension during invasive procedures such as heelsticks, but the data also showed negligible oxygen tension changes during neonatal assessments such as the Brazelton and during tactile stimulation procedures such as massage. Their results suggest that Brazelton assessments and massage stimulation are safe procedures at least for preterm infants who are being treated in intermediate care nurseries.

Chapter 9 by Debra Bendell-Estroff reviews the literature on the stress of Sudden Infant Death Syndrome (SIDS) and apnea monitoring on parents. Apneic infants (who are typically preterm infants with other medical complications) present a real stressor for parents, siblings, and extended family. Infants with interrupted Infantile Apnea are often discovered by their parents to be limp, pale, or cyanotic, and are revived only after vigorous manual or auditory stimulation and/or mouth-to-mouth resuscitation. The stress continues as the infant is hospitalized and placed on a monitor. Bendell-Estroff reports data suggesting that higher levels of distress are noted in parents who have previously lost a child to SIDS, mothers who are socially isolated, and those who have difficulty with monitor compliance. An additional stress is posed by the apneic infants typically being more demanding, wanting to be held more, and their more frequent crying and minor behavior problems, providing relatively little reinforcement for the mother's parenting the infant. Thus, apnea appears to be a significant stressor for both the infant and the infant's family.

In chapter 10, Danny Armstrong discusses the stress of childhood cancer and also presents ideas on how children and families can more effectively cope with cancer. Armstrong presents several examples of how most families of children with cancer are normal in their psychological functioning at the time of diagnosis, but their attempts to cope with the disease and treatment in a normal fashion often lead to ineffective or problematic behavior during and after the termination of treatment. For example, children with cancer often get extra attention, reassurance, and comfort. Their attempts to cope using accelerated distress behavior are responded to by increased comfort-giving and protection on the part of parents. This may in turn increase the stress by positively reinforcing and maintaining ineffective escape behaviors. The interventions Armstrong proposes are that the treatment be altered in some way to reduce its aversiveness, that strategies be taught to the patient to reduce the aversiveness of the treatment and its consequences, and that parents and children be taught to respond to this abnormal situation in ways that may seem abnormal to them but may be the most effective response for the situation.

Finally, Tiffany Field (chapter 11) reviews the literature on stress-reducing techniques for psychiatric patients. She then presents data from two studies on the use of relaxation therapy and massage with child and adolescent psychiatry patients. In the first study on relaxation therapy, decreases were noted in both self-reported anxiety and anxious behavior as well as increases in positive affect in child and adolescent patients diagnosed with adjustment disorder or depression. These patients also showed decreases in cortisol levels following relaxation therapy. Although both diagnostic groups appeared to benefit from the relaxation therapy, it was not clear what the effective treatment component was in that study because relaxation therapy consisted of yoga exercises, massage, progressive muscle relaxation, and visual imagery. In addition, although relaxation therapy clearly reduced stress and anxiety, at least in the short term, the study did not establish whether there were any longer term effects. Thus, the subsequent study was designed to examine the independent effects of massage as well as its short and longer term effects. Because child and adolescent psychiatric units in the United States have a no-touch policy, and these children and adolescents are typically hospitalized for as long as 2 to 3 months, they experience considerable touch deprivation. The data from this massage study showed that daily massage was beneficial in increasing positive affect and decreasing anxiety as well as cortisol levels. Over the longer term, nighttime sleep also increased. The consistency of the self-report, behavior observation, and physiological data support the use of this treatment for reducing stress in child and adolescent psychiatric patients.

Elsewhere, we have suggested that stress and coping begin at the moment of conception and continue across the life span. It is perhaps not surprising, then, that individual differences in responses to stress and individual styles of coping emerge early in infancy. For the same reason, it is not surprising that infants and children are able to cope with significant stressors such as invasive medical procedures and disease; they have had considerable experience with stress and practice with coping. Although this volume highlights individual differences and predispositions to stress responses and coping styles, it also reminds us of the role of the environment (most particularly parenting practices) in shaping these stress responses and facilitating coping.

ACKNOWLEDGMENTS

Several individuals, groups, and organizations helped make this symposium possible. First, we thank the participants, who gave freely of themselves and helped carry out the symposium on a modest budget. Second, we thank our postdoctoral fellows and graduate students, whose efforts attenuated the stress for all concerned. Third, we thank Ellie Schneiderman for her gracious hospitality. Fourth, we thank the staff of the Lowe Art Museum and the Mailman Center for Child Development for graciously allowing us to use their aesthetically pleasing surroundings. Finally, we thank, for their support and encouragement, David L. Wilson, Dean of the College of Arts and Sciences; Herbert C.

Quay, Chair of the Department of Psychology; Robert S. Stempfel, Jr., Vice Chair of the Department of Pediatrics and Director of the Mailman Center for Child Development; and Stephen Weiss, Chief of Behavioral Medicine, National Heart, Lung and Blood Institute. We gratefully acknowledge financial support from the University of Miami Graduate Student Association, the College of Arts and Sciences, The Mailman Center for Child Development, the Department of Psychology, and National Heart, Lung, and Blood Training grant HL07426.

T.F.
P.M.
N.S.

DEVELOPMENTAL STRESSORS

1

Infant Stress Reactions to Brief Maternal Separations in Human and Nonhuman Primates

Megan R. Gunnar
Laurie Brodersen
University of Minnesota

Maternal separation is one of the two most commonly studied psychosocial stressors of infancy. The other one, interaction with strangers, is frequently a component of separation (e.g., Ainsworth & Wittag, 1969). Developmental psychologists have focused on the behavior infants display during separation (e.g., Ainsworth, Blehar, Waters, & Wall, 1978; Schaffer & Emerson, 1964; Weinraub & Lewis, 1977). In contrast, developmental psychobiologists and neuroscientists have focused on the physiological consequences of maternal separation (e.g., Coe, Wiener, Rosenberg, & Levine, 1985; Hofer, 1987; Levine & Wiener, 1988; Reite, Kaemingk, & Boccia, 1989), and on the physiological substrates of separation behavior (e.g., Kalin, Shelton, & Barksdale, 1988; Kehoe & Blass, 1986; Kraemer, Ebert, Lake, & McKinney, 1984).

One conclusion from all of the research is that there are at least two distinct phases in the infant's response to maternal loss (Bowlby, 1969; Hofer, 1984). The initial minutes and hours of separation are termed the *protest phase,* during which the infant actively seeks to reestablish maternal contact. This phase may be followed 1 to 2 days later by a *despair phase* similar to the depression often noted during bereavement in adults. Although Bowlby proposed that both phases were regulated by the emotional response to loss, the data do not support this conclusion. The two phases can be decoupled. In addition, reactions occurring during each phase have different regulators (e.g., Hofer, 1984, 1987).

In this review, we focus on the protest phase, the only phase involved when separations are brief. We have chosen to focus on this phase because (a) most of the behavioral and physiological data on human infants deal with separations of only a few minutes; and (b) reactions to brief separations are of import these days because of concerns about infant day care. Emphasizing the protest phase, we

1

deal with the following questions: What are the physiological changes that occur during this phase of separation? How is the infant's affective behavior related to these physiological changes? What are the situational factors that make separations more and less stressful? And finally, what do we know about individual differences and developmental change?

PHYSIOLOGICAL CHANGES
DURING BRIEF SEPARATIONS

Separations of a few minutes to a few hours produce a set of physiological changes indicative of stress in the young of many mammalian species. Dramatic increases in heart rate, cortisol, and catecholamines have been documented in a number of species (see review by Hofer, 1987). For example, in the rhesus monkey, whose endocrine system is similar to our own, 30 minutes of separation can elicit increases of 40 to 60 μg/dl in circulating levels of cortisol (Gunnar, Gonzales, Goodlin, & Levine, 1981; Smotherman, Hunt, McGinnis, & Levine, 1979). This corresponds to increases of 100 to 200%. In juvenile squirrel monkeys, separations of 1 and 6 hours produce significant increases in cerebral spinal fluid metabolites of dopamine, serotonin, and norepinephrine that indicates heightened anxiety (Coe et al., 1985). In both macaque and squirrel monkeys, changes in immune functioning have been documented in separations lasting only a few hours, including decreases in white blood cell counts, increases in complement proteins, and decreases in thymic hormone (Friedman, Coe, & Ershler, under review).

There have been very few studies of physiological changes during brief separations in human infants. Nonetheless, the work that has been done suggests that similar physiological changes are produced. Thus, increases in heart rate have been noted during maternal separation, including tachycardia associated with intense crying (Donovan & Leavitt, 1985). Changes in brain activity have also been noted: Fox and Davidson (1988) showed an increase in right frontal activity associated with negative affect during separation in 10-month-olds. Many of these changes have been less dramatic than those produced in monkeys, perhaps because of differences in the quality of the separation environments.

For example, neuroendocrine changes have been more difficult to document. In an early study, Tennes and her colleagues (Tennes, Downey, & Vernadakis, 1977) examined cortisol excretion rates in year-old infants subjected to a one-hour separation in the home. They found a 22% increase in cortisol that was not statistically significant. Recently, we (Gunnar, Mangelsdorf, Larson, & Hertsgaard, 1989) examined salivary cortisol concentrations before and after administration of the Louisville Temperament Assessment to 9-month-old infants. The Louisville assessment involves two separations lasting about 30 minutes each, during which the baby interacts with two different strangers who administer a series of predetermined tasks. Like Tennes et al., we observed a

22% increase in cortisol that was statistically significant in our sample (see Table 1.1). However, to complicate matters, postassessment cortisol levels were not significantly different from levels obtained at home under basal conditions. Furthermore, using the same infants at 13 months, we examined responses to the Strange Situation assessment involving only a few minutes of separation. Here we obtained only a 10% increase that was not statistically significant. However, this may have been because we sampled the adrenocortical response too early, before it had reached its peak.

None of these studies provided unambiguous evidence of a neuroendocrine response to separation in human infants. The only unambiguous evidence comes from a study we (Larson, Gunnar, & Hertsgaard, 1991) recently completed in which the cortisol response to a 30 minute laboratory separation in 9-month-olds was compared to the response to 30 minutes of play with mother present. These data (see Fig. 1.1) clearly indicate that maternal separation elevates cortisol at

TABLE 1.1
Salivary Cortisol in µg/dl Means and Standard Errors

	Parent Home	Preseparation	Postseparation
9 months	0.53	0.42	0.51
	(0.03)	(0.03)	(.02)
13 months	0.57	0.50	0.55
	(0.03)	(0.02)	(0.03)

Note. Ns ranged from 52 to 61. Values expressed as µg/dl. Numbers in parentheses are standard errors. Adapted from Gunnar et al. (1989).

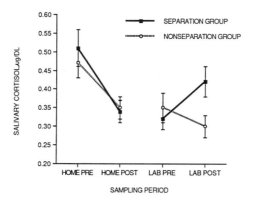

FIG. 1.1.   Salivary cortisol at home and in the laboratory during either a 30 minute separation or a 30 minute play period with mother. (Difference between Home Pre and Lab Pre reflects the calming effect of riding in the car.) Reprinted from Larson et al. (1991) *Child Development*.

this age over the levels observed when the mother is present. However, they also point to the problem of concluding that the separated infants were in a state of physiological stress. The cortisol response was small, and postseparation concentrations were not that different from cortisol levels obtained at home at the same time of day.

RELATIONS BETWEEN PHYSIOLOGICAL AND BEHAVIORAL REACTIONS

Brief separations produce a variety of behavioral effects. As noted, all of these effects were once viewed as reflecting a unitary emotional response to maternal loss (Bowlby, 1973). However, the current evidence suggests that, at the very least, during the protest phase we need to distinguish emotional behavior triggered by the enforced separation from emotional behavior reflecting infant reactions to the separation environment (Hofer, 1987). Furthermore, we argue that the emotional arousal produced during the protest phase of separation reflects the interaction among at least four emotion-behavior systems. First there are the attachment behaviors organized around attempts to elicit retrieval and reestablish contact. These include signaling and search behavior. Next there are withdrawal behaviors reflecting fear. These include freezing, inhibition of play and exploration, and sometimes threat gestures to fear-eliciting elements of the environment. Third, there are vocal and gestural reflections of frustration and anger at being blocked from achieving maternal contact. Finally, there are the behaviors organized around affect regulation, including clinging to surrogate caregivers, self-stimulation, and distraction. Only the first two of these, attachment (signaling/calling) and fear-anxiety (behavioral agitation and freezing), have received much attention in the neuroscience literature.

The endogenous opiate system appears to be most intimately involved in regulating the attachment behaviors of searching and signaling. Panksepp (e.g., Herman & Panksepp, 1978) has argued that this system plays a central role in affiliation and attachment. Consistent with this argument, it has now been demonstrated in several species that morphine reduces the number and intensity of the infant's "calls for mother" during separation, and that naloxone, an opiate antagonist, increases these calls and blocks the morphine effect (Herman & Panksepp, 1978; Kalin et al., 1988). Morphine also reduces the physiological stress of separation, producing significant reductions in the adrenocortical response (Kalin et al., 1988). These reductions can be blocked by prior treatment with naloxone.

Stimulation that triggers endogenous opioid activity reduces separation calls. Endogenous opioids can be triggered by pleasant social interactions (Panksepp, Herman, Vilberg, Bishop, & De Eskinazi, 1978), the consumption of milk, sugars, and fats (Blass, Shide, & Weller, 1989), and by stress (Akil, Madden, Patrick, & Barchas, 1976). As later discussed, stimulation of endogenous opioid system may partly explain why companionship during separation so potently reduces the stress of separation (Panksepp et al., 1978; but see also Blass, Fillion, Weller, & Brunson, in press, for a counterargument). Increases in endogenous opioids also may be one factor influencing the time-course of separation calling. During separation, calling and search behavior decreases. In infants who have been calling from the onset, the decrease in calling typically begins 20 to 30 minutes into separation. This is about the point when increases in endorphins triggered as part of the activation of the hypothalamic-pituitary-adrenocortical responses would be at high or peak concentrations. Anecdotally, this is also the time when, in human infants, one begins to notice the baby rubbing its eyes and acting sleepy. It may be that in a supportive environment, the combined effects of tiredness from increased energy expenditure, and endorphin-related reductions in the acute sense of loss are what allow some babies to quiet down and fall asleep (see Tennes et al., 1977).

Fear and anxiety, the second major emotion-behavior component of the separation response, appear strongly affected by the nature of the separation environment (Kalin & Shelton, 1989). Not surprisingly, manipulations of the neurochemical substrates of fear and anxiety have potent effects on the infant's fearful and anxious behavior. For example, Kalin et al. (1988) have provided evidence that the endogenous benzodiazepine system plays a role in regulating behavioral inactivity and social withdrawal as well as signaling behavior during brief separations. The major neurotransmittors may also be involved; however, their role in regulating separation vocalizations is still under debate. Kalin and Shelton (1988) have presented evidence that both the alpha and beta adrenergic systems may play a role in regulating behavioral agitation during separation. But, they noted that in order to reduce separation calling, pharmacological manipulations of the norepinephrine system had to be dramatic enough to produce general sedation.

Fear behaviors during separation may be regulated in part by the hypothalamic-pituitary-adrenocortical (HPA) system. Kalin, Shelton, and Barksdale (1989) found that intraventricular injections of corticotrophin releasing hormone (CRH) increased freezing and inactivity during a one-hour separation in rhesus infants. Similarly, Levine and his colleagues (Coe et al., 1985) found that pretreatment with metyrapone, which blocks cortisol production and produces hypersecretion of CRH under stress conditions, resulted in extreme behavioral inhibition in separated infant squirrel monkeys. The levels of CRH required to produce behavioral inhibition, however, are quite high and may naturally occur only with extremely intense activation of the HPA axis. Cortisol (and consequently CRH) levels produced during separation using typical monkey separation paradigms are positively correlated with behavioral agitation, not freezing (Gunnar et al., 1981).

So far, little attention has been paid to anger as a component of the protest response. Nonetheless, anger may be especially important in understanding the human infant's response. In a recent analysis of discrete facial expressions, Izard and his colleagues (Shiller, Izard, & Hembree, 1986) noted that few infants displayed fear and only a few infants displayed sadness in response to the brief separations in Ainsworth's Strange Situation. In contrast, anger was frequently noted. Anger is the emotion associated with goal-blocking and loss of anticipated control over desired outcomes. In monkeys, separation situations that should elicit anger are associated with heightened vocalizations, cage shaking, and moderate rather than extreme elevations in cortisol and cerebral spinal fluid concentrations of norepinephrine metabolites (Bayart, Hayashi, Faull, Barchas, & Levine, 1990). Such conditions have been created by placing a plexiglas barrier between mother and infant during separation: the baby thus can see but not get to the mother. Levine (Levine, Johnson, & Gonzalez, 1985) has argued that these conditions reduce the HPA response to separation because seeing the mother helps sustain the infant's active attempts to cope with or control the situation.

For ethical reasons, the situations used to study separation in human infants all contain cues that should prevent the baby from feeling helpless. The mother leaves the baby of her own accord (as opposed to being captured and removed); she frequently says goodbye and indicates that she will return soon (a pattern that Western infants should have experienced enough to associate with separations of a finite period); and the infant is rarely left without an alternative caregiver or babysitter. It would make sense, then, that much of the distress observed during brief, laboratory studies of separations in human infants may reflect anger.

This conclusion is consistent with available physiological and neuroendocrine data. Fox and Stifter (1989; Stifter & Fox, in press) have recently described the results of a longitudinal investigation of vagal tone in human infants. Infants with high vagal tone were shown to respond with more intense behavioral distress to limb restraint at 5 months, a manipulation that should elicit anger. By 13 months, these infants showed more intense and immediate crying to maternal separation than did infants with low vagal tone. Similarly, Davidson and Fox (1989) found that infants who were more right lateralized in frontal lobe EEG activity under baseline conditions were more likely to cry to a 1 minute separation from mother than were infants who were more left lateralized. Fox and Aaron (in preparation) have recently replicated these results. Anger elicited by frustration and goal-blocking should be associated with intense right frontal activity.

In several separation studies, we (Gunnar et al., 1989; Larson et al., 1991), have examined the relations between cortisol, crying, and parent-reported measures of temperamental fear of novelty and anger at limitations. We have consistently found that the modest adrenocortical activation noted in our research is greater for babies who typically show more anger to limitations and is not strongly related to measures of fear in response to novelty. Of course, in separation paradigms containing more novel and strange elements, temperamental fear of novelty may be more predictive of the infant's response.

Relatively little attention has been paid to the biobehavioral substrates of affect-regulatory behaviors during separation. In human infants, many of these behaviors appear to have their roots in social stimulation. They include non-nutritive sucking, clinging to a favorite blanket or toy, and seeking contact with babysitters. Blass and his coworkers (Blass et al., in press) have argued that nonopioid mechanisms mediate the distress-modulating effects of nonnutritive sucking and physical contact. Panksepp's (Panksepp et al., 1978) data, of course, would suggest that the distress-reducing effects of affiliation are mediated by opioid pathways. Whether opioid mechanisms mediate the effects of social support during separation in primate infants remains to be examined. It is possible, of course, that nonopioid pathways mediate the effects of contact comfort, whereas opioid pathways mediate the impact of pleasant social relations. Distraction and attention-regulation form another major category of affect-modulatory behavior in infancy. Rothbart and Posner (1985) recently have speculated on the neural substrates of these behaviors and their relation to individual differences in temperament and to developmental changes in negative affectivity. Anecdotally, giving the baby attractive toys to play with does seem to help reduce distress during brief separations. Playing with toys, of course, may help the baby to "tune out" the parent's absence if the separation is brief enough.

STRESS AND THE ENVIRONMENT
OF SEPARATION

The separation environment is a major determinant of the physiological stress of separation and it also affects behavioral reactions. However, the effects on behavior do not always mirror the physiological effects. As noted above, baby monkeys who can see their mothers during separation vocalize more and appear more agitated than infants who are completely isolated. Nonetheless, measures of cortisol and of brain monoamine metabolites indicate that the baby is less physically stressed when mother is visible (Bayart et al., 1990). Because crying and signaling are instrumental behaviors, they should be readily manipulated by altering environmental contingencies (Gewirtz & Pelaez-Nogueras, 1990). However, unless the manipulations increase the baby's control over stress-reducing elements of the separation environment, extinguishing crying and signaling by removing reinforcers should increase stress. This analysis is based on evidence that loss-of-control and helplessness are potent activators of physiological stress reactions (e.g., Hanson, Larson, & Snowdon, 1976).

Control is also a major determinant of fear in human infants by the last quarter of the first year. Babies who can self-activate a loud, mechanical toy cry less, smile more, and approach the toy more than yoked infants who have no control over activating the toy (Gunnar, 1980). Infants who can control the appearance of a stranger during peek-a-boo show more positive affect and less withdrawal than yoked, helpless babies (Levitt, 1980). Finally, 10-, 12-, and 18-month-old infants show less avoidance and more approach and positive affect when playing with controllable strangers who allow the baby to regulate the interaction as compared to controlling strangers who try to regulate the baby's actions (Mangelsdorf, Lehr, & Friedman, 1986; Mangelsdorf, Watkins, & Lehn, in preparation).

The behavioral and physiological effects of control over separation have not been experimentally examined in either human or nonhuman infants. However, perceived control over aversive stimulation is well known to reduce physical indices of stress in adult humans and animals (Seligman, 1975). Furthermore, sudden loss of control over a previously controllable event elicits even greater stress, as indexed by HPA activity, than never having control over the event (Hanson et al., 1976). A sense of sudden loss of control may characterize the infant's experience when forcibly separated from mother, and this loss of control may seem greater for infants from more rather than less responsive relationships. We (Gunnar et al., 1981) examined this prediction with rhesus infants who were observed in their social groups for several weeks prior to separation. We found that greater adrenocortical reactions to separation were produced in infants from more responsive mother-infant relationships, whereas separation produced a smaller HPA response in infants whose mothers were less responsive and more rejecting. Interestingly, upon reunion, the opposite pattern was noted, with infants from the most responsive relationships showing decreases in cortisol and those infants from unresponsive relationships actually showing a rise in cortisol to reunion (see Table 1.2).

Although control over separation has not been experimentally manipulated, there are a number of studies that have manipulated the controllability of the

TABLE 1.2
Relationship Quality and Plasma Cortisol Responses to Separation and Reunion in Rhesus Monkey Infants

Separated Pairs	% Approach-Leave[a]	Separation Cortisol[b]	Reunion Cortisol[c]
1	0.00	+29.8	- 0.7
2	0.19	+27.3	+ 1.0
3	0.29	+26.5	+20.5
4	0.31	+13.7	+12.7
5	0.46	+ 9.3	+27.1

Adapted from Gunnar et al., 1981.
[a]Higher scores indicate proximity of mother and infant regulated by infant approaching and mother leaving.
[b]Cortisol 3 hours after separation minus baseline.
[c]Cortisol 24 hours after reunion minus baseline. Separation period was 2 weeks.

separation environment. This manipulation of control, however, is typically produced through providing the infant with an alternative caregiver in the mother's absence. Thus the effects of control are confounded with the effects of social support.

The presence of familiar conspecifics is about the most potent situational factor determining the stress of separation. Levine and his colleagues (e.g., Levine & Wiener, 1988) have shown that the HPA response to separation can be reduced considerably, although not eliminated, in infant squirrel monkeys by leaving them in their social groups where they are often "aunted" by adult females during the separation. During prolonged separations, the presence of an "aunt" greatly reduces evidence of despair and moderates physiological reactions in macaque infants (e.g., Reite, Seiler, & Short, 1978). In human infants, even the presence of a strange adult female greatly reduces crying during brief separations in the Strange Situation (Ainsworth et al., 1978).

Physiologically, as noted, both opioid and nonopioid pathways may be involved in regulating the effects of companions on the infant's reactions to separation. Psychologically, there is growing evidence that the controllability of the social other is also important. For example, we (Gunnar et al., in preparation) recently manipulated babysitter responsiveness to 9-month-olds during separations lasting 30 minutes. In one condition the babysitter was moderately responsive and controllable: She responded warmly and sensitively to the baby if he became upset, but otherwise was preoccupied reading a magazine (caretaker condition). In the other condition, the babysitter was highly responsive and controllable. Throughout the separation period she interacted with the baby, playing with the baby if he was happy and comforting him if he became upset (playmate condition). Remarkably, this relatively small increase in the babysitter's controllability and responsiveness was enough to eliminate the HPA response to separation (see Fig. 1.2).

Because we believe that these data have important implications for discriminating low- from high-stress daycare environments, we decided to determine whether adding additional infants eliminated the buffering effect of high babysitter playfulness and responsiveness. Using the highly responsive/playful babysitter paradigm, we compared behavioral and adrenocortical responses of infants separated singly with the babysitter (1 : 1) to infants who shared the babysitter with two other infants of the same sex. As before, in the 1 : 1 condition, no evidence of a stress reaction was obtained. Furthermore, even when two "strange" babies were added to the separation environment, the availability of a playful and responsive babysitter still buffered the HPA response (see Fig. 1.3).

Control was probably not the only psychological variable affecting infant reactions to separation in our "playful/responsive" babysitter studies. The playful, responsive babysitter may have helped the baby use distraction as a coping strategy. In addition, her behavior may have been more predictable and under-

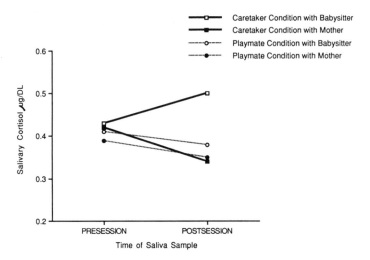

FIG. 1.2. Salivary cortisol under two care conditions, caretaker or playmate, with mother versus a babysitter as the caregiver. Gunnar et al., in preparation.

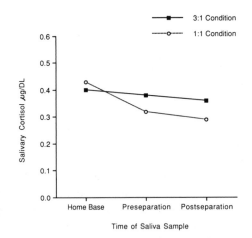

FIG. 1.3. Salivary cortisol during a 30 minute separation in either group care (3 babies: 1 caregiver) or singleton care (1 baby: 1 caregiver).

standable to the baby. In the stress literature, predictability has also been shown to reduce adverse reactions to noxious stimulation (Seligman & Binik, 1977). There are mixed data, however, on whether predictability increases or decreases the infant's negative reactions to separation. On the positive side, Kagan (1974) has demonstrated that infants cry and protest less when separated at home if the mother leaves by a familiar exit (the front door) than by an unfamiliar one (the closet). On the negative side, Levine and his colleagues (Jordan, Coe, Patterson, & Levine, 1984) found that increasing the predictability of the separation period by fixing its duration in squirrel monkeys increased, rather than reduced, agitated behavior and vocalizations while having no effect on cortisol.

As these data suggest, increasing predictability does not always reduce fear and stress. What appears to matter is whether the information the individual obtains increases the salience of threatening or safe elements of the situation (Miller, 1981; Seligman & Binik, 1977). With one-year-old human infants, we (Gunnar, 1980; Gunnar, Leighten, & Peleaux, 1984) found that neither providing warning signals nor fixing the periods of aversive stimulation reduced crying, withdrawal, and other fearful behaviors towards a noise-producing, mechanical toy. Indeed, these manipulations often increased fear behaviors. In contrast, fixing the duration of the safe or "toy-not-on" periods did reduce fear. With regard to separation, the research on fear and predictability would suggest that increasing the salience of cues associated with reunion and those associated with safe, pleasant experiences should reduce fear and distress reactions. This may be why Kagan's (1974) manipulation worked. The infants associated the front door with reunion as well as leave-taking. They had no experience with the mother returning through the closet door.

Predictability should also be increased by repeating the separation in the same environment. However, there are also mixed data on whether this reduces physiological reactions. Distress vocalizations are reduced with repeated separations, although this may merely reflect extinction of the response (Levine & Wiener, 1988). Using repeated, 6-hour separations in squirrel monkeys, Levine and his colleagues (Coe et al., 1985) showed no habituation of the cortisol response after 6 separations. Hennessy (1986) did note a reduction in cortisol after 28 separations, but even after 80 separations, the response was still measurable. Does this mean that human children, too, will not adapt to separations when the separation situation becomes highly familiar and predictable? Probably not. The separation environments used in the monkey research provided the baby with few means of coping with separation. Unfortunately, there have been no studies of repeated, brief separations in monkeys in which the baby is left in the social group and is "aunted" during separation. Although repeated brief separations have not been studied in human infants, Field (personal communication), has found that preschoolers adapt to repeated, prolonged separations of several days.

To summarize, the stress of separation is strongly affected by the separation context. The major situational variable appears to be the presence of a responsive, supportive alternative caregiver. Physiologically, the effects of a responsive caregiver may be mediated, in part, by the opioid-affiliative system. Psychologically, the effect may be due to an increase in the controllability of the separation environment. Predictability may also be increased when a responsive caregiver is available to the infant and when the infant is separated repeatedly under the same conditions. Whether repetitions decrease, increase, or have no effects on separation stress may depend, however, on whether the infant learns that the separation environment is safe and that his or her needs will be met.

INDIVIDUAL DIFFERENCES
AND DEVELOPMENTAL CHANGE

Stress research in humans has been focused largely on individual differences (Tennes & Mason, 1982). This is certainly the case for research on infant separation responses (e.g., Tennes et al., 1977). In our own studies, we have noted large differences among babies in both their behavioral and adrenocortical responses to maternal separation. Unfortunately, as yet, there is no coherent explanation for why some infants are more behaviorally and physiologically stressed than others by brief separations from caregivers. The quality of the parent-infant relationship does not appear to predict crying and other indices of behavioral upset to separation (e.g., Belsky & Rovine, 1987). Some securely attached infants show intense behavioral distress (e.g., the B4 classification, see Ainsworth et al., 1978), whereas others show little behavioral distress (e.g., the B1 classification). Similarly, some insecurely attached babies show little distress (the A classification) and others show intense distress (the C classification).

The impact of relationship history on physiological, as opposed to behavioral, responses to separation has not been adequately assessed. What data there are suggest that infants from both secure and insecure relationships show similar increases in heart rate (Donovan & Leavitt, 1985) and cortisol (Gunnar et al., 1989) to brief separations. Because relationship quality and separation reactions have typically been explored at the same time using the Strange Situation, these data are far from conclusive. Furthermore, of greater interest may be the association between relationship quality and the infant's response to more naturalistic separations. For example, in separations lasting more than one or two minutes, hypothesized differences in social competence among attachment groups might predict differences among infants in their ability to use and gain solace from responsive, alternative caregivers.

Although there is little evidence that behavioral distress is determined by the emotional security of the attachment relationship, there is evidence that temperament plays a role. As noted, distress to limitations, as reported by mother, has predicted greater adrenocortical responses to separation in our own research (Gunnar et al., 1989; Gunnar, in preparation). Likewise, Belsky and Rovine (1987), have reported that infants described as less difficult during the first few months of life later cry less during the Strange Situation at one year. There is now considerable interest in the development of emotional reactivity and stress vulnerability during the first year (Fox & Stifter, 1989). Unfortunately, although there is good evidence of association between behavioral and physiological reactions to psychosocial stressors during infancy, there is little evidence that physiological differences in reactivity form the basis for these behavioral differences (see review by Gunnar, 1990). There is, however, increasing evidence that some aspect(s) of emotional reactivity may be heritable (Matheny, 1989). Whether this heritability of behavioral reactions extends to physiological reactions to separation, however, is not known.

Separation history is another factor believed to affect the infant's reactivity to separation. A number of researchers have suggested that the Strange Situation, for example, is an inappropriate tool for assessing quality of attachment in day-care children because their history of separation should make the situation less strange to them. Belsky and his colleagues (Belsky & Braungart, in press) have recently shown, however, that insecure avoidant infants with day-care experience actually show more rather than less behavioral upset in the Strange Situation than do insecure avoidant infants with little nonparental care experience. Thus, if anything, more experience with nonparental care in the first year may heighten separation distress.

We also have examined nonparental care and reactions to separation in our own research. The majority of babies in our studies have averaged less than 10 hours per week in nonparental care; however, a few in each study have been in full time care of 40 hours per week or more. So far we have not found any consistent or significant relations between hours in nonparental care and either behavior or cortisol during 30-minute separations. Our earlier discussion of predictability, nonetheless, suggests that the amount of separation experience may be less important than the quality of the experience. More experience with low-stress nonparental care might actually reduce later stress reactions to separation by leading the baby to expect a pleasant or at least neutral experience, whereas more experience with high-stress nonparental care might increase later stress reactions.

Along with individual differences, behavioral research on separation has emphasized the study of normative, developmental change. Studies of protest behavior suggest that crying and resisting separation begins around 8 months, peaks at around 18 months, and then wanes thereafter (Weinraub & Lewis, 1977). There have been no developmental studies of physiological reactions to separation in human infants. As noted, separation protest may not always reflect the intensity of physiological stress. Furthermore, separation may be a different type of stressor at different points in development. Hofer (1987) has argued that biological homeostasis is a function of all close relationships and that much of the separation reaction of young organisms can be explained by the loss of regulation typically provided by the mother. Pipp and Harmon (1987) have taken Hofer's regulation argument to be especially applicable to parent-infant relations during the first months of life. To the extent that homeostatic regulation is largely accomplished via the infant's interactions with mother early in the first year, then we might expect to see physiological responses to separation long before the baby organizes a behavioral protest response. Further, our developmental studies of protest behavior have typically examined extremely brief separations (1–3 minutes) in relatively noncomplex environments. Perhaps the 2-year-old has grown to be less threatened by the idea that mother may leave for 2 minutes while she plays alone with some new toys, but this may not mean that the same child now protests less and is less stressed when mother leaves her for several hours in nursery school or day care with new children and new caregivers. Waters and his colleagues (Waters, Kondi-Ikemara, Posada, & Richters, 1990) have recently argued that 12- to 18-month-olds are only beginning to organize their security seeking around remaining in proximity to mother. Indeed, their data suggest that this type of secure-base behavior does not peak in intensity until about 3 years. If accurate, this may mean that separations into naturalistic, complex environments may be more stressful for the 3-year-old than for the infant.

A final developmental issue that has not been adequately addressed is the long-term consequences of repeated, brief separations. In nonhuman primates and in humans there are data suggesting that experiences with prolonged separation and loss early in life predisposes the individual to later psychopathology (Kalin & Carnes, 1984, for review). What about repeated, frequent, brief separations? This question is being addressed with regard to infant day care. As reviewed previously, there are currently no data indicating that physiological reactions to brief separations are affected during infancy by repeated and frequent separation experiences. With regard to behavior, there is some evidence that attachment behaviors may be reorganized and that slightly greater, rather than less, distress may be elicited by a history of brief separations. These data, however, deal with effects emerging within the infancy period. We do not know the long-term effects on stress-reactivity of these kinds of experiences in human infants.

Recently Levine and his students (Mody, 1989; Lin, 1990) have noted significant long-term effects in their squirrel monkey subjects. They examined adolescent squirrel monkeys who had served during infancy in studies of repeated, 6-hour separations. At 2 years and again at 3 years of age they repeatedly isolated these animals from their social groups for 6 hours. Compared to subjects with no history of early separations, the previously separated adolescent squirrel monkeys showed a blunted cortisol response to social isolation at both 2 and 3 years. Furthermore, the experience of repeated social isolations at 2 years did not modify the adrenocortical response to isolation at 3 years. Thus, the infancy period appeared particularly sensitive to the modifying effects of repeated, stressful stimulation. Finally, reminiscent of the literature on early handling stress, the previously separated animals also reached puberty earlier than did the animals who were not separated in infancy. Unfortunately, at this point we do not know whether the previously separated animals would show a blunted stress reaction to other, nonsocial types of stressors. Nor do we know whether similar long-term effects would be obtained if the separation environment had been made less stressful in infancy by leaving the baby in its social group. However, these data raise the provocative possibility that the effects of early, repeated brief separations on stress-reactivity may not become apparent until the child is older.

In summary, although babies differ markedly in their physiological reactivity to brief separations, we have no adequate models to account for these individual differences. Relationship history has not yet been shown to influence stress reactions to extremely brief separations of only a few minutes, and there are no data on relations between attachment security and the infant's physiological or behavioral reactions to more normative brief separations of one to a few hours. There does appear to be a heritable component to negative emotional behavior elicited by separation and strangers; however, there are no data indicating that this heritability of reactivity extends to physiological responses. With regard to developmental issues, although there have been a number of studies of developmental changes in behavior to extremely brief separations, we do not know whether the developmental pattern extends to separations lasting more than a few minutes and whether the behavioral pattern mirrors the pattern for physiological stress reactions. Finally, we have no data on the long-term consequences of early separations on physiological responses to later stressors in human children. All of these areas would seem ripe for research.

CONCLUSIONS

In humans as well as the young of many mammalian species, brief separations from attachment figures can provoke intense physiological stress reactions. These reactions are sometimes correlated with the intensity of the infant's protest behavior, but protest behavior can be extinguished by manipulating environmental cues and reinforcers without reducing the physiological response. In monkey and human infants, the stress of separation reflects both responses to maternal loss and to the separation environment. Providing high quality, responsive, alternative care during separation can reduce, and in some instances, completely buffer the physiological stress of separation. Unfortunately, many human infants probably repeatedly experience separations in much less supportive environments than those studied in our laboratory paradigms. The effects of such separations on stress physiology is not known. Indeed, as noted previously, there is a great deal about the stress of separation for human infants and children that is still unknown. The day care debate has focused attention on the impact of early care arrangements on later social and psychological development. It is hoped that this review will encourage greater attention to the physiological stress of early separations and the potential such stress may have, if repeated and intense, for the child's later physiological reactivity and health.

ACKNOWLEDGMENTS

This research was supported by NICHD grants R01-HD16494 and K04-HD00712 to Megan Gunnar.

REFERENCES

Ainsworth, M. D. S., & Wittig, B. A. (1969). Attachment and the exploratory behavior of one-year-olds in a strange situation. In B. M. Foss (Ed.), *Determinants of infant behavior* (Vol. 4, pp. 113–136). London: Methuen.

Ainsworth, M. D. S., Blehar, M. C., Waters, E., & Wall, S. (1978). *Patterns of attachment: A psychological study of the strange situation.* Hillsdale, NJ: Lawrence Erlbaum Associates.

Akil, H., Madden, J., Patrick, R. L., & Barchas, J. D. (1976). Stress-induced increase in endogenous opiate peptides: Concurrent analgesia and its partial reversal by naloxone. In H. Kosterlitz (Ed.), *Opiate and endogenous opiate peptides* (pp. 63–70). Amsterdam: Elsevier.

Bayart, F., Hayashi, K. T. Faull, K. F., Barchas, J. D., & Levine, S. (1990). Influence of maternal proximity on behavioral and physiological responses to separation in infant rhesus monkeys (Macaca mulatta). *Behavioral Neuroscience, 104*(1), 98–107.

Belsky, J., & Braungart, I. (in press). Are insecure-avoidant infants with extensive daycare experience less stressed by and more independent in the strange situation? *Child Development.*

Belsky, M., & Rovine, M. (1987). Temperament and attachment security in the strange situation: An empirical rapprochement. *Child Development, 58,* 787–795.

Blass, E. M., Fillion, T. F., Weller, A., & Brunson, L. (in press). Separation of opioid from nonopioid mediation of affect in neonatal rats: Nonopioid mechanisms mediate maternal contact influences. *Behavioral Neuroscience.*

Blass, E. M., Shide, D. J., & Weller, A. (1989). Stress-reducing effects of ingesting milk, sugars, and fats: A developmental perspective. *Annals of the New York Academy of Sciences, 575,* 292–305.

Bowlby, J. (1969). *Attachment and loss: Attachment* (Vol. 1). New York: Basic Books.

Bowlby, J. (1973). *Attachment and loss: Separation* (Vol. 2). New York: Basic Books.

Coe, C. L., Wiener, S. G., Rosenberg, L. T., & Levine, S. (1985). Endocrine and immune responses to separation and maternal loss in nonhuman primates. In M. Reite & T. Field (Eds.), *The psychobiology of attachment* (pp. 163–199). New York: Academic Press.

Davidson, R. J., & Fox, N. A. (1989). Frontal brain asymmetry predicts infants' response to maternal separation. *Journal of Abnormal Psychology, 98*(2), 127–131.

Donovan, W. L., & Leavitt, L. A. (1985). Physiologic assessment of mother-infant attachment. *Journal of the American Academy of Child Psychiatry, 24*(1), 65–70.

Fox, N. A., & Aaron, N. *The relation of frontal brain asymmetry to attachment behavior and behavioral inhibition in 14- to 24-month-old children.* Manuscript submitted for publication.

Fox, N. A., & Davidson, R. J. (1988). Patterns of brain electrical activity during the expression of discrete emotions in 10-month-old infants. *Developmental Psychology, 24,* 230–236.

Fox, N. A., & Stifter, C. A. (1989). Biological and behavioral differences in infant reactivity and regulation. In G. A. Kohnstamm, J. E. Bates, & M. K. Rothbart (Eds.), *Temperament in childhood* (pp. 169–183). New York: Wiley.

Friedman, E. M., Coe, C., & Ershler, W. B. (in preparation). *Time-dependent effects of peer separation on lymphocyte proliferation responses in juvenile squirrel monkeys.*

Gewirtz, J., Pelaez-Nogueras, M. (1990, April). *Complications of uncontrolled mother/stranger contingencies in maternal departures and in the strange situation: A functional analysis.* Paper presented at the Seventh International Conference on Infant Studies, Montreal, Canada.

Gunnar, M. (1980). Control, warning signals, and distress in infancy. *Developmental Psychology,* *16*(4), 281–289.

Gunnar, M. (1990). The psychobiology of infant temperament. In J. Colombo & J. W. Fagan (Eds.), *Individual differences in infancy: Reliability, stability, prediction* (pp. 387–410). Hillsdale, NJ: Lawrence Erlbaum Associates.

Gunnar, M., Gonzales, C., Goodlin, B., & Levine, S. (1981). Behavioral and pituitary-adrenal responses during a prolonged separation period in infant rhesus macaques. *Psychoneuroendocrinology, 6*(1), 65–75.

Gunnar, M., Leighton, K., & Peleaux, R. (1984). The effects of stimulus predictability on fear reactions in year-old infants. *Developmental Psychology, 20,* 449–458.

Gunnar, M., Mangelsdorf, S., Larson, M., & Hertsgaard, L. (1989). Attachment, temperament and adrenocortical activity in infancy: A study of psychoendocrine regulation. *Developmental Psychology, 25,* 355–363.

Hanson, J. D., Larson, M. E., & Snowdon, C. T. (1976). The effects of control over high intensity noise on plasma cortisol levels in rhesus monkeys. *Behavioral Biology, 16,* 333–338.

Hennessy, M. B. (1986). Multiple, brief maternal separations in the squirrel monkey: Changes in hormonal and behavioral responsiveness. *Physiology and Behavior, 36,* 245–250.

Herman, B. H., & Panksepp, J. (1978). Effects of morphine and naloxone on separation distress and approach attachment: Evidence for opiate mediation of social affect. *Pharmacology, Biochemistry, and Behavior, 9*(2), 213–220.

Hofer, M. A. (1984). Relationships as regulators: A psychobiologic perspective on bereavement. *Psychosomatic Medicine, 46*(3), 183–197.

Hofer, M. A. (1987). Early social relationships: A psychobiologists' view. *Child Development, 58,* 633–647.

Jordan, T. C., Coe, C. L., Patterson, J., & Levine, S. (1984). Predictability and coping with separation in infant squirrel monkeys. *Behavioral Neuroscience, 98*(3), 556–560.

Kagan, J. (1974). Discrepancy, temperament, and infant distress. In M. Lewis & L. Rosenblum (Eds.), *The origins of fear* (229–248). New York: Wiley.

Kalin, N. H., & Carnes, M. (1984). Biological correlates of attachment bond disruption in humans and nonhuman primates. *Progress in Neuro-Psychopharmacology and Biological Psychiatry, 8*(3), 459–469.

Kalin, N. H., & Shelton, S. E. (1988). Effects of clonidine and propranolol on separation-induced distress in infant rhesus monkeys. *Brain Research, 470*(2), 289–295.

Kalin, N. H., & Shelton, S. E. (1989). Defensive behavior in infant rhesus monkeys: Environmental cues and neurochemical regulation. *Science, 243,* 1718–1721.

Kalin, N. H., Shelton, S. E., & Barksdale, C. M. (1988). Opiate modulation of separation-induced distress in nonhuman primates. *Brain Research, 440*(2), 285–292.

Kalin, N. H., Shelton, S. E., & Barksdale, C. M. (1989). Behavioral and physiologic effects of CRH administered to infant primates undergoing maternal separation. *Neuropsychopharmacology, 2*(2), 97–104.

Kehoe, P., & Blass, E. M. (1986). Opioid-mediation of separation distress in 10-day-old rats: Reversal of stress with maternal stimuli. *Developmental Psychobiology, 19*(4), 385–398.

Kraemer, G. W., Ebert, M. H., Lake, C. R., & McKinney, W. T. (1984). Cerebrospinal fluid measures of neurotransmitter changes associated with pharmacological alteration of the despair response to social separation in rhesus monkeys. *Psychiatry Research, 11*(4), 303–315.

Larson, M., Gunnar, M., & Hertsgaard, L. (1991). The effects of morning naps, car trips, and maternal separation on adrenocortical activity in human infants. *Child Development, 62,* 362–372.

Levine, S., Johnson, D. F., & Gonzalez, C. A. (1985). Behavioral and hormonal responses to separation in infant rhesus monkeys and mothers. *Behavioral Neuroscience, 99*(3), 399–410.

Levine, S., & Wiener, S. G. (1988). Psychoendocrine aspects of mother-infant relationships in nonhuman primates. *Psychoneuroendocrinology, 13*(1–2), 143–154.

Levitt, M. J. (1980). Contingent feedback, familiarization, and infant affect: How a stranger becomes a friend. *Developmental Psychology, 16*(5), 425–432.

Lin, R. Y. (1990). *Effects of maternal separation on pubertal development in the squirrel monkey.* Unpublished honors thesis, Stanford University, Stanford, CA.

Mangelsdorf, S., Lehr, C., & Friedman, J. (1986, April). *Control predictability and the infants' appraisal of strangers.* Paper presented at the Fifth International Conference on Infant Studies, Los Angeles.

Mangelsdorf, S., Watkins, S., & Lehn, L. (in preparation). *The role of control in infants' appraisal of strangers.*

Matheny, A. P., Jr. (1989). Children's behavioral inhibition over age and across situations. *Journal of Personality, 57*, 215–235.

Miller, S. (1981). Predictability and human stress: Towards a clarification of evidence and theory. *Advances in Experimental Social Psychology, 14*, 203–256.

Mody, T. M. (1989). *Influence of early maternal separation on the behavioral and physiological responses to social isolation in adolescent squirrel monkeys.* Unpublished honors thesis, Stanford University, Stanford, CA.

Panksepp, J., Herman, B., Vilberg, T., Bishop, P., & De Eskinazi, F. G. (1978). Endogenous opioids and social behavior. *Neuroscience and behavioral reviews, 4*, 473–487.

Pipp, S., & Harmon, R. J. (1987). Attachment as regulation: A commentary. *Child Development, 58*(3), 648–652.

Reite, M., Kaemingk, K., & Boccia, M. L. (1989). Maternal separation in bonnet monkey infants: Altered attachment and social support. *Child Development, 60*(2), 473–480.

Reite, M., Seiler, C., & Short, R. (1978). Loss of your mother is more than loss of your mother. *American Journal of Psychiatry, 135*(3), 370–371.

Rothbart, M. K., & Posner, M. I. (1985). Temperament and the development of self-regulation. In H. Hartlage & C. G. Telzrow (Eds.), *Neuropsychology of individual differences: A developmental perspective* (pp. 93–123). New York: Plenum Press.

Schaffer, H. R., & Emerson, P. E. (1964). The development of social attachments in infancy. *Monographs of the Society for Research in Child Development, 29*(3, Serial No. 94).

Seligman, M. (1975). *Learned helplessness: On development, depression, and death.* San Francisco: Freeman & Co.

Seligman, M., & Binik, Y. (1977). The safety-signal hypothesis. In H. Davis & H. Hurwitz (Eds.), *Pavlovian-operant interactions* (pp 165–188). Hillsdale, NJ: Lawrence Erlbaum Associates.

Shiller, V. M., Izard, C. E., Hembree, E. A. (1986). Pattern of emotion expression during separation in the Strange Situation. *Developmental Psychology, 22*, 378–383.

Smotherman, W., Hunt, L., McGinnis, V., & Levine, S. (1979). *Developmental Psychobiology, 12*, 211–217.

Stifter, C. A., & Fox, N. A. (in press). Behavioral and psychophepilogical indices of temperament in infancy. *Developmental Psychology.*

Tennes, K., Downey, K., & Vernadakis, A. (1977). Urinary cortisol excretion rates and anxiety in normal one-year-old infants. *Psychosomatic Medicine, 39*, 178–187.

Tennes, K., & Mason, J. (1982). Developmental psychoendocrinology: An approach to the study of emotions. In C. Izard (Ed.), *Measuring emotions in infants and children* (pp. 21–37). Cambridge, England: Cambridge University Press.

Waters, E., Kondi-Ikemara, K., Posada, G., & Richters, J. E. (1990). Learning to love: Mechanisms and milestones. In M. Gunnar & L. A. Sroufe (Eds.), *Self processes and development, Vol. 23, Minnesota Symposia on Child Psychology* (pp. 217–256). Hillsdale, NJ: Lawrence Erlbaum Associates.

Weinraub, M., & Lewis, M. (1977). The determinants of children's responses to separation. *Monograph of the Society for Research in Child Development, 42*(4, Serial No. 172).

2 Infants' Separation Difficulties and Distress Due to Misplaced Maternal Contingencies

Jacob L. Gewirtz
Martha Peláez-Nogueras
Florida International University

Infant protests during maternal/caregiver departures and separations are not observed during the early months of life. Our thesis here is that those cued responses emerge in the infant's repertory later in the first year due to learning, due to inadvertent training by mothers in the very departure and separation settings in which the protests are found. The research being reported in this chapter was mounted to ascertain how infant protests can come under the control of cues and contingencies generated by a mother's responses during her departures and after brief separations from her infant. These cued protests have served to denote *distress* for some theorists, *separation anxiety* for others, and an unlearned index of *attachment* for still others. A demonstration that such cued infant protests can be trained/encouraged by contingent maternal responding would provide evidence for the learned basis of the protests during departures and separations, and hence for the conditioned basis of the distress or attachment they have indexed. A by-product of the research being described identifies procedures that parents might employ to minimize separation difficulties, thus precluding their children's protests and distress in these settings.

ETIOLOGY OF INFANT DEPARTURE AND SEPARATION PROTESTS

In everyday settings, there are often found patterns of infant protests cued by maternal preparations for distancing and/or separating herself from her infant, by actual departures from the infant's vicinity, and by the ensuing short- or long-term separations. In infants during the first year, these protests may be comprised

In T.M. FIELD, P.M. McCABE, & N, SCHNEIDERMAN (Eds.) (1992). Stress and coping in infancy and childhood (pp. 19-46) H illsdale, N.J.: Lawrence Erlbaum Associates Publishers.

of cries, screams, fusses, whines, and/or whimpers; in older children, protests may additionally involve such responses as grabbing the parent's body or clothing, pleading, and/or imploring. The response elements denoting protests that have just been enumerated seem to be functional equivalents for delaying departures of, and for cutting short, separations from parents. On this basis, the passive- or reactive-expressive behavior elements and the active behavior elements denoting child protests that have been listed should function as members of a class of cued instrumental (discriminated operant) responses, conditionable by their effectiveness in delaying or precluding parental departures, or in shortening separations from them (Gewirtz & Peláez-Nogueras, 1987).

Major problems occur typically when children have their first experiences leaving their mothers and family settings, as when they are placed for the first time in preschools, day-care centers, or kindergartens. Such problems can (a) cause distress in infants/children, parents, and teachers; (b) distort the quality of the relationships involved; and/or (c) disorganize school settings, often for lengthy periods. The absence of behavioral problems at separation is thought to provide a basis for the later social and cognitive competence of the child.

There has been some work on separation symptoms and their disappearance in the early weeks of school (Bloom-Feshbach & Blatt, 1981), and separation stress due to transferring from one nursery-school group or school to another (Field, 1984; Field, Vega-Lahr, & Jagadish, 1984). Moreover, from a factor analysis, three factors were distinguished in the responses of two-years-olds during the initial 15 sec. of their mothers' standardized *departures* from a room: "protests" (e.g., direct actions to block departure), "passive distress" (e.g., fretting, but without an attempt to impede mother's departure), and "active distress" (e.g., crying with active attempts to prevent departure) (Weinraub & Lewis, 1977). The crying on this last factor was taken to denote either an active-distress call for the mother or an index of severe distress and/or frustration. Besides the distress observed during maternal departures, Weinraub and Lewis also identified a distress response to maternal postdeparture separation. Regrettably, on the basis that once upset, 2-year-old subjects were unlikely to process what their mothers say or do, those researchers did not consider maternal responses contingent on the child's protests during departures or after separations as potential reinforcer determinants of the protest/distress behavior patterns in those contexts.

Weinraub and Lewis did note, however, that some children who show distress during maternal departures may adjust rapidly to mothers' actual absences, and that some children who do not seem distressed during their mothers' preparations and steps to depart may protest once the door is closed and the mother is out of the room. Gewirtz and Peláez-Nogueras (1989) demonstrated experimentally that the latter outcome pattern can result from conditional-discrimination training. That is, under concurrent treatments (i.e., multiple schedules of reinforcement), 18 six- to 10-month-old infants learned to respond differentially to departure than to separation cues, and vice versa. A related study reported that 40% of the mothers and none of the fathers interviewed worried about their infants impending responses to departures, with 75% of mothers and 35% of fathers expecting their infants to cry (Weinraub & Frankel, 1977). Discussing these data, Field, Gewirtz, Cohen, Garcia, Greenberg, and Collins (1984) noted that parents may behave differentially in ways consistent with their beliefs to produce the outcomes called for by their beliefs.

MATERNAL RESPONDING AND ITS IMPLICATIONS

To date, little attention has been devoted to the role of the parent and caregiver behaviors in departure and separation difficulties their children manifest in home, day care, or other settings. The results of studies in which measures of maternal responsivity are related to measures of child protests/crying seem contradictory, particularly those results obtained in contexts of departure or brief separation where no operational distinction between those contexts is made and where the maternal behaviors contingent on the child's responses are not monitored. On one hand, Blurton-Jones and Leach (1972), Gewirtz and Peláez-Nogueras (1987), and Schaffer and Emerson (1964) have reported that infant departure/separation protests can be positively related to maternal responsivity. On the other hand, Stayton and Ainsworth (1973) found a higher rate of infant separation protests associated with maternal "unresponsiveness" to protests or "signals." Fleener and Cairns (1970) found no association between maternal responsivity and infant crying at separation. At the same time, it has been reported that 10-month-olds would leave the room in which they were with their mothers to venture alone into an adjoining strange room, whereas comparable infants protested when their mothers left them alone in the room (Rheingold & Eckerman, 1970, 1971), suggesting that infants are less likely to protest a separation that they initiate than when their mothers separate from them.

In this frame, an investigation to clarify the role of maternal/caregiver behavior in child departure and separation problems was thought necessary, including protests and distress during her preparations to depart and her brief separations from the child and of procedures to eliminate them. Such experimental analysis could provide a more adequate basis for understanding infant social development and the parent–child interaction process, specifically children's self-reliance or dependence, as well as the basis for applying these principles and procedures to alleviate departure and separation problems in family and school settings.

SEPARATION PROTESTS AS AN ATTACHMENT INDEX

Cued protests at maternal departures (often termed "separation protests" and indicators of "separation anxiety"), in addition to providing an index of "distress," have also served as an unlearned index of attachment (Stayton & Ainsworth, 1973). Thus, Bowlby (1960) proposed that the infant's protesting at maternal departures was the inverse of the proximity-seeking core of attachment. Based on this Bowlby proposal and Piaget's (1954) conception of object permanency, a widely cited report by Schaffer and Emerson (1964) of the age course in the first 18 months and the onset and intensity of infants' focused attachments to their mothers used measures based on what was essentially a single cued-protest response index of attachment. Their index was derived from Glasgow workingclass maternal reports that summarized the reported incidence, intensity, and direction of infant protests after seven types of *departures* from them. Schaffer and Emerson plotted means of those measures by monthly age. On this index, Fig. 2.1 shows that attachment intensity to mother began at 25 to 28 weeks and peaked at 41 to 44 weeks. By the same departure-protest index, 60% of the Schaffer and Emerson sample showed the *onset* of an attachment-to-mother by 29 to 32 weeks. On the other hand, Kagan, Kearsley, and Zelazo (1978) reported the rates of crying/fretting cued by maternal departures and separations in several cultural groups, which they took to denote not attachment but separation anxiety, fear, and/or distress. Kagan et al. reported that crying/fretting (or play inhibition) cued by maternal departures and separations ". . . is low prior to 8 months of age, rises rapidly from 9 to 18 months and then begins to decline" (p. 106). For the first 12 to 18 months of life, it appears that the infant cry/fret index of Kagan et al is the same as what Schaffer and Emerson (1964) and we in this chapter have termed *protests*.

On the basis of the maternal reports about characteristic intensity of protests at departure, Schaffer and Emerson reported that the intensity of infant attachment-to-mother at 18 months was a positive function of the speed of the mother's responding to her infant's crying. In this frame, Schaffer and Emerson themselves noted the possibility that the mothers, by their consistent, rapid reactions to the protest cries of their offspring in the very departure settings from which their measures were collected, may have expedited the learning of the cued protest response on which their attachment index was based. Thus, stimuli pro-

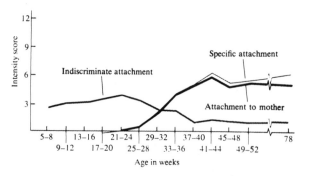

FIG. 2.1.   The age course of cued departure protests (termed "separation protests") reported by Schaffer and Emerson (1964). Reprinted by permission of the Society for Research in Child Development, Inc.

vided by a mother's preparations for departure from her infant may have cued the infant's protests. Even so, Schaffer and Emerson discounted this conditioning possibility, arguing that cause and effect could not be disentangled in their study in the context of their maternal reports, and concluded that their results could just as likely have reflected the infants' demands or mothers' having learned to "give in" to persistent infant protest crying.

Yet, regardless of Schaffer's and Emerson's commendable restraint in identifying cause and effect and the Weinraub and Lewis choice not to monitor maternal responding to infant protests during departures and after brief separations, the possibility remains that the pattern of infant protests cued by maternal departure behaviors, and the attachment index based on it, may result simply from *operant learning,* produced by well-intentioned, contingent maternal reactions to those protests in the departure setting itself. This possibility impeaches interpretations of the Schaffer and Emerson use of cued protests as their index of attachment because that index is hostage to the idiosyncratic patterns of maternal contingent reactions to cued protests (Gewirtz, 1972b, 1976). In particular, the process variables manipulated in the experiment reported here include the provision of *contingent* stimuli by the mother during her departure by a standard set of her reactions. These maternal behaviors are of the same class as the mother stopping, retracing her steps, hesitating, vacillating, turning to, speaking to, reasoning with, demonstrating verbal concern about leaving, or returning after separation to hug or pick up her protesting child. Any of these contingent events potentially can function as reinforcing stimuli that raise the relative incidence of the child's protests, denoting that those protests are conditioned to the cues provided by the mother's preparations to leave, and her separations from, her child. The research reported later in this chapter sheds light on this thesis.

THE SOCIAL-CONDITIONING APPROACH
TO ATTACHMENT

As in the ethological approach, the attachment *metaphor* has also served as a convenient process label in social–conditioning theory (cf. Gewirtz, 1961, 1972a, 1972b, 1977, 1978, 1991; Gewirtz & Boyd, 1977; Gewirtz & Peláez-Nogueras, 1987). However, unlike its usage in the ethological approach, in the social-conditioning approach attachment involves the acquisition of a close reliance, typically concurrent, of one individual's behavior upon the appearance and behavior stimuli of another, expressed in a variety of cued-response patterns of the former. The attachment metaphor has served to label this influence process that is denoted by the complex of child-response patterns coming to be cued and reinforced/maintained by stimuli provided by the appearance and behavior of an attachment figure/object; in early life primarily the mother, but can also include the father, siblings, grandparents, and/or servants. The child-response pattern might maintain contact proximity, produce attention, comfort, or the like. In this frame, attachment also has labeled concurrent reflections of the aforementioned process, such as the child's differential responding favoring the maternal attachment figure, or by increases in child exploratory behavior in her presence, as well as a child's protests upon a mother's departures. Also, the term *attachment* may be applied to organize a child's behavior upon its disruption due to rejection by, separation from, or the death of, the attached figure, when that behavior can become highly disorganized and may be accompanied by intense emotional/affective responding (distress) often with a concomitant failure to thrive. The cued-response patterns denoting attachment are pervasive and may occur in any segment of the life span, from infancy through late adulthood, and with any interaction partners, for instance, mother and child, wife and husband, person and animal, as well as friends or lovers.

In this social-conditioning account, the dyadic functional relations between the discriminative (cue) and reinforcing stimuli from an attachment figure/object and the child's responses to that figure (that those stimuli cue) that connote attachment, may involve several object persons concurrently, as well as concurrent influence (i.e., bidirectional) patterns; for instance, mother-to-child and child-to-mother. Moreover, initiations could be maintained if only intermittently reciprocated across occasions by an attachment figure. The discriminated operants denoting attachments are not to be conceived as cross-situational traits. By definition, they are controlled by particular cue and reinforcing stimuli from the attachment object, as well as by contextual stimuli (including setting conditions), so their occurrence will vary across situations otherwise defined.

Under this conception, the cued departure/separation protest may well be a prototypic learned behavior during the child's socialization that is, at the same time, representative of the pattern of infant responses cued and reinforced by stimuli provided by the appearance and behavior of the mother (or a significant other). In the frame of this social-conditioning approach, the infant departure/separation protest can serve as one of a number of reasonable indices of infant attachment to its mother (as object), insofar as attachment is seen as a metaphoric abstraction for such discriminated operants of the infant under the control of maternal stimuli (Gewirtz, 1972b, 1978).

In life settings, mothers are often found who, instead of responding immediately, appropriately, and consistently to their infant's initiations or protest-precursor signals, typically do not respond until the infant makes an intense expressive response, for example, by crying. If such cued infant responses were to be monitored in these contexts and found to increase in rate (or another response attribute), one might suspect that the mothers have been reinforcing lengthy, intense protest patterns in their infants. Numerous mother-infant dyads may adopt this pattern of interaction as their normal mode of communication. This interactive pattern often implies bidirectional influence, with the mechanism maintaining the maternal responding to infant protests in these situations that of *negative reinforcement* (Gewirtz, 1977; Gewirtz & Peláez-Nogueras, 1987). The same maternal responses that reinforce positively the infant behavior can come under the close negative–reinforcer control of the *cessation* of the infant's (aversive) protests contingent on these maternal responses.

Reported here are early results from a laboratory study mounted to ascertain if, and how, infant protests can come under the acquired control of maternal and contextual stimuli generated by mothers' contingent behaviors during departures and after brief separations. The demonstration that infant protests cued by maternal departures and brief separations can be maintained by contingent maternal responding would provide presumptive evidence for the *learned* basis of the departure/separation protests that have served as attachment and "distress" indices in life settings. This demonstration would also detail an important instance of social learning in early life, as well as provide some understanding of the case where the very same pattern of maternal responding to the infant's cued protests (that appeals to some conceptions of loving mothering) can generate problems of infant-behavior management that prevent the constructive fostering of developmentally–appropriate, healthy behaviors.

METHOD

Research Tactics

This experiment was mounted to illustrate in detail how departure and separation conditions, separately, can acquire stimulus control over the infant's protests by providing discriminable cues that denote (a) a mother's departure including her preparations to leave the infant's vicinity: saying "bye, bye," touching the infant, picking up her purse, walking towards the door, and/or waving her hand; and (b) a mother's separation, including the sight and sound of her opening the door, exiting, and closing the door, and the loss of sight of the mother. The infant protest response manifested in the presence of these discriminative stimuli was shaped differentially by the contingent stimuli. For instance, during departures the frequent responding of a mother contingent on her infant's protests or their precursors should shape and condition (i.e., affect more frequently and/or intensely) her infant's protests; and during separations by her contingent return to her infant from outside the room.

Shaping and Differential Reinforcement.   The shaping procedure involves systematic provision of the maternal responses contingent upon *successive approximations* of the infant responses to the target response, in this case, protesting. For instance, an infant's vocalizations may be shaped into an intense protest across sessions by the mother responding only to successive increases in their duration, amplitude, or some other response feature. In this way, what originally may have started as an incidental vocalization or protest precursor during preseparation events might be shaped ultimately into an intense protest. The protest response involved is then routinely followed by contingent maternal responding and is sometimes termed *CRF* (*continuous reinforcement*). On the other hand, if a mother were to cue her child that she is departing (e.g., "Bye bye, I'll be right back") and to leave her infant's vicinity without vacillation or apparent concern (whether or not the infant were to protest in reaction to the maternal departure cues), the infant's responses would not be shaped into a protest pattern and conditioned to maternal departure cues.

Another procedure (sometimes termed *DRO*) involves *differential reinforcement of behaviors other than the target,* in which the target protest is ignored and other more desirable responses are followed by contingent maternal responding. The differential–reinforcement–of–behaviors–other–than–the–target procedure can be combined with shaping. In this way, for each instance of the protest response, increasingly lengthy pauses are required for the mother to respond, until the nonoccurrence of a protest cues the mother's response to her infant. Then, the mother responds contingently only to alternative infant behaviors (e.g., vocalizations, smiles, and/or play). Using this procedure for several training sessions in laboratory settings, a conditioned high protest rate can be reduced, even discontinued, with the child then exhibiting behaviors incompatible with protests.

The experimental paradigm employed here facilitates maximizing between-treatment differences (effects) while minimizing interindividual and intraindividual differences. Between-treatment differences were heightened by establishing the two treatments as logical opposites at extremes of the dimension ranging from contingent to noncontingent maternal stimulation. Intrasubject score variability was minimized by using a within-subject repeated-measures design, in which each subject is subjected to the same treatment for several sessions, until the response stabilizes (Barlow & Hayes, 1979; Kazdin, 1982). Intersubject differences (such as differences in temperament, history of experiences in separation contexts, age, and cognitive abilities) should be minimized by requiring that a behavioral *criterion* be attained by each subject. In this way, every infant subject received a maximal dose of each treatment that could contribute to override (or at least minimize) each subject's unique reinforcement history, thresholds, capacities, and experiences. Under the research plan outlined, treatments were implemented and behavior outcomes examined in a laboratory setting in which relatively much control was exercised over the proximate conditions thought to be causal (i.e., the independent variables).

Subjects and Setting

The research procedure involved bringing 23 middle-class infant-mother pairs into the laboratory for successive, daily sessions (ranging from 6 to 11), each lasting about 35 minutes. The normal middle-class babies ranged in age from 6 to 11 months at the start of their participation in the study. The sample included 15 males and 8 females. Mothers of participating subjects reported them capable of remaining in a playpen comfortably for at least 20 minutes without crying. Seven infants dropped out the study at different points; four because their mothers stated they found the daily visits too taxing, and three because their mothers took part-time jobs and thus had not the time to continue the daily visits. A daily session was postponed when a mother reported that her child was "out of sorts" or off schedule, that she had rushed to get him/her to the laboratory on time, or that the subject or subject's sibling was ill.

Infants were placed in a 1–meter–square playpen, containing several simple toys (e.g., blocks, plastic animals), located in the far corner from the entrance/exit door of a yellow, windowless, 15–meter–long by 5–meter–wide room with children's paintings decorating the wall. An easy chair on which the mother sat at the start of a trial was positioned adjacent to the playpen. Two television cameras located in the room concurrently monitored the expressions and behavior of the infant in the playpen and of the mother as she sat near the playpen and then walked from her seat to and through the door while cueing and responding either contingently or noncontingently to her infant's protests, depending on the treatment in force. In an adjacent observation room, the synchronized behavior of infant and mother in interaction was displayed on a video monitor in split-screen format and recorded on videotape. From the observation room video monitor, two experimenters could view the mother-infant interaction in the laboratory, at the same time as one of them was directing the mother's actions via earphone, instructing her on when and how to give the departure cues and when and how to respond to the infant initiations. (For each of the 23 mothers, a routine departure style was requested and noted in a preliminary trial.)

Response Definitions

The outcome measure used under both conditions was the proportion of trials-per-daily session on which the infant made a cued protest. Infant protests during the departure, separation and reunion, and control periods were scored, with the exact time of occurrence noted. The proportion of play activity was also scored separately for each treatment condition.

A *protest* was defined as a whine, whimper, fuss, or cry sound emitted by the infant in response to the cues provided by a mother's departure or separation.

A *cry* was defined as a shrill, intense, continuing, or lengthy duration rhythmic wail, typically accompanied by tears and a grimace, furrowed brow, red face, and/or sad expression. When an *elicited* (respondent, reflexive) cry occurred (due putatively to physical discomfort, pain, sleepiness, hunger), a session was terminated. Nonintense, short-latency, cries that were emitted in response to the maternal departure or separation cues (when the infant had not been engaged in elicited crying at all during the preceding period) were taken to be *instrumental* (operant) protests.

Play behavior was defined as any action of the child that employed playpen toys as distal (for looking/examining) or proximal (for manipulating) stimuli, not dependent on the mother. Play acts usually involved manipulating a toy or object of interest, searching for an object other than the mother, or viewing or focusing on surroundings, without actively focusing on or searching for the mother. During the occurrence of a protest, play was not scored even if a child had been manipulating a toy.

Dependent Measures

Proportion measures for protests and crying were calculated for each session across trials, separately for departure and separation settings. (To produce percentage measures, proportions were multiplied by 100.) Proportion of protests was determined by dividing the total number of trials that included a protest by the total number of trials in that session. Proportion of play was calculated by dividing total playing time by duration of the departure or separation setting condition. The number of trials per session ranged from five to eight, and was determined by each infant's tolerance of being in the playpen, registered during the first two sessions. (A trial consisted of departure, separation, reunion, and control periods; see procedure).

Interobserver Agreement. Pairs of independent observers scored the time and events as they occurred. Five observers were involved in all. One of the observers helped the experimenter in the timing of instructions to the mother, particularly on when the mother should leave/return to the room, and in determining whether or not the subject's response pattern attained the criterion. Observer–reliability determinations in the scoring of protests, amount of playing, crying in each session, and latencies for protests were made subsequently from the videotape records. Percentage of agreement on a behavior category was obtained by dividing the total number of agreements between the two independent observers by the total number of observations (agreements plus disagreements). An agreement was scored when both observers recorded a given behavior occurrence aligned within 1 sec under the same behavior category. A disagreement of commission was scored when two observers scored a behavior event under two categories. A disagreement of omission involved a tally being entered by one observer but not by the other. Whenever a disagreement between two independent observers occurred, a third observer scored the segment in question for consensus for definitive record.

Two observers independently scored 573 trials comprising 103 sessions for 13 of the 23 subjects, on whether or not a cued protest occurred during a trial under each treatment, separately during departures and separations, whether or not it included a cry element, and the proportion of play per trial. Overall percentage observer agreement on cued protests was determined to be 94% for protests emitted during maternal departures, and 95% for protests emitted during brief separations. Overall percentage observer agreement on amount of play was found to be 85% during maternal departures, and 86% during the brief separations.

Procedure

Three repeated measures designs with two orders of treatment presentation were implemented. Nine infants served in an A–B–A (i.e., DRO–CRF–DRO) design; one infant served in an AB (i.e., an incomplete ABA) design; and 13 subjects served in a BA design (i.e., CRF-DRO). Mother–infant dyads were assigned randomly to either an ABA or a BA design group, in which the two treatments (contingent vs. noncontingent responding) were introduced sequentially. The two groups differed only in treatment order, and were used to counterbalance for order-of-treatment presentation.

The *departure* condition began when a mother first cued her infant that she was leaving, and ended when she closed the room's door after exiting. The *separation* condition began at that point and lasted until the mother opened the door and reentered the room. Before the start of the first session (during a preliminary trial), mothers were instructed to leave the room as naturally as possible, as they would during routine departures in a familiar setting. The pattern of maternal behaviors was noted on this trial, and subsequently emphasized in experimenter's instructions via earphones to mothers during departure and separation settings across all treatment trial sessions.

There was a 5 min habituation period before the first trial of each daily session. Afterward, the experimenter signaled the mother to leave the room, initiating a trial. A trial consisted of a departure period ($M = 28$ sec), a period of maternal absence (5 min maximum), and a standard reunion period (15 sec). Infant protests during maternal departures (when the mother was responding to the infant and in full view), were considered operationally different from the protests occurring during separations (when the mother was out of sight and earshot), and were assumed to be independent (uncorrelated). (An empirical demonstration of the independence between the departure and separation contexts for infant responding is presented in Gewirtz and Peláez-Nogueras, 1989.) Each subsequent trial began after 1 min of a control period between trials had elapsed, and only if no observation of any infant protest or potential distress was noted during that period. This procedure was useful in precluding carry-over effects from one trial to the next.

The content and number of maternal cue and contingent stimuli (auditory, visual, tactile) presented to the infant subjects during the departure, separation, and reunion, and during the control period between trials, was under the close instructional earphone control of the experimenter. On every trial, the mother signaled her departures from the room explicitly and redundantly three times: first, by picking up her purse, standing up, and waving (e.g., she said "Bye bye,

I'll be right back") while turning toward the exit door; second, by starting to walk slowly to the door while giving the child a second verbal cue; and, third, once she had opened the door, by turning to look at her child and once more verbally signaling her departure in her usual style (as assessed in the preliminary trial), closing the door, and exiting the room. All maternal behaviors were under the moment-to-moment control of a sequence of instructions from the experimenter given via earphone.

In the *contingent*-stimulation treatment sessions, infant protests or precursors of protests to the departure cues were *always* followed immediately (within 2 sec) by maternal auditory and visual stimuli provided by her contingent responses (e.g., orienting towards the infant and saying "It's all right, Mommy will be right back" or "What's the matter?"), until the infant's response was shaped to a protest and the criterion was met. The criteria for terminating the contingent treatment and initiating the reversal treatment was for a protest to occur in at least 80% of the trials of a session, both for departures and separations, and the protest latency (i.e., the elapsed time between the onset of a maternal cue [S^D] and the onset of a protest) during departures had to be less than 5 sec on each of the last 3 trials of the last session. When the mother was outside of the room with the door closed during the separation condition, the baby's protest brought on contingent maternal responding, that is her immediate return to the room and approach to her infant while emitting her routine verbal responses.

Under the noncontingent-stimulation treatment on the other hand, the maternal response occurred either when the infant was *not* protesting or after at least 10 sec had elapsed from the offset of the most recent protest while the mother was departing. (It is recalled that this maternal response pattern can also be termed a *Variable DRO* schedule of reinforcement, wherein behaviors other than the target response are followed by maternal contingencies. In most instances, these other–than–protest behaviors were playing and vocalizing.)

After the protest criterion was attained under the contingent treatment in both the departure and separation contexts, the treatment was reversed. From that point on, the cued infant protest rate was decreased by providing *non*contingent maternal responding relative to protests for several sessions until a reversal criterion (< 17% of the protest trials) was met. In instances where a protest began during a maternal departure and continued into the ensuing separation context, that response was scored as a departure protest. A subsequent protest was scored as occurring during separation only after there had been at least a 10-sec pause after the previous departure protest and the mother was already outside the room. Under the noncontingent treatment in the separation setting, mothers were instructed initially to return to the infant only after there had been a 10–sec pause without protest and, when feasible, were sent back to their infants on successive trials with systematically increasing nonprotest pauses (30, 60, 90,

120, 150 sec, etc.). In this way, the pause or nonprotest period required for maternal responding (i.e:, her return to the infant) was increased gradually from 10 sec to 5 min. This time lapse served as one criterion for ending the noncontingent–separation treatment sessions. In the rare cases where elicited crying persisted for longer than 45 sec, the session was terminated.

In the event a protest did not occur under the contingent stimulation treatment when the separated mother was outside the experimental room, the maximum time of her absence was 5 min. In such cases of maximum elapsed time without protests, the mother was instructed to return to the room without looking at, or talking to, the infant. A new discrete trial began as usual after a 1-min between–trials *control period* had elapsed without an infant protest. This control period allowed the experimenter to insure that the baby, who was in the playpen, was in good form (not protesting), and not responding emotionally on apparently unconditioned grounds due to hunger, pain, or sleepiness, and, as indicated above, precluded potential carryover effects from one trial to the next, thus making the effects of the departure cues (S^Ds) more salient.

The *density* of maternal stimuli refers to the number and content of maternal responses (providing the cues and contingent or noncontingent stimuli either for protests or for alternative behaviors). For all subjects, the density of maternal stimulation provided was made comparable in both the contingent and the noncontingent treatments in the departure context and in the separation context. To equate the pattern and density of discriminative *cues* in the two treatments under experimenter instructions, both under the contingent and the noncontingent treatments, during a *departure* trial a mother emitted the same three short statements (each lasting approximately 3 sec) as *cues* (e.g., "Bye, bye, mommy will be right back," while looking towards her infant) and usually emitted the same number of similar short statements as either *contingent* or *non*contingent responses, depending on the treatment (e.g., "It's all right, Mommy will be back soon"; "Don't worry!"). For the *separation* trials, the mother's exiting, closing of the door, and absence were the only cues, and there was only one contingent or noncontingent response possible in each trial—the mother's return to the child. This procedure of equating the pattern of cues and contingencies precluded the possibility that the different effects of the treatments on the child-behavior pattern could be due to differential elicitation/stimulation/arousal resulting from the incidental fact of the maternal stimulation preceding the infant responses and not from the contingent responding (reinforcement) itself.

Additional Criteria for Terminating Treatments.   For both treatment–sequence groups, the final noncontingent–exposure session allowed for the reversal of the rate of cued protests before the infant left the project. Under the noncontingent reversal treatment, an infant's protest rate had to reduce to occur on one sixth or fewer of the total trials of a session, before the treatment was terminated. (Even so, it was necessary occasionally to shift treatments before these criteria were met in cases where the number of daily sessions reached six under one of the treatments.)

RESULTS

Protests

Results are based on 23 individual infant subjects, each of whom received a sequence of either two or three treatment conditions. The individual conditioning records of nine of these subjects, who were studied under conditions of the ABA design, are displayed in Fig. 2.2. Within–group analyses are presented for patterns of gross effects for individual subjects using nonparametric one–tail chi–square tests with 1 *df*. It makes sense to compare final–session–within–a–treatment scores between treatments for our repeated measures procedure in which a response criterion was employed to reverse or terminate a treatment. This logic of using a criterion to terminate a treatment and switch to a second one emphasizes the final–session score level (that represents the acquisition-curve asymptote) and deemphasizes such factors as the rate/rapidity (i.e., total number of trials or sessions per subject) in attaining the criterion level. Thus, the outcome measure used under all conditions was the percentage of trials–per–daily–session (range 5 to 8 trials per session, mode 6 trials) on which the infant made a cued protest.

In the contingent-responding-*second* sequence group (ABA), during departures 10 of 10 (1 df $X^2 = 10.00$, $p < .0025$, 1 tail) infants showed a rise in the percentage of trials with protests from the final noncontingent (A1) to the final contingent (B) session; and, during separations, 10 of 10 (1 df $X^2 = 10.00$, $p < .0025$, 1 tail) of these infants showed such a rise. Of these 10 subjects, 9 showed a rise in protests of 50% or more during departures (1 df $X^2 = 6.4$, $p < .01$, 1 tail) and all 10 showed a rise of 60% or more during separations (1 df $X^2 = 10$, $p < .0025$, 1 tail). In addition, for the 9 infants of the contingent-second sequence subjected to a final noncontingent (A2) condition series after the contingent (B) condition, 9 out of 9 (1 df $X^2 = 9.0$, $p < .0025$, 1 tail) showed a decline in the percentage of trials with protests from the final contingent to the final noncontingent session, during *both* departures and separations. Of these 9 subjects, 100% showed a decline of 50% or more during departures (1 df $X^2 = 9.0$, $p < .0025$, 1 tail) and 100% showed a decline of at least 60% during separations (1 df $X^2 = 9.0$, $p < .0025$, 1 tail).

In the contingent-responding *first* (of two) treatment sequence (BA), during maternal *departures,* 12 of 13 infant subjects (1 df $X^2 = 9.3$, $p < .0025$, 1 tail) showed a decline in the percentage-of-trials-with-protests from the final Contingent to the final Noncontingent session; and during maternal *separations,* 13

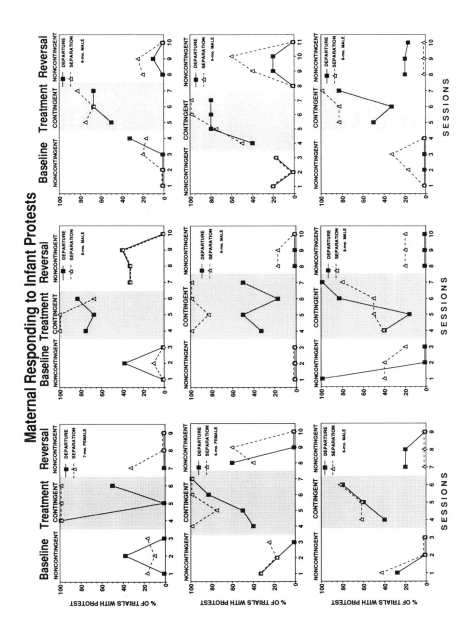

FIG. 2.2. Cued protest curves under each treatment for maternal departures and separations of each of the nine infant subjects of the ABA
(i.e., Noncontingent-Contingent-Noncontingent) design group.

33

of 13 (1 df $X^2 = 13$, $p < .0005$, 1 tail) of those infants showed such a decline. Of these 13 subjects, 10 (77%) showed a decline of 50% or more in the percentage of trials with protests during departures (range 00 to 100) (1 df $X^2 = 3.77$, $p < .03$, 1 tail) and all 13 subjects (100%) (1 df $X^2 = 13$, $p < .0005$, 1 tail) showed such a decline during the separations.

A composite conditioning curve based on the medians of the infant scores is presented separately for each of the two order-of-treatment groups, Noncontingent-stimulation first (Fig. 2.3, ABA, N=9) (the single AB subject is excluded from this composite figure), and Contingent–stimulation first (Fig. 2.4, BA, N=13). The composite patterns clearly indicate that protest conditioning and reversal have occurred for each treatment sequence, during both departures and separations.

In summary, it was found for all nine infants subjected to the Noncontingent-Contingent-Noncontingent (ABA) sequence, both before and after Contingent stimulation, both during departures and separations, as well as for the 13 infants subjected to the Contingent-Noncontingent (BA) sequence, that 12 during maternal departures and all 13 during maternal separations manifested cued–separation-protest patterns in accordance with an operant-learning interpretation: Infant cued-separation protests increased under maternal contingent responding, de-

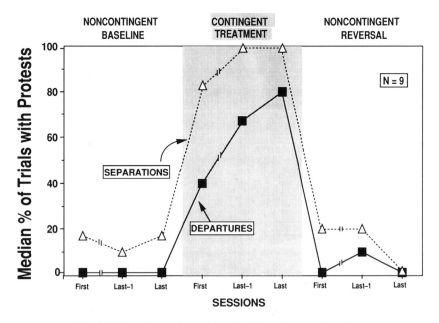

FIG. 2.3. Median Percentage Protest trials per session, for First, Last-1 (next-to-last), and Last session scores under each of the three mother-responding treatments, for maternal departures and for separations, based on the nine infants of the ABA design group.

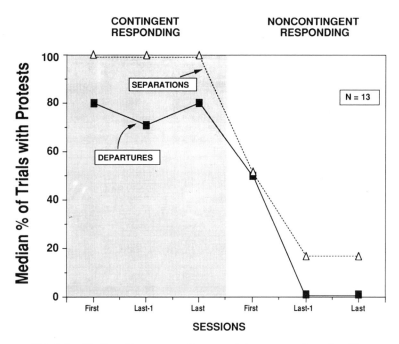

FIG. 2.4. Median Percentage Protest trials per session, for First, Last-1 (i.e., next-to-last), and Last sessions under each of the two mother-responding treatments, for maternal departures and separations, based on the 13 infants of the BA (i.e., Contingent-Noncontingent) design group.

creased under maternal noncontingent responding, and shifted upwards from noncontingent to contingent maternal responding and downwards from contingent to noncontingent maternal responding. As was noted in Fig. 2.3 and 2.4, the median pattern of changes manifested by the individual subjects in the aggregate was supported by statistically reliable chi square analyses from treatment to treatment.

Order of Treatment. Using the same gross-change statistical analysis focused on individuals, *no* reliable differences were found in the dependent measure being reported either between Contingent–first [B(A)] and Contingent–second [(A)B] sequences, or between Noncontingent–first [A(B)] and Noncontingent–second [(B)A] sequences. By this gross measure, the sequence of treatment presentation played no role at all in the findings.

Durations of Maternal Separation. Toward the end of the Noncontingent-stimulation treatment series during separations, mothers tended to remain outside the room reliably longer than under the Contingent-stimulation treatment and with minimal infant protesting. Thus, the mothers of every one of the nine ABA and the one AB infants (1 df $X^2 = 10.0$, $p < .0025$, 1 tail) showed a marked *decline* in the time they remained outside the room from the final Noncontingent-first to the final Contingent-second session. And the mothers of 18 of the 22 infants (pooling ABA and BA design group infants, but omitting the single AB design subject) (1 df $X^2 = 6.54$, $p < .01$, 1 tail) showed a marked *increase* in the time they remained outside the room from the final Contingent-second to the final Noncontingent-third session.

Play and Distress.   In this study, elicited infant crying occurred almost not at all. In this circumstance, an alternative-to-elicited-crying distress index was required. Such an index employed by earlier researchers for separation distress used the percentage of time during departure trials that the children engage in play activity, with lower play-time percentages assumed to denote distress (e.g., Weinraub & Lewis, 1977).

Infant's play performances were scored during both maternal departures and separations. For the pooled order-of-treatment groups, median percentage play scores are charted in Fig. 2.5 for departures and in Fig. 2.6 for separations. The composite pattern during maternal departures (Fig. 2.5) suggests that median

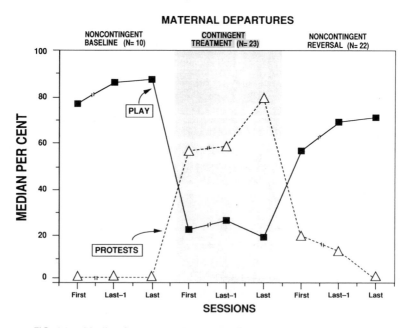

FIG. 2.5.   Median Percentage Play, and Median Percentage Protests, per session during Maternal *Departures,* for First, Last-1 (next-to-last) and Last sessions under each of the three treatments, based on all 23 infant subjects.

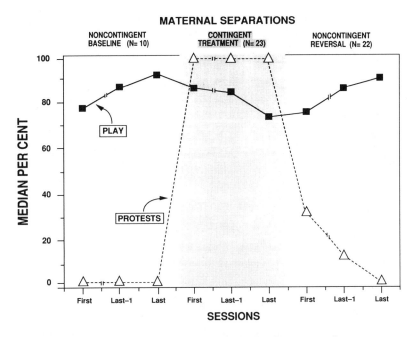

FIG. 2.6. Median Percentage Play, and Median Percentage Protests, per session during *Separations* from mother, for First, Last-1 (next-to-last) and Last sessions under each of the three treatments, based on all 23 infant subjects.

percentage play scores, possibly denoting distress, decrease concurrently with the increase in the median rate of protests that results from contingent maternal stimulation, and increase concurrently with the decrease in median protest rate resulting from noncontingent maternal stimulation. Although dramatic in the case of *departures*, that pattern is not at all pronounced in the case of *separations* (see the subsequent discussion).

To flesh out this inverse association between protests and play behavior, an analysis was done of changes in play of the noncontingent to and from the contingent stimulation treatments using 1 df chi squres. During *departures*, it was found that 9 of 10 infants of the ABA design showed a *decline* in play from the last Noncontingent–first (A1) session to the first, and to the last, Contingent–second (B) session (1 df X^2 = 6.4, p < .02, 2 tails in both instances), and that 22 infants pooled for BA and (A)BA designs manifested a rise in play from the last Contingent (B) session to the first, and to the last, Noncontingent–second (A2) session (1 df X^2 = 22, p < .0005, 2 tails in both instances). Hence, the composite inverse-association pattern clearly holds for departures.

The same inverse-association pattern holds more loosely during the brief *separations*. Six of nine (with one tie, p = ns) infants showed a decline in play from the *last* Noncontingent–first (A1) session to the *first* Contingent–second (B) session, and 7 of 10 infants (1 df $X^2 = 1.6$, $p > .20$, 2 tails) showed such a decline in play from the *last* Noncontingent–first (A1) to the *last* Contingent–second (B) session. Also, with one tie, 14 of the 22 pooled ABA plus BA infants exhibited a rise in play during separations from the *last* Contingent (B) session to the *first* Noncontingent–last (A2) session (1 df $X^2 = 2.34$, $p < .20$, 2 tails) and 20 of the 22 cases showed a play increase from the *last* Contingent (B) to the *last* Noncontingent (A2) session (1 df $X^2 = 14.72$, $p < .0005$, 2 tails). Thus, the between-treatments difference pattern in which play declines as protests rise during contingent stimulation holds saliently for departures and less dramatically for brief separations.

DISCUSSION

Separation Protests as a Learned Response Class

The result patterns reported support the assumption that, in life settings, infant protests separately to maternal departures and to maternal separations can be learned, trained by the mother incidentally to her purposes, in the departure and separation settings themselves. Further, the results support the assumption that such protests can be minimized or reversed by eliminating the contingencies that maintain them. These results from our laboratory-research program indicate that 6– to 11–month-old infants (actually closer to 7– to 12–month olds when their participation concluded) can be trained differentially to protest, and not to protest, to maternal departure or separation cues by the reinforcing contingencies produced by maternal responding. This learning/training could be occurring on similar bases in home or day care settings, though due there inadvertently to well–intentioned maternal/caregiver responding contingent on those infant protests in the departure or separation contexts. These contingencies might involve such behaviors as speaking to, explaining, or reasoning with the infant, as well as the mother vacillating, backtracking, or hesitating during her departure, showing concern, and/or returning to pick up or hug her infant after he/she emits a protest.

The Age Course of Protests

The results of the training reported put into question the assumed-unlearned "separation-protest" attachment index used by Schaffer and Emerson (1964) to chart the age course of attachment in the first 18 months of life (Fig. 2.1). In the 26 years since its publication, the interview-derived Schaffer and Emerson chart has been emphasized, nearly without exception, to represent the developmental course of attachment in introductory child-developmental psychology textbooks. For some examples, see Hall, Lamb, and Perlmutter (1986), Hetherington and

Parke (1986), Helms and Turner (1986), Liebert and Wicks-Nelson (1981), Santrock (1988), Santrock and Bartlett (1986), Santrock and Yussen (1987), and Schaffer (1979; 1985; 1988). There is also a similar question about the 9-month or so age–of–onset and the temporal course of separation fear/anxiety/distress, as denoted by observed separation protests, summarized for several cultural groups by Kagan et al. (1978).

In the laboratory research we have reported here, high rates of departure protests and of separation protests were conditioned in infants as young as 6 months of age; an age at which infants ordinarily would not protest at separations according to Kagan et al. and to Schaffer and Emerson (1964). Under the contingent–maternal responding treatment, at 6 months 100% (i.e., all six) of our infant subjects protested their mother's departures, as did 100% of our three subjects age 7 months, three subjects age 8 months, seven subjects age 9 months, three subjects age 10 months, and one subject age 11 months. In the more natural nontraining circumstances reported by Kagan et al. for four culture groups and in the home-care and day-care groups at ages 5 to 10 months, as well as for the Schaffer and Emerson data, far lower percentages of infants manifested departure/separation protests at our subjects' age points. Moreover, no significant differences were detected between the 6– plus 7–month–old infant subjects and the 10– plus 11–month-old infant subjects of this study in the number of treatment sessions required for them to reach criterion responding.

With respect to the Schaffer and Emerson (1964) and the Kagan et al. (1978) reports of the age course of protests at separation, our view is that there should be continuity in an infant's protest pattern across age as long as there is continuity across age in the contingent maternal behavior maintaining that protest pattern. Declines in protests, for instance like that observed by Kagan et al. after 18 months, simply may reflect a change in the style of maternal responding to infant departure/separation protests, perhaps due to developmental advances in the infant's behavior repertory.

This research has reported that (a) protests during departures were conditioned on an operant basis in 22 of 23 infants; and (b) protests during brief separations from the mother were conditioned on the same basis in all 23 infants. The infant subjects ranged in age from 6 to 11 months. As with other demographic-type variables (e.g., culture group, social status, sibling position, geographic location), the *age-in-months* (against which the separation-protest scores were plotted by Schaffer and Emerson and by Kagan et al.) is not, in itself, a psychological variable; it must be reduced to the causal variables required by the extant psychological theories to function as proper input variables (Baer, 1970; Gewirtz, 1969). Hence, in a process analysis the infants' age could not be considered to be the causal process variable responsible for the developmental changes observed.

Schaffer and Emerson had reported the onset and rise in separation protests within the 6- to 12-month age range, which they took to denote focused attachment. Under our methodology, *no* age differences were found in the conditioning and reversibility of infant protests either to maternal departure or to separation cues. Protests were conditioned in every boy and girl subject in the 6- to 11-month range, the age span in which Schaffer and Emerson and Kagan et al. detected the onset and rise of such protest patterns. The findings we have reported, showing that separation protests and departure protests can be operant conditioned throughout the 6- to 11-month age range both for girls and boys, is compatible with the logic cited earlier that age, *not* a proximal causal variable, cannot explain the process involved in the learning of such infant outcome patterns. (In the present study, the main proximal variable was contingent vs. noncontingent maternal responding). This finding suggests that infants can learn to protest, or not to protest, maternal departures or separations, due to differential contingent maternal responding (as reinforcers).

Cued Protests and Attachment

A corollary of our finding that protests can be conditioned on an operant basis is that, by using separation protests to index attachment, Schaffer and Emerson made their conception of attachment hostage to the idiosyncratic factors underlying whether or not, and how, mothers respond to their infants' departure or separation protests. Schaffer and Emerson did not propose that such idiosyncratic maternal factors as maternal responding contingent on the infant protests during separations were at all relevant to their attachment conception.

On the other hand, it was noted for the social–conditioning approach that infant attachment is a metaphor for infant discriminated operants being under maternal–stimulus control. In this context, cued departure or separation protests like those trained in this experiment may be prototypic *learned behaviors* during socialization that can represent the pattern of infant responses cued and reinforced by stimuli provided by the mother's appearance and behavior. On this basis, in the first 18 months of life, cued protests can serve well as a representative index of infant attachment to mother (Gewirtz, 1972b, 1978).

Infant Distress

Elicited intense crying resulting from identified antecedent causes (e.g., hunger, discomfort, or pain) or the treatments of this experiment was found almost not at all in this study. On a very few occasions, such intense infant crying was elicited by apparent physical hurt due to falling from a standing position or hitting self in face with a toy or an object. Further, insofar as protests included brief cries, emphasis in the study being reported here was on nonelicited instrumental or operant cries and their considerable potential for controlling maternal behavior. (As components of the operant protest–response class, such instrumental cries represented 18% of protest–response class occurrences.).

The emphasis of this research has been upon the child's protest response and how it can be reinforced/encouraged by contingent maternal responding and nonreinforced/discouraged by *non*contingent maternal responding, both during departures and after brief separations. The question that remains is: Are the children experiencing distress at the times their protests, cued by maternal departures or separations, are being manifested? Elicited crying like that due to pain might be taken as one index of distress (Kagan et al. 1978; Weinraub & Lewis, 1977). However, as earlier noted, elicited crying appears not to have occurred due to the treatments of this experiment and, on those few occasions when it did occur, appeared elicited only by physical hurt (falling over, hitting self in face with a block). On the basis of the incidence of elicited crying as a distress index, therefore, there was little if any overt distress manifested in the research contexts.

Based on the fact that the treatments of this study seem not to have produced elicited crying, it was reasonable to use an alternative-to-crying distress index: the percentage of time during departure and separation trials that the children engaged in *play activity*, with lower play-time percentages taken to denote distress (after Weinraub & Lewis, 1977; Kagan et al., 1978). Infant subjects' play performances were scored during both departures and separations, for both contingent and noncontingent treatments. However, once infant protests came under the differential control of the maternal contingencies, play time was necessarily greater in the noncontingent (DRO) than in the contingent (CRF) departure and separation settings, with increases in play associated with decreases in protests.

One explanation of finding little if any distress manifested in this study is that, in contexts where maternal responding is contingent on infant protests, those cued protests necessarily reflect close stimulus control that could preclude the occurrence of incompatible behavior like play. The child was simply involved in protesting and, hence, could not be playing. Therefore, lower play-time percentages do not necessarily reflect distress in strong stimulus-control circumstances. At the same time, it was seen that another presumptive distress index, elicited crying, almost never occurred in this study. On both grounds, distress may not have been manifested in this study.

Implications

It has long been assumed in the child-care literature that proper caregiving requires that the mother or caregiver respond to alleviate the physical distress underlying various elicited (unconditioned, reflexive, expressive) behaviors, such as intense crying (resulting from identified antecedent causes, e.g., hunger, pain). The core aspect of maternal sensitivity as defined by Ainsworth's attachment theory is responsiveness to the infant's signals in communication (Ainsworth & Bell, 1977). Nevertheless, a sensitive caregiver should be able to discriminate between her child's instrumental (manipulative) protests and her child's pained, elicited crying (Gustafson & Harris, 1990). The problem emphasized in this paper is that, in caregiving situations in life, mothers often provide an abundance of *misplaced* contingencies to their infants' behaviors, which can encourage developmentally inappropriate behaviors. A remedy is provided by maternal *discriminated responsiveness* to their infant's behaviors. A sensitive mother responds differentially to her infant's protests, cries, or other initiations, based on her knowledge of antecedents of the response, of the particular context, and of her infant's idiosyncrasies.

Noncontingent Responding is not Unresponsiveness

To date, the profound effect of contingent events on children's behavior and on their socio-cognitive development is unquestionable. We conceive a *responsive mother* to be one who is sensitive in responding differentially contingent to her infant's behaviors, with appropriate, timely, and consistent reactions. This mother would be unlikely to provide misplaced contingencies. Thus, the discrepancy between the Stayton and Ainsworth (1973) interpretation of their findings that the infant's separation protest was positively associated with maternal "unresponsiveness to," "ignoring of," or delay in responding to, her child's cries, and Gewirtz and Peláez-Nogueras (1987) behavior-analytic view of those same maternal behaviors, seems to be attributable to the different a) conceptualizations of "maternal unresponsiveness" to protest/crying in the separation context, b) methodologies employed by the theorists, and c) conceptions of the role, and units, of time. Stayton and Ainsworth equated an unresponsive mother with a mother whose response or return to her infant is delayed, constituting "ignoring" (as did Bell & Ainsworth, 1972, in the report that infant crying results from maternal unresponsiveness). Such a view is not possible within a behavior–functional analytic account, where a delay in responding to an initiation (e.g., a protest) is very different from being unresponsive to the initiation; and where the conditions of returning after a delay may relate to new/different behavior omitted by the child. Thus also, an "unresponsive" mother (using the Stayton and Ainsworth term) could shape effectively the infant's loud, lengthy, protests and/or cries by ignoring short, low–intensity protest/cries and responding *only* to high–intensity and long–duration protest/cries of her child. The inclination of this mother actually may be to ignore her infant's protest when its needs have been met, but she may be inconsistent and sometimes respond to the protest only intermittently, particularly when it is lengthy or intense.

In yet another contrast, a consistently responsive mother may foster behavior incompatible with her infant's protest (e.g., smiles, vocalizations, playing); she may respond with dispatch only to short, low–intensity precursors of her infant's crying or to nonprotesting behavior, this way rearing a child who protests or cries rarely. This last instance is like the one described by Bell and Ainsworth (1972) and Stayton and Ainsworth, (1973) of a mother "sensitively responsive" to the signals of her infant. The infant, therefore, has less occasion to protest but more occasion for effectively emitting signals to the mother. At a gross level, a pattern of *delayed maternal responding,* like the pattern reported by Stayton and Ainsworth, could have contributed to finding a positive correlation between infant separation protests and maternal "ignoring" or "unresponsiveness."

The analysis of the dyadic interaction provides detailed information of the potential effects of both *contingent* and *noncontingent* maternal responding to infant protests in departure and separation contexts. An illustration was presented of some of the potential pathways to the child's development of inappropriate behavior patterns (e.g., fussing, instrumental crying, rage, and protests) that may flow from these early mother-infant patterns of interaction and eventually interfere with the child's social competence. The significant results of the research reported here provide some basis for designing preventive interventions that parents and/or caregivers might use to preclude, eliminate, or minimize problem behavior of the child while potentially increasing incompatible and more developmentally-appropriate behavior patterns. The extent to which maternal responses are contingent on infant protests more than on other infant behaviors (e.g., exploratory play, smiles, vocalizations) will result in an increase in the infant's protest rate and in a reduction in latencies of these responses to the mother's cues. In contrast, mothers who are contingently responsive to their babies' smiles or vocalizations, or who talk to their infants at play, tend to produce babies that protest neither to her departure cues nor her separation cues.

CONCLUSIONS

The laboratory analysis of contingent maternal behavior that can condition/train and maintain infant departure and separation protests has generated:

1. A basis for understanding features of social conditioning in early human life, in particular social discriminative operants that can index the attachment process.

2. An instance of early infant social learning, namely of protests cued by departures and by separations, and of some maternally–mediated proximal environmental conditions responsible for their acquisition and maintenance.

3. A basis for minimizing or eliminating unconstructive infant behaviors, such as departure or separation protests and the potential distress involved; in this instance by mothers employing noncontingent (differential responding to behaviors other than protests) rather than contingent maternal responding to the protests.

4. An illustration of the place of laboratory experiments in providing leverage over questions and solutions for problems that exist in the real world.

In addition to detailing an important instance of social learning in early life, the study provides some understanding of the case where the very pattern of maternal responding to the infant's cued protests (that appeals to some conceptions of "positive/loving mothering") can generate problems of infant-behavior management that preclude the constructive fostering of developmentally-appropriate and more advanced infant social and cognitive behaviors.

Appreciating the maternal/caregiver role in separation problems and in procedures to eliminate them provides a basis for understanding early child social development and the parent-child interaction process, and for applying these principles/procedures to family, day care, and school settings. It is conceivable that, in such other settings as the home and day–care center, other of the child's instrumental responses emitted during maternal departures and separations could also be trained inadvertently by caregiver reactions like those provided contingent upon infant protests. Understanding the mechanisms involved in the infants' and adults' contingent responses in interaction can illuminate the "pathological" as well as the "normal" development of the child.

REFERENCES

Ainsworth, M. D. S., & Bell, S. M. (1977). Infant and maternal responsiveness: A rejoinder to Gewirtz and Boyd. *Child Development, 48,* 1208–1216.

Baer, D. M. (1970). An age-irrelevant concept of development. *Merrill-Palmer Quarterly of Behavior and Development, 16,* 238–246.

Barlow, D. H., & Hayes, S. C. (1979). Alternating treatments design: One strategy for comparing the effects of two treatments in a single subject. *Journal of Applied Behavior Analysis, 12,* 199–210.

Bell, S. M., & Ainsworth, M. D. S. (1972). Infant crying and maternal responsiveness. *Child Development, 43,* 1171–1190.

Bloom-Feshbach, S., & Blatt, S. J. (1981). Separation response and nursery school adaptation. *Journal of the American Academy of Child Psychiatry, 21,* 58–64.

Blurton-Jones, N., & Leach, G. (1972). Behaviour of children and their mothers at separation and greeting. In N. Blurton-Jones (Ed.), *Ethological studies of child behavior* (217–247). Cambridge: Cambridge University Press.

Bowlby, J. (1960). Separation anxiety. *International Journal of Psychoanalysis, 41,* 89–113.

Field, T. (1984). Separation stress of young children transferring to new schools. *Developmental Psychology, 20,* 786–792.

Field, T., Gewirtz, J. L., Cohen, D., Garcia, R., Greenberg, R., & Collins, K. (1984). Leave-takings and reunions of infants, toddlers, preschoolers, and their parents. *Child Development, 55,* 628–635.

Field, T., Vega-Lahr, N., & Jagadish, S. (1984). Separation stress of nursery school infants and toddlers graduating to new classes. *Infant Behavior & Development, 7,* 277–284.

Fleener, D. E., & Cairns, R. B. (1970). Attachment behavior in human infants: Discriminative vocalization upon maternal separation. *Developmental Psychology, 2,* 215–223.

Gewirtz, J. L. (1961). A learning analysis of the effects of normal stimulation, privation and deprivation on the acquisition of social motivation and attachment. In B. M. Foss (Ed.), *Determinants of infant behaviour* (pp. 213–299). London: Methuen. (New York: Wiley).

Gewirtz, J. L. (1969). Mechanisms of social learning: Some roles of stimulation and behavior in early human development. In D. A. Goslin (Ed.), *Handbook of socialization theory and research* (pp. 57–212). Chicago: Rand-McNally.

Gewirtz, J. L. (1972a). Attachment, dependence, and a distinction in terms of stimulus control. In J. L. Gewirtz (Ed.), *Attachment and dependency* (pp. 179–215). Washington, DC: Winston.

Gewirtz, J. L. (1972b). On the selection and use of attachment and dependence indices. In J. L. Gewirtz (Ed.), *Attachment and dependency* (pp. 179–215). Washington, DC: Winston.

Gewirtz, J. L. (1976). The attachment acquisition process as evidenced in the maternal conditioning of cued infant responding (particularly crying). *Human Development, 19*, 143–155.

Gewirtz, J. L. (1977). Maternal responding and the conditioning of infant crying: Directions of influence within the attachment-acquisition process. In B. C. Etzel, J. M. LeBlanc, & D. M. Baer (Eds.), *New developments in behavioral research: Theories, methods, and applications.* Hillsdale, NJ: Lawrence Erlbaum Associates, Inc.

Gewirtz, J. L. (1978). Social learning in early human development. In A. C. Catania & T. Brigham (Eds.), *Handbook of applied behavior research: Social and instructional processes* (pp. 105–141). New York: Irvington Press.

Gewirtz, J. L. (1991). Social influence on child and parent via stimulation and operant-learning mechanisms. In M. Lewis & S. Feinman (Eds.), *Social influences and socialization in infancy,* (pp. 137–163). New York: Plenum Press.

Gewirtz, J. L., & Boyd, E. F. (1977). In reply to the rejoinder to our critique of the 1972 Bell and Ainsworth report. *Child Development, 48*, 1217–1218.

Gewirtz, J. L., & Peláez-Nogueras, M. (1987). Social-conditioning theory applied to metaphors like "attachment": The conditioning of infant separation protests by mothers. *Revista Mexicana de Análisis de la Conducta, 13*, 87–103.

Gewirtz, J. L., & Peláez-Nogueras, M. (1989, April). Infant protesting to maternal departures and separations: A conditional discrimination process. Paper presented at the biennial meeting, Society for Research in Child Development, Kansas City, Missouri.

Gustafson, G. E., & Harris, K. L. (1990). Woman responses to young infants' cries. *Developmental Psychology, 26*, 144–152.

Hall, E., Lamb, M. E., & Perlmutter, M. (1986). *Child psychology today* (2nd. ed.). New York: Random House.

Helms, D. B., & Turner, J. S. (1986). *Exploring child behavior* (3rd. ed.). Monterey, CA: Brooks/Cole.

Hetherington, E. M., & Parke, R. D. (1986). *Child psychology: A contemporary viewpoint* (3rd. ed.). New York: McGraw-Hill.

Kagan, J., Kearsley, R. B., & Zelazo, P. R. (1978). *Infancy: Its place in human development.* Cambridge, MA: Harvard University Press.

Kazdin, A. E. (1982). *Single-case research designs: Methods for clinical and applied settings.* New York: Oxford University Press.

Liebert, R. M., & Wicks-Nelson, R. (1981). *Developmental psychology* (3rd.ed.). Englewood Cliffs, NJ: Prentice-Hall.

Piaget, J. (1954). *The construction of reality in the child* (M. Cook Trans.). New York: Basic Books.

Rheingold, H. L., & Eckerman, C. D. (1970). The infant separates himself from his mother. *Science, 1968*, 78–83.

Rheingold, H. L., & Eckerman, C. D. (1971). Departures from mother. In H. R. Schaffer (Ed.), *The origins of human social relations* (pp. 73–82). London: Academic Press.

Santrock, J. W. (1988). *Children.* Dubuque, IA: W. C. Brown.

Santrock, J. W., & Bartlett, J. C. (1986). *Developmental psychology: A life-cycle perspective.* Dubuque, IA: W. C. Brown.

Santrock, J. W., & Yussen, S. R. (1987). *Child development: An introduction* (3rd ed.). Dubuque, IA: W. C. Brown.

Schaffer, H. R., & Emerson, P. E. (1964). The development of social attachments in infancy. *Monographs of the Society for Research in Child Development, 29*(3, Serial No. 94).

Shaffer, D. R. (1979, 1988). *Social and personality development* (1st and 2nd ed.) Monterey, CA: Brooks/Cole.

Shaffer, D. R. (1985). *Developmental psychology: Theory, research, and applications.* Monterey, CA: Brooks/Cole.

Stayton, D. J., & Ainsworth, M. S. (1973). Individual differences in infant responses to brief, everyday separations as related to other infant and maternal behaviors. *Developmental Psychology, 9,* 226–235.

Weinraub, M., & Frankel, J. (1977). Sex differences in parent-infant interaction during free play, departure, and separation. *Child Development, 48,* 1240–1249.

Weinraub, M., & Lewis, M. (1977). The determinants of children's responses to separation. *Monographs of the Society for Research in Child Development, 42,* 4, (Serial No. 172).

3 Maternal Self-Efficacy and Response to Stress: Laboratory Studies of Coping With a Crying Infant

Wilberta L. Donovan
Lewis A. Leavitt
University of Wisconsin-Madison

Among the most stressful and vexing child-care tasks is attending to a crying infant. In recent years, our laboratory has tried to understand how infant caregivers' response to infant crying is affected by (a) their perceptions and expectations of their infants, and (b) their experience in dealing with child-care tasks. Our findings suggest that a mother's response to the stress of attending to a crying infant is related to her perception of how effective she is in addressing the task of managing a crying infant. She may respond appropriately, and by controlling the cry she will feel successful in her childrearing endeavor. Her self-efficacy in turn influences her ability to respond in a sensitive, contingent manner as she continues to parent. Alternatively, she may be unsuccessful and thereby develop feelings of inefficacy. Our research suggests that to the degree that the mother believes she is ineffective in managing infant crying, nonoptimal caregiving can arise that in turn may result in negative consequences for the infant (Donovan & Leavitt, 1989).

Because response to infant crying has such important ramifications for parent-infant interaction, an understanding of variables affecting response to this signal is essential. We have used laboratory simulations of child-care tasks to better understand the coping processes activated in response to a crying infant and to the demands of childcare in general. We have tried to delineate the psychological and physiological processes evoked in the development of effective versus ineffective coping during childcare. We have been particularly interested in the antecedents and consequences of variations in perception of control in the development of our model of maternal self-efficacy. The construct of self-efficacy is based on the notion that people who experience success develop the expectation that certain important events are controllable (Bandura, 1982). In this chapter we begin by presenting our model of maternal self-efficacy. This is followed by a presentation of those experimental studies conducted in our laboratory that contributed to the construction and testing of the model. We conclude with a discussion of the implications of our research for clinical studies of parent-infant interaction and response of parents to the stresses of daily child-care tasks.

MODEL OF MATERNAL SELF-EFFICACY

In our model of maternal self-efficacy, we view maternal response as being multiply determined by the mother's attributions about success and failure, her mood state, the availability of social support, and perception of infant temperament (see Fig. 3.1).

Borrowing from attribution theory (Heider, 1958; Kelley, 1973), we propose that the mother's response to her infant will be affected by her attributions about success and failure, especially in child-care situations. The concept of *attributional style* lends itself to the description of coping strategies. Attributional style refers to how one attributes motives and causes for behavior and outcome and encompasses three dimensions—internal/external, stable/unstable, and global/specific. A *self-serving attributional style* is a characteristic of individuals who perceive themselves to be effective actors in everyday life and reflects making internal, stable, and global attributions for positive outcomes; that is, ascribing good things to factors within oneself (internal), to factors that will occur again (stable), and to factors in other situations as well (global). For negative outcomes, the self-serving attributional style is comprised of making external, unstable, and specific attributions; that is, ascribing bad things to factors such as chance (external), a single episode (unstable), and in this situation only (specific). In contrast, making external, unstable, and specific attributions for positive outcomes, and internal, stable, and global attributions for negative outcomes has been labeled a *depression-prone attributional style* (Abramson, Seligman, & Teasdale, 1978).

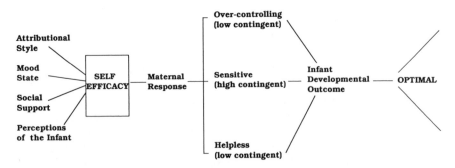

FIG. 3.1. Our model of maternal self-efficacy, its determinants and effects.

Varying attributions have been shown to be related to parental concepts of development (Sameroff & Feil, 1985), children's math performance (Holloway & Hess, 1985), and the socialization process of children (Dix & Grusec, 1985; Manusco & Handin, 1985). In response to the demands of childrearing, a parent's attribution about success or failure during parenting appears to act as a selective filter or sensitizer to child behaviors, with a mother with low self-perceived efficacy reacting negatively to the unresponsive child in a manner that reinforces unresponsiveness in the child (Bugental & Shennum, 1984).

In addition to attributional style, mood state may also adversely affect a mother's responsiveness to her infant. Depressed mood state has been associated with low self-efficacy (McCabe & Schneidermann, 1985) and has been shown to interfere with optimal caregiving behavior (Field, Sandberg, Garcia, Vega-Lahr, Goldstein, & Guy, 1985). Because parental mental health is particularly relevant in predicting the social competence of the child (Sameroff & Feil, 1985), clinicians are becoming increasingly concerned with the effect of less severe maternal depressive symptoms on the child's developmental outcome (Zuckerman & Beardslee, 1987).

Social support frequently counters less than optimal environments and is associated with increased sensitive, responsive, and involved maternal behavior (Crnic, Ragozin, Greenberg, Robinson, & Basham, 1983; Crockenberg, 1981, 1987). It appears that social support facilitates the maintenance of self-esteem in times of stress (Cohen & McKay, 1984), and exerts a protective function against maternal depression by enabling the mother to perceive herself as more effective (Cutrona & Troutman, 1986).

Lastly, infant temperament affects maternal response, including her perceptions and her physiological and behavioral responses. Studies indicate that parents perceive the cries of difficult infants to be more aversive, demanding and "spoiled sounding" (Lounsbury & Bates, 1982), as well as more grating, arousing, and piercing (Boukydis & Burgess, 1982) than the cries of easy infants. Boukydis and Burgess report that difficult infant cries elicit greater physiologic arousal than easy infant cries. Evidence is mixed as to the effect of perceptions of infant difficulty on maternal behavioral responsiveness. Although there are reports of lowered responsiveness of mothers who perceive their infants as difficult (Campbell, 1979; Milliones, 1978), others have found that the difficult infant elicits attentive behavior from the mother (Klein, 1984), or has no noticeable impact (Daniels, Plomin, & Greenhalgh, 1984).

Our model postulates that perceived self-efficacy is the mediating link between these determinants and maternal response, which in turn affects the developmental progress of the infant. Therefore, perceptions of *inefficacy* should lead to deviations from an optimal level of responding during caregiving, which then adversely affect developmental outcome. Those deviations proposed by the model involve variation in perception of control and can be characterized by either loss of control (withdrawal), or by greatly overestimating control (high illusory control). The model predicts that both manifestations of inefficacy create interaction patterns that interfere with the developmental progress of the infant.

In our research program, we have found that indexing physiologic substrates of the psychological processes activated while attending to environmental stimuli can enhance our understanding of the mother's perception of control as it relates to her self-efficacy. For a mother, being attentive to cues that signal the impending cry (CS), as well as to the cry itself (UCS), is an essential first step in controlling infant crying, and as such, reveals something about the mother's sense of competency in managing her crying infant. Therefore, in a two-stimulus paradigm (CS-UCS) such as ours, we look at this anticipatory cardiac response following CS onset because the anticipatory period can be divided into different phasic components which are identified as correlates of signal processing activity (Bohlin & Kjellberg, 1979). Increased magnitude of the accelerative component is interpreted as a measure of the UCS (i.e., cry) aversiveness, whereas increased magnitude of the second decelerative component is interpreted as a measure of "attentive" processing. Thus to measure the physiological concomitants of processing infant signals, we have turned to an analogue strategy as a means to study maternal coping during simulated child-care tasks.

EMPIRICAL TESTING OF THE MODEL

An abundance of data indicate that a mother's decreased responsiveness during social interaction with her infant decreases the infant's expectation of effectiveness and hence exploration and mastery of the environment. Therefore, we initially investigated how maternal perceptions of inefficacy associated with feelings of helplessness lead to withdrawal and reduced responsiveness. To this end, we turned to learned helplessness theory (Seligman, 1975) as a working model. The theory of learned helplessness holds that individuals exposed to uncontrollable events learn that responding is futile. Such learning undermines the incentive to respond. Decreased motivation to act is accompanied by feelings of failure and the inability to cope with future events.

Applying this theory to parenting behavior, it followed that as a mother learns to parent, her sense of competency during interaction with her child is related to learning that her efforts during interaction with her child are effective. With specific reference to coping with infant crying we proposed that a mother's history of success in controlling crying episodes is a reliable predictor determining her attention to and her ability to terminate infant crying. To the extent she has previously been unsuccessful, the resulting state of helplessness will interfere with current and future attempts to control crying.

In addressing this issue, we devised a simulated child-care task by modifying the helplessness paradigm and, as predicted by helplessness theory, we demonstrated that the mother's past experience with failure in terminating infant crying proactively interfered with performance on a second child-care task (Donovan,

1981). Mothers were first randomly assigned to one of three pretreatment groups designed to induce varying levels of helplessness by manipulating the control exercised over cry termination. Following exposure to the pretreatment, each mother was tested for susceptibility to learned helplessness on a second learning task. As predicted, when given the opportunity to terminate the cry on the second task, those mothers pretreated with inescapable infant crying (i.e., attempted but failed to stop the cry) showed debilitated performance measured by several learning criteria (see Fig. 3.2).

Importantly, different psychological processes appear to be activated during coping with the cry for these mothers on the helplessness task. The cardiac data demonstrated a positive relation between an "attentive" cardiac response and successful attempts by the mother at terminating the cry. During the session when all mothers had the opportunity to stop the cry, only mothers with prior experience controlling the cry showed the "attentive" response to the impending cry. These data indicate that differential processing of cues signaling the onset of crying may be a contributing factor to the observed behavioral differences in the ability to stop infant crying.

Thus, by employing the helplessness model in our study of maternal coping, we were able to assess factors potentially responsible for the proactive interference with the mother's sensitivity to her infant's signals. Following these findings, we were eager to assess the effect of an intervention designed to reduce the debilitating effects of prior experience with failure. For an intervention strategy, we drew upon attribution theory that predicts that an attribution for failure that is specific to a particular situation will be less likely to produce a state of helplessness than an attribution for failure that entails failing in many situations—a global attribution (Abramson et al., 1978). To test the effect of altering the mothers' attributions for failure, we told an intervention group that performance on the second task was unrelated to performance on the first. As predicted, the debilitating effects of prior experience with failure were countered in

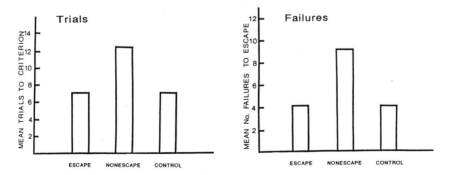

FIG. 3.2.   Mean number of trials to criterion and failures to escape for the three pretreatment groups.

the intervention group. These data have important implications in that, with this model, we are able to selectively manipulate variables, such as attributions about success and failure, and thus determine appropriate intervention strategies to prevent the adverse long-term developmental consequences predicted for the infant receiving unresponsive caregiving.

Our discussion so far has focused on delayed infant developmental outcome via interaction with mothers who are relatively less sensitive and more withdrawn due to feelings of helplessness. We now turn our attention to our most recent work that has focused on the second proposed pathway leading to developmental delay—over-controlling maternal behaviors—in our endeavor to define the antecedents and consequences of variations in perception of control as they relate to maternal self-efficacy.

In testing this second proposed pathway of nonoptimal responding resulting from perceptions of inefficacy, a second paradigm was employed to assess self-efficacy. Rather than expose mothers to failure and then test for susceptibility to helplessness, we eliminated exposure to failure and directly measured maternal perception of control over the termination of an infant cry. In contrast to the development of helplessness following failure, individuals who experience success should develop the expectation that important outcomes are controllable; and in fact, people often treat noncontingent events as if they were contingent, thus overestimating their own control and thereby exhibiting an *illusion of control* (Alloy & Abramson, 1979).

The simulated child-care task we use to assess perception of control is a modification of the illusion of control paradigm developed by Alloy and Abramson. Experimentally, control can be defined by the individual's estimation of the contingency between outcome and response. Hence the relation between experimentally controlled objective contingencies and a person's subjective judgment about contingencies can be studied in the laboratory. The illusion of control task involves making one of two responses to an event after which the subject is asked to estimate their perceived control over the event. In our simulated child-care task, the mothers responded to an audiotaped infant cry, their goal being the termination of the cry.

In our study (Donovan & Leavitt, 1989), each mother received 42 30-sec trials. Each trial was initiated by the onset of a 10-sec red light (CS) followed by cry onset (UCS). For the first 40 trials and for Trial 42, the onset of the UCS was simultaneous with CS offset. The cry stimulus was omitted on Trial 41 and then readmitted on Trial 42. The elicitation of cardiac deceleration at the omission of an anticipated event is used as an index of an "expectancy" process. Response to the readmitted UCS is of interest because the CS has acquired new meaning due to the uncertainty generated by the omitted UCS (Öhman, 1979; Siddle, 1985). Instructions stated that this was a problem-solving task, and that after the presentation of each cry, the mother had the option of either pressing or not pressing the button. Her response was followed by a fixed schedule of cry termination at 5 sec (success) on half of the trials or cry continuation for 20 sec (failure) on the other half (see Fig. 3.3).

Following the 42 trials, each mother estimated how much control she thought she had over the termination of the cry; that is, was one response more effective than the other. The task was designed as a zero contingency task in which neither response was more effective than the other in terminating the cry. Therefore, the mother's estimate of perceived control constituted her *illusion of control* score. Based upon illusion of control scores, mothers were divided into three groups: low, moderate, and high illusory control.

Before presenting the results from our study, let us state that illusory control is commonly viewed as an adaptive coping strategy of the healthy individual (Alloy & Abramson, 1979). However, based upon our results, we contend that illusory control has its limitations as a coping strategy in situations involving interpersonal interaction—a contention to be developed more fully after presenting our data. In fact, we argue that in these situations involving interpersonal interaction, *greatly* overestimating control, instead of being adaptive, actually masks inefficacy.

We found that mothers who *greatly* overestimated their control (i.e., exhibited high illusory control) had a depression-prone attributional style, were the most depressed, and reported the father as participating least in childcare. Physiologically, they alone exhibited an augmented accelerative component across trials to the impending cry (CS), interpreted as aversive conditioning, which is characteristic of a defensive response (see Fig. 3.4). Our argument that this is a defensive reaction is consistent with the proposal that the process of cardiac acceleration diminishes the effect of aversive stimuli (Lacey & Lacey, 1974) and furthermore, that this perceptual gating process reflects defensive behavior (Hare & Blevings, 1975). In contrast, mothers with low and moderate illusory control exhibited moderate attentive responses indicative of efficient signal processing.

PARADIGM:

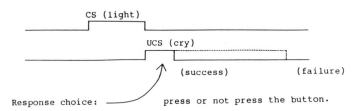

FIG. 3.3. Illusion of Control paradigm for the simulated child-care task.

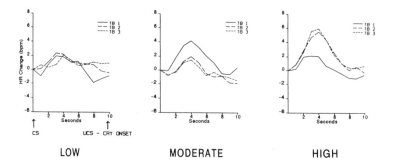

FIG. 3.4. Mean second-by-second changes in heart rate during the 10-sec CS period on the first six trials, blocked by two, as a function of illusion group.

We also looked at physiologic response to the cry signal (UCS). As expected, all mothers showed activation in response to the cry. However, with response habituation being recognized as an important aspect of behavioral plasticity (Siddle, 1985) and being linked to efficient processing, it is important to note that varying rates of habituation across trials differentiated mothers in the three groups. In contrast to the response habituation of mothers with low and moderate illusory control, mothers with high illusory control exhibited response modulation across trials that we interpreted as being associated with an ineffective coping process. Furthermore, mothers with high illusory control required more time to reach peak deceleration during the omission of the cry on Trial 41, indicating that these mothers were delayed (i.e., ineffective processing) in their recognition of the change in anticipated events (i.e., CS-UCS pairing).

It was this defensive responding, indexed physiologically, that led us to argue that high illusory control, instead of being adaptive, actually masks perceived inefficacy. Several studies link perceived inefficacy and physiologic indices of arousal. In anticipation of an aversive event, elevated blood pressure and cardiac acceleration are correlated with low perceived self-efficacy (Bandura, 1982). Knowing when an aversive event will occur without being able to exercise control increases anticipatory stress reactions (Gunnar, 1980; Miller, 1981). In contrast, the ability to exercise behavioral control over potentially aversive events eliminates or decreases autonomic reactions to them (Miller, 1981) and manipulations involving enhanced self-efficacy are followed by changes in physiologic responding (Bandura, 1982).

The finding that high illusory control appears to be limited in its effectiveness as a way of coping with child-care tasks prompted our next study in which we asked: Is the ability to learn to respond effectively and appropriately to infant signals more easily disrupted for mothers with high illusory control? To test this hypothesis, we turned back to the learned helplessness paradigm to test the prediction that inefficacy, this time masked by high illusory control, is marked by the mother's inability to learn appropriate responses during childcare. Would mothers with high illusory control show greater susceptibility to learned helplessness in our simulated child-care task as compared to mothers with low or moderate illusory control?

Mothers of 5-month-old infants participated in two simulated child-care tasks to examine differences in response to the performance demands of childcare (Donovan, Leavitt, & Walsh, 1990b). They first participated in the illusion of control task in which they estimated their perception of control over stopping an infant cry. One week later, they participated in the learned helplessness task to assess their ability to learn effective responses in stopping the cry.

As predicted, mothers who exhibited high illusory control over stopping an infant cry showed increased susceptibility to learned helplessness on three learning criteria (see Fig. 3.5). The increased susceptibility of these mothers provided further evidence that high illusory control, while indicating that the mother believed she was effective, is actually a masking of inefficacy.

Again, the physiologic data enhance our understanding of the benefits and limitations associated with the illusion of control phenomenon. The "attentive" response of cardiac deceleration to the impending cry during the solvable task of the helplessness session was clearly evident in mothers with moderate illusory control (see Fig. 3.6). Cardiac deceleration in anticipation of the cry was not seen in mothers with either low or high illusory control. However, because mothers with low illusory control performed very well on the solvable task (see Fig. 3.5), and because we find that mothers in this group are in most instances physiologically the least responsive (Donovan & Leavitt, 1989), we attribute this lack of deceleration to the impending cry to a consistently attenuated level of physiologic responding. On the other hand, mothers with high illusory control are typically reactive physiologically; thus their failure to exhibit a decelerative response to the impending cry cannot be attributed to attenuated responding.

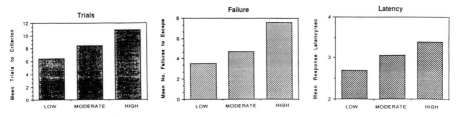

FIG. 3.5. Mean scores for each illusion group on the three learned helplessness measures.

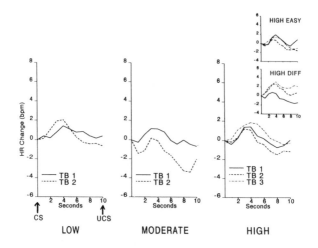

FIG. 3.6. Mean second-by-second changes in heart rate during the 10-sec CS period on trials, blocked by three, prior to reaching success criterion on the helplessness task as a function of illusion group, with detail for the High group as a function of infant temperament.

Instead, their failure to exhibit a decelerative response, coupled with poor performance on the helplessness task, is interpreted as "inattentiveness."

INFANT TEMPERAMENT AND ILLUSORY CONTROL

There is considerable agreement that temperament reflects an early-appearing, somewhat stable trait of the child's behavior, with considerable support for the assertion that the temperament-like variable of difficultness can be measured with validity (Bates, 1987). As stated, a number of studies have explored the link between the mother's perception of her infant's temperament and maternal responsiveness. Because the evidence is mixed as to the effect of infant difficulty on maternal response, Crockenberg (1986) has urged that we turn our attention to possible maternal measures or other contextual variables that interact with infant temperament to predict the outcome measure of interest. Indeed, we have consistently found that perception of control interacts with perception of infant temperament to predict maternal response.

In the studies described earlier, mothers with high illusory control with easy versus difficult infants are differentiated by their attitudinal and cardiac responses. On the illusion of control task, on Trial 42 when the cry was readmitted, mothers paired with difficult infants responded to the impending cry with cardiac acceleration, interpreted as aversive conditioning (see Fig. 3.7); furthermore, these mothers exhibited a depression-prone attributional style (Donovan & Leavitt, 1989). On the helplessness task, only mothers with high illusory control paired with a difficult infant exhibited aversive conditioning, as they reached success criterion (see Fig. 3.6) (Donovan et al., 1990b). Although mothers with moderate illusory control paired with a difficult versus an easy infant do not show differential physiological responses, they do show attitudinal and behavioral differences, in that those paired with a difficult infant showed a more depression-prone attributional style (Donovan & Leavitt, 1989) and greater susceptibility to helplessness (Donovan et al., 1990b).

On the other hand, mothers with low illusory control are not adversely affected if paired with a difficult rather than an easy infant. In fact, they not only exhibited a more self-serving attributional style, but also at the physiologic level these mothers were found to be more "attentive" if paired with a difficult infant; as demonstrated by the cardiac data from the illusion of control task (Donovan & Leavitt, 1989) (see Fig. 3.7). On the helplessness task, they were less susceptible to helplessness than those paired with easy infants (Donovan et al., 1990b). Together these data support the theoretical "goodness of fit" model (Lerner & Lerner, 1983; Thomas & Chess, 1977) by suggesting that, for a mother with low illusory control, difficulty may be construed in terms of a "challenge" rather than raise doubts about her capabilities.

Undoubtedly, temperament effects will best be understood when they are studied in conjunction with maternal variables (Crockenberg, 1986); yet, as researchers, we are confronted with the task of measuring infant temperament and maternal behavior independently to assess the contribution of each to the developing relationship. Most studies designed to assess the relation between infant temperament and interaction patterns lack this independence. Crockenberg has outlined three alternatives to untangle the confounding of these two variables, with one approach being the use of the experimental method to assess whether and how infant temperament affects caregiving behavior. Studies em-

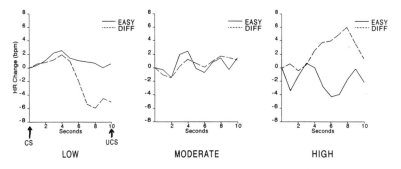

FIG. 3.7. Mean second-by-second changes in heart rate during the 10-sec CS period on Trial 42, following cry omission on Trial 41, as a function of illusion group and infant temperament.

ploying an experimental approach share in common the assessment of mothers' responses (e.g., physiological, psychological, or behavioral) while she interacts with "infants" identified (i.e., labeled) as differing reliably on some measure of temperament. With this approach, the powerful experimental techniques of random assignment to groups and control over stimulus presentation become available.

We have recently used the experimental approach to manipulate infant "difficulty" to study the effects of infant temperament on maternal perception of control and autonomic responding. In order to "mirror" differences in infant temperament, mothers were randomly assigned to one of two conditions in the illusion of control task: The cry stopped 75% of the time for the "easy infant" manipulation, or 25% of the time for the "difficult infant" manipulation. Our initial findings show that illusory control interacted with experimental condition to predict physiologic response. Mothers with high illusory control in both conditions exhibited the characteristic defensive response, thus indicating an insensitivity in these mothers to the experimental manipulation. Conversely, mothers with low and moderate illusory control did exhibit sensitivity to the manipulation as indicated by a differential response as a function of condition. For mothers with moderate illusory control, exposure to the "difficult" infant manipulation resulted in delayed habituation, indicating less efficient processing of the stimulus, whereas habituation for mothers with low illusory control was not adversely affected by "difficulty" (Donovan, Leavitt, & Walsh, 1990a). We interpret these differences in maternal response to temperamental differences among infants as evidence that experience with infant crying plays an important role in the determination of differing coping strategies adopted by mothers during childcare.

To summarize these data on temperament effects, predictions about temperament effects on maternal response must take into account variations in perception of control. We find that the mother's perception of her own infant's temperament interacts with illusory control to affect her attitudinal, behavioral and physiological responses. Importantly, with the manipulation of infant temperament, we find that mothers varying on the illusory control variable are differentially sensitive to the experiences afforded by frequency of cry termination. Specifically, mothers with high illusory control are not sensitive to the differing experiences afforded them, whereas mothers with moderate or low illusory control appear to process their experience with a crying infant in a manner that helps determine their response.

DEVELOPMENTAL OUTCOME

These findings shed some light on the value of contrasting styles of coping with child-care tasks. High illusory control is consistently associated with defensive responding, which we believe interferes with the ability to learn appropriate responses during childcare. Similar physiologic insensitivity has been linked to later behavioral insensitivity of the mother and delayed cognitive development for the infant. Therefore, we reasoned that if less attentive behavioral response characterized mothers with high illusory control, then high illusory control, limited in its effectiveness as a way of coping, would, as a consequence, interfere with the infant's developmental progress. To test this hypothesis, we have studied the relation between illusory control and one aspect of the infant's developmental outcome—security of attachment.

In the study reported earlier (Donovan & Leavitt, 1989) in which mothers' response patterns were assessed on the illusion of control task when infants were 5 months old, mother-infant dyads returned when the infants were 15 months old to assess the infants' attachment status in the Strange Situation (Ainsworth & Wittig, 1969). This procedure is comprised of a standard sequence of episodes designed to assess the balance between the infant's exploratory and attachment behavioral systems. Observations are made of the infant's reaction to a novel environment, to interaction with a stranger, and to separation from and reunion with its mother.

As predicted, the distribution of securely versus insecurely attached (avoidant and ambivalent) infants was not random. Significantly more insecurely attached infants were paired with mothers with high illusory control. These mothers were no longer more depressed than mothers with low or moderate illusory control as they had been at the 5-month session, however, they still perceived the father as participating less in childcare. Physiologically, mothers of insecurely attached infants had exhibited aversive conditioning to the impending cry at the 5-month period (see Fig. 3.8).

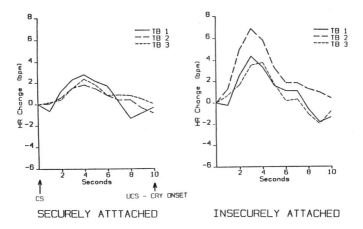

FIG. 3.8. Mean second-by-second changes in maternal heart rate response, recorded at the 5-month session, to the 10-sec CS on the first six trials, blocked by two, as a function of infant attachment assessed at the 15-month session.

More recently we have replicated this finding associating illusory control and attachment status (Donovan, Leavitt, & Walsh, 1989). When we grouped on attachment status, we found that mothers of avoidant insecure infants had greatly overestimated their control over terminating infant crying and, furthermore, showed a tendency to be more susceptible to learned helplessness at the 5-month session entailing participation in the simulated child-care tasks. Physiologically, mothers of the avoidant insecure infants at 14 months had, at the 5-month period, exhibited an aversive response to the impending cry during the solvable task of the helplessness session.

Although we believe that the data support our model of mother-infant interaction in which maternal perception of "self-efficacy" is a central influence on infant developmental outcome, equally important, we believe, are the data indicating that there is no single description of an optimal environment for an infant's development. Rather, any attempt to describe an optimal environment within which an infant can thrive will most likely include not only variables described as main effects, but also variables represented by interaction effects between mother and child variables. To date, this has been reflected in our studies in the statistical interaction between illusory control and infant temperament.

Both physiological and attitudinal data indicate that interaction with a difficult infant need not adversely affect the relationship. Mothers with both low illusory control and a perception of their infant as more difficult exhibited the more self-serving attributional style, and physiologically, exhibited the more "attentive" response. Whereas others have reported that response to infant difficulty is dependent upon resources available to the caregiver, such as social support (Crockenberg, 1981), our data have further demonstrated that reactions to infant behaviors will also depend upon particular characteristics of the caregiver, specifically, perceptions of control, that are brought to the situation. We ask, to what degree does the perception of "difficulty" arise in part from a mother's realization that her need for control exceeds what is likely to occur in a particular situation? It appears that a noncontrolling mother works well with an infant, seen by others as difficult, who draws forth attentive behavior from her. Given these data, it is understandable, indeed predictable, that assessment of infant temperament alone may fail to predict developmental outcome, such as later attachment classification (Bates, Maslin, & Frankel, 1985).

GENERAL CONSIDERATIONS

We have presented a model of maternal self-efficacy that was developed to better understand maternal coping processes activated in response to the demands of childcare. Several hypotheses generated from our model have been confirmed by experiments conducted in our laboratory, and are reviewed here. We have focused on deviations from an optimal level of responding during caregiving that result from perceptions of inefficacy, with special emphasis in this review on perceptions of inefficacy characterized by greatly overestimating control (high illusory control). We further show how these perceptions of inefficacy are translated into behavioral patterns during interaction that interfere with the developmental progress of the infant.

We have argued that high illusory control, as a means of coping with stress, is a defensive response that masks inefficacy. This limits the mother's ability to learn effective responses while engaged in interaction with her infant. Experimentally, this was demonstrated by finding that mothers with high illusory control were more susceptible to helplessness following exposure to failure on a simulated child-care task in which mothers attempted to terminate an infant cry. We believe that this inability to learn appropriate responses occurs for these mothers because experience with failure is disruptive when one's expectation for control is very high and that expectation is not realized.

We further believe that circumstances surrounding parenting activities may, under certain conditions, evoke this defensive response, because parenting, unlike other activities, may not allow withdrawal. Although withdrawal can be seen in parenting situations, for those for whom certain attitudes or values preclude the possibility of withdrawal, we propose that, when parenting efficacy is tested, high illusory control may be employed as a defensive coping mechanism.

To date, the precursors to the withdrawn versus the overcontrolling coping style have yet to be delineated. Although a depressive mood state has been associated with both helplessness (Seligman, 1975) and high illusory control (Donovan & Leavitt, 1989), these different coping strategies can be discriminated physiologically. Whereas attentional deficits are associated with both coping styles, defensive response patterns were present only under conditions of high illusory control (Donovan & Leavitt, 1989), not under conditions of helplessness and withdrawal (Donovan, 1981). Other differentiating predictors may include maternal characteristics, such as internal expectations of success, or other circumstantial factors that allow for or restrict the possibility of withdrawal. The appearance of withdrawal may only require continued failure when striving for desired outcomes. On the other hand, the appearance of high illusory control masking inefficacy may require that the mother has placed excessively high demands on herself and the defensive response surfaces when she falls short of her exacting standards. To the degree that these two distinct coping styles have different causes and remedial implications, additional research is necessary to further clarify conditions leading to one style over the other.

A consideration of attributional style in our formulation of the coping style represented by high illusory control has been particularly fruitful. Whether or not the mother adopts a self-serving or a depression-prone attributional style in response to life's demands, including those of childcare, has consistently differentiated mothers with high illusory control from mothers with a more self-efficacious coping style. Mothers with high illusory control consistently exhibit a depression-prone attributional style (Donovan & Leavitt, 1989; Donovan et al., 1990b). In contrast, mothers with a more self-efficacious coping style, those who exhibited low and moderate illusory control in our task, express a more self-serving attributional style.

These data on the role of attributional style in determining maternal self-efficacy suggest simple, concrete clinical approaches that may be effective in helping mothers cope with stressful child-care tasks. It is possible that over-controlling behavior under stress may be a result of the depression-prone attributional style arising from her stringent standards of self-evaluation and a devaluation of accomplishments because she falls short of her exacting standards (Kanfer & Hagerman, 1980). An intervention could involve a modification of the mother's present attributions assigned to interaction patterns with her infant.

Because Bugental and colleagues have reported that adults with "high-control" attributions (i.e., those who attributed more importance to ability than to luck as a determinant of interaction success) showed more positive patterns of interaction than adults who express "low-control" attributions (Bugental & Shennum, 1984), a careful distinction must be made between their concept of "high-control" and ours of "high *illusory* control." High-control refers to believing and receiving confirmation that actions are effective, whereas high illusory control refers to a self-deception stemming from perceiving far more control than actually exists. Thus high-control denoting actual control is a correlate of a self-serving attributional style and predicts positive interaction patterns, and high illusory control is a correlate of a depression-prone attributional style and defensive responding that predicts negative interaction patterns.

For our last consideration, we return to the statement made earlier that contends that illusory control has its limitations, even though to date, illusory control is commonly viewed as an adaptive coping strategy of the healthy individual. Alloy and Abramson (1979) find that nondepressed persons exhibit illusory control, whereas we find that mothers with high illusory control not only exhibit a depression-prone attributional style but also were the most depressed (Donovan & Leavitt, 1989). Because we have consistently found high illusory control to be maladaptive, we believe the discrepancy between their findings and ours is due to that fact that, whereas Alloy and Abramson measure illusory control over inanimate events, we are interested in control over a social signal (i.e., infant crying). We have previously argued that in the interpersonal domain, high illusory control, in contrast with low or moderate illusory control, is not characteristic of the person with high perceived self-efficacy. Whereas control over environmental events is considered a positive accomplishment in our culture, in the interpersonal domain, high levels of control may interfere with social exchange, and indeed may hinder the establishment of meaningful relationships (Donovan & Leavitt, 1989). In support of this argument, others report that mothers experiencing pregnancy problems (marital difficulties and ambivalence about the child) were postpartum, more depressed, expressed more punitive, controlling child-rearing attitudes, and showed less optimal interaction patterns with their infants (e.g., fewer contingent responses) (Field et al., 1985). Also, social power attributed to the child is as important as self-perceived power of the caregiver in predicting positive social interaction between parent and child (Bugental & Shennum, 1984). Thus if, as we believe, successful interpersonal relationships depend upon the ability to allow the other to change as a function of the interaction, then high levels of control over the other could be counterproductive.

However, in agreement with Alloy and Abramson's data, we find that in some instances a mother may benefit from operating under an illusion of control when interacting with her infant. Moderate illusory control may sustain certain interactional sequences that are viewed as mutually rewarding for the mother and the infant. Likewise, moderate illusory control may prevent the mother from defining certain consequences as personal failure (e.g., "I can't stop the baby's crying"). It may provide the continuity needed for competent caregiving throughout the parenting years and may sustain her through the more trying times. Thus moderate illusory control is viewed as advantageous, whereas excessive illusory control may be a precursor to overcontrolling, interfering behavior that subsequently produces deleterious effects for the relationship.

IMPLICATIONS

Clinicians who work with parents with infants who are at risk for developmental problems have a need for a theoretical framework that informs intervention strategies affecting the welfare of the child and its family. For mothers who have developed ineffective coping strategies with their infants, our data points to the strategy of helping mothers reinterpret their infant's behavior in a more positive mode as well as interpreting their success more optimistically.

Concretely this accents the use of educational materials that describe the transitions of infancy in a positive manner as well as modeling coping strategies that enhance success at well-defined, small parts of the global activity of infant care. An example of the reinterpretation process is the reported success of programs that use the newborn physical examination in the mother's presence to give her an understanding (positive interpretation) of the infant's neurobehavioral repertoire (Widmayer & Field, 1980).

Our findings to date have led us to speculate that the early attributional/behavioral/physiological style characteristic of high illusory control may be a possible precursor to later overcontrolling, interfering behaviors observed during the toddler years (Crockenberg, 1987; Lee & Bates, 1985; Pettit & Bates, 1984). Indeed, consistent with our earlier finding that linked high illusory control in mothers to insecurity of attachment in infants (Donovan & Leavitt, 1989), others have reported that a controlling maternal style is negatively related to the infant's mastery motivation (Frodi, Bridges, & Grolnick, 1985) and that security of attachment is promoted by moderate as opposed to high levels of maternal involvement (Belsky, Rovine, & Taylor, 1984).

It is with some caution that we discuss the relation between our findings of maternal illusion of control over infant crying at the 5-month period and those data describing coercive patterns of parenting at age 2–4 years of age. However, perceived difficult temperament and early control conflicts are two factors frequently involved in the development of behavior problems. Lee and Bates (1985) report a link between early temperament and later problem behavior. Two-year-old children rated by their mother as difficult were found to approach "mild trouble" more frequently than easy or average children, their mothers used intrusive control tactics more frequently, and the more difficult toddler then resisted their mother's control attempts significantly more often. Bates regards this interaction pattern as similar to the coercive pattern of behavior described by Patterson (1980, 1982), who found that socially aggressive boys often responded with resistive or noxious behavior in the face of maternal control attempts. Perhaps not surprisingly, mothers who see their toddlers as difficult tend to have more problems in the discipline area than other mothers and exhibit ineffective parenting. Indeed, our data indicate that the perception of control variable may aid in predicting when the temperamentally difficult infant will pose significant problems for the mother. If our contention that high illusory control and its defensive physiologic correlate is a maladaptive coping strategy is valid, it may prove to be useful clinically for detecting dyads at risk for later problems during social interaction.

CONCLUDING REMARKS

Infant crying and parental response to that cry is of particular concern because an infant who cries a lot can create considerable stress for its parents. The inability to soothe and quiet one's crying infant may lead to feelings of rejection that are then countered by rejecting the baby. However, when crying is successfully managed, the parent is not only rewarded for having stopped the cry, but also views the positive interactions that follow as evidence of successful parenting.

We have presented evidence that differing *perceptions of control* are implicated in the development of effective versus ineffective coping styles in response to the demands of childcare. The differing coping strategies of low, moderate, and high illusory control, reflected by their attitudinal, behavioral, and physiological responses, indicate a self-efficacious coping style for mothers with low or moderate illusory control, in contrast to the defensive style of mothers with high illusory control. Specifically, mothers with low and moderate illusory control exhibit a self-serving attributional style and their behavioral and physiological responses in our simulated childcare tasks indicate that they are more attentive and are more effective learners of appropriate responses to the demands of childcare. In contrast, mothers with high illusory control exhibit a depression-prone attributional style, show aversive conditioning, and are less effective learners in the simulated child-care task. Furthermore, mothers with high illusory control are more adversely affected by being paired with a difficult infant, and they alone failed to show differential responding to the infant temperament variable when it was experimentally manipulated.

Lastly, our finding that high illusory control, characterized by a depression-prone attributional style, aversive conditioning, and less effective learning, is a maladaptive coping strategy that adversely affects infant developmental outcome—security of infant-mother attachment, allows us to argue that the introduction of the *perception of control* variable into our models of mother-infant interaction will increase their explanatory and predictive power.

We believe that our model of maternal self-efficacy will aid investigators assessing the relative effectiveness of various intervention strategies for use with at risk mother-infant pairs by finding the illusion of control measure, in addition to the alleviation of the helplessness measure, a useful criterion to compare the relative success of various intervention strategies for at-risk dyads.

ACKNOWLEDGMENTS

This research was supported in part by NIH grant HD03352 awarded to the Waisman Center and by grant MH42479 awarded to the authors. We thank Reghan Walsh, whose assistance was invaluable in the preparation of this chapter.

REFERENCES

Abramson, L. Y., Seligman, M. E. P., & Teasdale, J. D. (1978). Learned helplessness in humans: Critique and reformulation. *Journal of Abnormal Psychology, 87,* 49–74.

Ainsworth, M. D. S., & Wittig, B. A. (1969). Attachment and exploratory behavior of one-year-olds in a strange situation. In B. M. Foss (Ed.), *Determinants of infant behavior IV* (pp. 113–136). London: Methuen.

Alloy, L. B., & Abramson, L. Y. (1979). Judgment of contingency in depressed and nondepressed students: Sadder but wiser? *Journal of Experimental Psychology: General, 108,* 441–487.

Bandura, A. (1982). Self-efficacy mechanism in human agency. *American Psychologist, 37,* 122–147.

Bates, J. E. (1987). Temperament in infancy. In J. D. Osofsky (Ed.), *Handbook of infant development* (pp. 1101–1149). New York: Wiley.

Bates, J. E., Maslin, C. A., & Frankel, K. A. (1985). Attachment security, mother-child interaction, and temperament as predictors of behavior problem ratings at age three years. In I. Bretherton and E. Waters (Eds.), Growing points in attachment theory and research. *Monographs of the Society for Research in Child Development, 45,* (1-2, Serial No. 209), 167–193.

Belsky, J., Rovine, M., & Taylor, D. G. (1984). The Pennsylvania infant and family development project, III: The origins of individual differences in infant-mother attachment: Maternal and infant contributions. *Child Development, 55,* 718–728.

Bohlin, G., & Kjellberg, A. (1979). Orienting activity in two-stimulus paradigms as reflected in heart rate. In H. D. Kimmel, E. H. Van Olst, & J. F. Orlebeke (Eds.), *The orienting reflex in humans* (pp. 169–197). Hillsdale, NJ: Lawrence Erlbaum Associates.

Boukydis, C. F. Z., & Burgess, R. L. (1982). Adult physiological response to infant cries: Effects of temperament of infant. *Child Development, 53,* 1291–1298.

Bugental, D. B., & Shennum, W. A. (1984). "Difficult" children as elicitors and targets of adult communication patterns: An attributional-behavioral transactional analysis. *Monographs of the Society for Research in Child Development, 49,* (1, Serial No. 205).

Campbell, S. B. G. (1979). Mother-infant interaction as a function of maternal ratings of temperament. *Child Psychiatry and Human Development, 10,* 67–76.

Cohen, S., & McKay, G. (1984). Social support, stress, and the buffering hypothesis: A theoretical analysis. In A. Baum, S. E. Taylor, & J. E. Singer (Eds.), *Handbook of psychology and health (Vol. 4).* Hillsdale, NJ: Lawrence Erlbaum Associates.

Crnic, K. A., Ragozin, A. S., Greenberg, M. T., Robinson, N. M., & Basham, R. B. (1983). Social interaction and developmental competence of preterm and full-term infants during the first year of life. *Child Development, 54,* 1199–1210.

Crockenberg, S. B. (1981). Infant irritability, mother responsiveness, and social support influences on security of infant-mother attachment. *Child Development, 52,* 857–865.

Crockenberg, S. B. (1986). Are temperamental differences in babies associated with predictable differences in care giving? In J. V. Lerner & R. M. Lerner (Eds.), *Temperament and social interaction in infants and children* (pp. 53–73). San Francisco: Jossey-Bass.

Crockenberg, S. (1987). Predictors and correlates of anger toward and punitive control of toddlers by adolescent mothers. *Child Development, 58,* 964–975.

Cutrona, C. E., & Troutman, B. R. (1986). Social support, infant temperament, and parenting self-efficacy: A mediational model of postpartum depression. *Child Development, 57,* 1507–1518.

Daniels, D., Plomin, R., & Greenhalgh, J. (1984). Correlates of difficult temperament in infancy. *Child Development, 55,* 1184–1194.

Dix, T. H., & Grusec, J. E. (1985). Parent attribution process in the socialization of children. In I. E. Sigel (Ed.), *Parental belief systems* (pp. 201–233). Hillsdale, NJ: Lawrence Erlbaum Associates.

Donovan, W. L. (1981). Maternal learned helplessness and physiologic response to infant crying. *Journal of Personality and Social Psychology, 40,* 919–926.

Donovan, W. L., & Leavitt, L. A. (1989). Maternal self-efficacy and infant attachment: Integrating physiology, perceptions, and behavior. *Child Development, 60,* 460–472.

Donovan, W. L., Leavitt, L. A., & Walsh, R. O. (1989). *Measures of maternal control and security of infant attachment.* Paper presented at the annual meeting of the Society for Psychophysiological Research, New Orleans, LA.

Donovan, W. L., Leavitt, L. A., & Walsh, R. O. (1990a). *The effects of perception of control and infant temperament on maternal physiologic response.* Paper presented at the Seventh International Conference on Infant Studies, Montreal, Canada.

Donovan, W. L., Leavitt, L. A., & Walsh, R. O. (1990b). Maternal self-efficacy: Illusory control and its effect on susceptibility to learned helplessness. *Child Development, 61,* 1638–1647.

Field, T., Sandberg, D., Garcia, R., Vega-Lahr, N., Goldstein, S., & Guy, L. (1985). Pregnancy problems, postpartum depression, and early mother-infant interactions. *Developmental Psychology, 21,* 1152–1156.

Frodi, A., Bridges, L., & Grolnick, W. (1985). Correlates of mastery-related behavior: A short-term longitudinal study of infants in their second year. *Child Development, 56,* 1291–1298.

Gunnar, M. R. (1980). Control, warning signals, and distress in infancy. *Developmental Psychology, 16,* 281–289.

Hare, R. D., & Blevings, G. (1975). Defensive responses to phobic stimuli. *Biological Psychology,* *3,* 1–13.

Heider, F. (1958). *The psychology of interpersonal relations.* New York: Wiley.

Holloway, S. D., & Hess, R. D. (1985). Mothers' and teachers' attributions about children's mathematics performance. In I. E. Sigel (Ed.), *Parental belief systems* (pp. 177–199). Hillsdale, NJ: Lawrence Erlbaum Associates.

Kanfer, F. H., & Hagerman, S. (1980). The role of self-regulation. In L. P. Rehm (Ed.), *Behavior therapy and depression: Present status and future directions* (pp. 143–179). New York: Academic Press.

Kelley, H. H. (1973). The process of causal attribution. *American Psychologist, 28,* 107–128.

Klein, P. S. (1984). Behavior of Israeli mothers toward infants in relation to infants' perceived temperament. *Child Development, 55,* 1212–1218.

Lacey, B. C., & Lacey, J. I. (1974). Studies of heart rate and other bodily processes in sensorimotor behavior. In P. A. Obrist, A. H. Black, J. Brener, & L. V. DiCara (Eds.), *Cardiovascular psychophysiology* (pp. 538–564). Chicago: Aldine.

Lee, C. L., & Bates, J. E. (1985). Mother-child interaction at age two years and perceived difficult temperament. *Child Development, 56,* 1314–1325.

Lerner, J. V., & Lerner, R. M. (1983). Lifespan development and behavior. In P. B. Baltes & J. O. G. Brim (Eds.), *Temperament and adaptation across life: Theoretical and empirical issues* (Vol. 5, pp. 197–231). New York: Academic Press.

Lester, B. M., & Boukydis, C. F. Z. (1985). *Infant crying: Theoretical and research perspectives.* New York: Plenum.

Lounsbury, M. L., & Bates, J. E. (1982). The cries of infants of differing levels of perceived temperamental difficultness: Acoustic properties and effects on listeners. *Child Development, 53,* 677–686.

Manusco, J. C., & Handin, K. H. (1985). Reprimanding: Acting on one's implicit theory of behavior change. In I. E. Sigel (Ed.), *Parental belief systems* (pp. 143–176). Hillsdale, NJ: Lawrence Erlbaum Associates.

McCabe, P., & Schneiderman, N. (1985). Psychophysiological reactions to stress. In N. Schneiderman & J. Tapp (Eds.), *Behavioral medicine: The biopsychology approach* (pp. 99–131). Hillsdale, NJ: Lawrence Erlbaum Associates.

Miller, S. M. (1981). Predictability and human stress: Towards a clarification of evidence and theory. In L. Berkowitz (Ed.), *Advances in experimental social psychology* (Vol. 14, pp. 204–256). New York: Academic Press.

Milliones, J. (1978). Relationship between perceived child temperament and maternal behaviors. *Child Development, 49,* 1255–1257.

Öhman, A. (1979). The orienting response, attention, and learning: An information-processing perspective. In H. D. Kimmel (Ed.), *The orienting reflex in humans* (pp. 443–471). Hillsdale, NJ: Lawrence Erlbaum Associates.

Patterson, G. R. (1980). Mothers: The unacknowledged victims. *Monographs of the Society for Research in Child Development, 45,* (5, Serial No. 186).

Patterson, G. R. (1982). *Coercive family process, social learning approach series (Vol. 3).* Eugene, OR: Castalia.

Pettit, G. S., & Bates, J. E. (1984). Continuity of individual differences in the mother-infant relationship from 6 to 13 months. *Child Development, 55,* 729–739.

Sameroff, A. J., & Feil, L. A. (1985). Parental concepts of development. In I. E. Sigel (Ed.), *Parental belief systems* (pp. 83–105). Hillsdale, NJ: Lawrence Erlbaum Associates.

Seligman, M. E. P. (1975). *Helplessness: On depression, development, and death.* San Francisco: Freeman.

Siddle, D. T. (1985). Effects of stimulus omission and stimulus change on dishabituation of the skin conductance response. *Journal of Experimental Psychology: Learning, Memory, and Cognition, 11*, 206–216.

Thomas, A., & Chess, S. (1977). *Temperament and development.* New York: Brunner/Mazel.

Widmayer, S. M., & Field, T. M. (1980). Effects of Brazelton demonstrations on early interactions of preterm infants and their teenage mothers. *Infant Behavior and Development, 3*, 79–89.

Zuckerman, B. S., & Beardslee, W. R. (1987). Maternal depression: A concern for pediatricians. *Pediatrics, 79*, 110–117.

4 The Heritability of Autonomic Nervous System Processes

Brian T. Healy
Ithaca College

The discussions of laboratory stressor task effects (e.g., cold pressor tasks, shock avoidance reaction time tasks, etc.) on autonomic nervous system (ANS) activity have typically emphasized their effects on sympathetic (i.e., beta-adrenergic) responses (Porges, 1983). For example, increases in heart rate, respiration, blood pressure, or oxygen consumption during active coping tasks within the laboratory have been used as a physiological marker of stress. As Grossman and Svebak (1987) have noted, laboratory paradigms have typically used pharmacological blockade of beta-adrenergic activity (i.e., sympathetic influences) to assess which branch of the ANS is associated with the physiological response. If, for example, heart rate does not increase during the task while sympathetic effects are pharmacologically blocked, yet it shows an increase during the task when the sympathetic blocker is removed, this is seen as evidence that sympathetic effects predominate.

Unfortunately, the effects of stress on parasympathetic activity, or parasympathetic-sympathetic nervous system interaction, has received less attention. Recent work, however, has emphasized the parasympathetic contribution to the stress response (Grossman & Svebak, 1987; Porges, 1983). This line of research has shown that a specific stressor may cause an increase in heart rate or blood pressure, yet this response may be viewed not only as an indication of sympathetic activation but also as parasympathetic inhibition. As Porges has noted, vagal inhibition may occur 300 milliseconds prior to sympathetic activation when assessing the cardiovascular effects of stress.

The purpose of this paper is to: (a) provide evidence for the significance of vagal tone as it relates to behavioral differences in young children; (b) address issues relating to the genetic basis of cardiovascluar activity; and (c) present data that have examined the possible heritable basis for vagal tone.

The Autonomic Nervous System and Behavior

Recent studies have stressed the relation between physiological response patterns and the development of individual differences in temperament (Boomsma & Plomin, 1986; Coll, Kagan, & Resnick, 1984; Kagan, 1982; Rothbart & Derryberry, 1981). Although some investigators have studied the relation between both endocrine and neurotransmitter activity and temperamental behaviors (Rappaport, Pandari, Renfield, Lake, & Zieglar, 1977; Tennes, Downey, & Vernadakis, 1977) the majority of recent work has focused on the use of peripheral recordings of autonomic nervous system processes. The selection of ANS measures is often based on the practical point that these physiological processes may be easily assessed and generally involve noninvasive recording procedures (Campos, 1976). On a theoretical level, ANS measures are linked to direct central neurophysiological systems that mediate behaviors associated with state regulation. For example, research has demonstrated that variations in autonomic tone are paralleled by individual differences in behavior (Gellhorn & Loofbourrow, 1963; Porges, 1976; Wenger, 1941).

Recent studies (Coll et al., 1984; Kagan, 1982; Resnick, Kagan, Snidman, Gerstan, Baak, & Rosenberg, 1986) have demonstrated a relation between approach/withdrawal behavior in young children and heart rate patterns. Specifically, children who were more inhibited (i.e., less likely to approach either unfamiliar persons or novel objects within a laboratory setting) had fast and stable heart rates. Because low vagal tone reflecting either a tonic or situational neural state results in fast stable heart rate, the inhibited child may be characterized by low vagal tone. An alternative hypothesis offered by Kagan and colleagues is that inhibited children present a pattern of greater sympathetic arousal.

A measure of vagal tone may be extracted from the heart rate pattern by analyzing only that portion of the cardiac cycle associated with spontaneous breathing. For example, the variability in the rate at which the heart beats is not only a function of increases and decreases in respiration, but also a function of blood pressure changes, somatic activity, and temperature regulation (Porges, 1974). Because the increases and decreases in heart rate as a function of breathing are primarily influenced by the gating of vagal nuclei within the medulla in the brain stem, the extent of heart rate change as a function of respiration indirectly measures vagal influences.

Quantification Issues

Heart rate variability has typically been measured by calculating descriptive statistics on continuous heart rate data recorded for varying lengths of time. Such measures as the range of heart rate values (i.e., the highest minus the lowest value) or the standard deviation of the heart rate values have been used to assess variability. Because various physiological processes affect heart rate variability, more precise methods of quantification have been developed to control for extraneous variance not associated with vagal influence.

One method used to extract vagal effects is Time Series analysis. This procedure decomposes continuous heart rate data into its component frequencies. Detrending methods are often employed to remove slow aperiodic changes in heart rate (such as blood pressure changes) or linear trends (i.e., increases or decreases in heart rate over time) not associated with respiration. These detrending methods are significant in that they underly an important criterion for the Time Series procedures: that being that the data are stationary (i.e., there is an equal mean and variance over time). The statistical removal of such effects (especially the removal of slow aperiodic fluctuations) results in a residual data set consisting predominantly of heart rate fluctuations associated with breathing. If Time Series analysis is then used on this residual data set, one may quantify the degree of "power" (i.e., spectral density) within the residual time series associated with respiratory activity. The greater the amplitude of increases and decreases in heart rate associated with breathing the greater is the vagal influence on heart rate. This process may be better understood from a study by Sroufe (1971) in which changes in tidal volume (i.e., depth of breathing) influenced estimates of heart rate variability. In this case, as tidal volume increased so did the estimates of heart rate variance.

Rhythmic cardiac patterns associated with respiration are vagally mediated and associated with the influence of parasympathetic processes (Katona & Jih, 1975). The influence of respiration on heart rate has been termed *respiratory sinus arrhythmia* (Porges, McCabe, & Yongue, 1982). Greater respiratory sinus arrhythmia is associated with a heart rate pattern marked by slow rate and high variance; lower respiratory sinus arrhythmia would produce the opposite pattern, that is, fast rate and low variance.

Individual differences in tonic levels of respiratory sinus arrhythmia have been found to be associated with different attentional states as well as levels of anxiety (Grossman, 1985; Porges, 1976). Several studies have also demonstrated that decreases in heart rate variability are associated with sustained attention to visual stimuli (Porges, 1974; Richards, 1987). Fox (Fox & Gelles, 1984; Stifter, Fox, & Porges, 1987) has reported that infants with greater vagal tone were more facially expressive and reactive to novel events. Similarly, DiPietro, Larson, & Porges (1987) found that breast-fed infants had greater vagal tone and were more likely to be rated as irritable on the Neonatal Behavioral Assessment Scale (Brazelton, 1973). The common dimension across these studies may be that the degree of infant reactivity to novel or mildly stressful events is associated with higher parasympathetic tone.

In addition, recent work (Healy, 1989) has demonstrated a relation between tonic estimates of parasympathetic activity and certain behavior that may reflect temperamental variation in young children. In this study, tonic estimates of heart rate variance were related to the reactive nature of one– to three–year–old children based on maternal perceptions of the child's mood. For example, those children who reacted strongly to such things as face washing, cold symptoms, etc., also had greater tonic estimates of vagal tone recorded in a laboratory setting. Healy interpreted these findings as related to the child's sensory threshold such that those children with greater tonic parasympathetic dominance were those who were more attentive and reactive to various changes in their environment.

The Heritability of Autonomic Nervous System Functioning

Several studies have examined the genetic contribution to measures of autonomic nervous system activity (Block, 1967; Boomsma & Plomin, 1986; Lader & Wing, 1966; Shapiro, Nicotero, Sapira, & Schieb, 1968; Vandenberg, Clark, & Samuels, 1965). The majority of these studies, aside from Boomsma and Plomin (1986), have used adult twin samples and compared concordance between monozygotic and dizygotic twins on measures of heart rate, blood pressure, and respiratory activity. The consensus of these studies is that these physiological processes are influenced by genetic factors based on higher concordance among monozygotic versus dyzygotic twin pairs. The study by Boomsma and Plomin found a genetic basis for heart rate in a sample of young children.

The finding of a heritable basis for the rate at which the heart beats is not surprising due to the similarity of the structural characteristics of the cardiovascular system in identical twins. Although both sympathetic and parasympathetic nervous system activity are involved in increasing and decreasing heart rate, the heart also has its own pacemaking ability (Vanhoutte & Levy, 1979). With regard to the cardiovascular response to a stressor, however, the study by Shapiro et al. (1968) is of particular interest. In this study, both heart rate and biochemical assays (epinephrine and norepinephrine) were collected from pairs of identical and fraternal adult twin pairs during a frustrating mental exercise (the Stroop color test) and following induced ischemic pain to the arm (i.e., the subject had to open and close his/her hand in time to a metronome while blood flow to the arm was occluded). The results showed that heart rate remained concordant for the identical pairs and less concordant for the fraternal pairs under both conditions. For example, heart rate tended to increase to a similar level in the identical pairs following the ischemic pain yet remained discordant in the fraternal pairs. However, an analysis of catecholamine activity both prior to and following the induced pain showed discordance for both the identical and fraternal twins. This may indicate that the biochemical assay was more sensitive to individual differences in response to the applied stressor and was not influenced by genetic factors. Although the identical twins responded to the stressor with a similar increase in heart rate, individual differences in anticipatory anxiety and the influence of the test environment may have influenced rates of catecholamine excretion.

The following is a description of a research project whose methodology has been described in detail elsewhere (Healy, 1989). This portion of the project addressed issues related to the genetic basis for heart rate, heart rate variance, and estimates of vagal tone, in addition to the relation among these physiological measures and approach/withdrawal behavior.

METHOD

Subjects

Forty-five same-sexed twin pairs (25 monozygotic and 20 dizygotic; N = 90) between 11 and 35 months of age (with age corrected for prematurity) were subjects in this study. The monozygotic (MZ) group consisted of 13 male pairs with a mean age of 19.5 months (SD = 6.3) and 12 female pairs with a mean age of 22.6 months (SD = 5.2). The dizygotic (DZ) group consisted of 9 male pairs with a mean age of 19.1 months (SD = 7.9) and 11 female pairs with a mean age of 17.8 months (SD = 6.9). Subjects were recruited from various Mothers of Twins clubs located within the Washington, D.C. area.

The children were from middle to upper-middle class families. The mean age for mothers of these children was 31.9 years (SD = 3.9). The mean educational level for mothers was 14.9 years (SD = 2.3). The mean age for fathers of the children was 34.8 years (SD = 5.4). The mean educational level for fathers was 15.2 years (SD = 2.1). There were no significant differences in either age or educational level between the parents of the MZ and DZ twins.

Determination of Zygosity. The majority of twin studies have relied on blood typing techniques to determine zygosity. A more recent, expedient, and reliable technique has been developed by Cohen, Dibble, Grawe, and Pollin (1973), in which physical markers such as eye color, hair color and texture, skin complexion, height, and weight may be used to determine zygosity. This method has an accuracy of over 90% when validated against blood samples. Measurement error when using physical criteria is usually due to a misclassification of a fraternal pair as identical. Thus, estimates of differences between MZ and DZ pairs with this method are conservative. The information using this method is obtained using a 10-item questionnaire. The questionnaire includes items regarding physical characteristics and twin pair identity, such as the frequency of identity confusion by the parents, relatives, and unfamiliar persons. Similar diagnostic criteria have been used in other twin studies to determine zygosity

(Boomsma & Plomin, 1986; Plomin & Rowe, 1979; Plomin, Willerman, & Loehlin, 1976; Torgersen & Kringlin, 1971).

The zygosity of the twins in this study was not determined until all experimental procedures had been completed.

Perinatal Characteristics of the Sample.   Parents reported the incidence of medical complications as well as the birth weight and gestational ages of their twins. The Postnatal Complications Scale (PCS) (Littman & Parmele, 1978) was used to determine the incidence of medical risk within both the MZ and the DZ groups. The mean PCS score for the MZ group was 143.8 (SD = 29.3) and the score for the DZ group was 143.0 (SD = 28.6). The difference between the groups was not significant.

It is possible that the parents may have underestimated the severity of their child's medical complications at birth and the degree of medical compromise that might affect the physiological data. However, all parents reported that their child was in good health at the time of the study and had not undergone any significant medical complications since birth. No significant relations were found between the PCS scores and the physiological measures reported in this study. There were no differences in gestational age between groups. The fraternal twins were lower in birth weight (F $(1,75)$ = 5.51, p < .05) than the identical twins although there was no relation between birth weight and any of the physiological measures reported in this study.

Experimental Design

The experiment required one laboratory visit. The experimental sequence included the recording of EKG during a baseline condition, during the presentation of a "Sesame Street" video, a videotaping of social behavior, and a post recording of EKG. The observation of social behavior has been described in detail elsewhere (Healy, in press). In general, it consisted of a series of separations from mother, reunion episodes, interaction sequences with unfamiliar adults, and latencies to approach a novel toy.

Heart Rate Recording

Baseline Condition.   Two pregelled disposable electrodes were placed across the chests of each child. Once the leads were in place, 3 to 5 minutes of EKG were recorded simultaneously from each twin. The EKG signal was amplified via a Grass model #7P5B wide band AC preamplifier and recorded on a Vetter model D FM instrumentation recorder. The EKG signal was also displayed on polygraph paper.

"Sesame Street" Condition.   Following the baseline condition, the experi-

menter entered the playroom and played a recorded tape of "Sesame Street" on the video monitor situated in front of the mother and her children. Three to 5 minutes of EKG were recorded simultaneously from each child as they watched the video monitor.

Approach/Withdrawal Behavior

The behavior of each twin was also observed during the presentation of a novel toy. The toy was a small mechanical robot that was manipulated by a research assistant from behind a one-way screen. Such a presentation made it seem as if the robot was moving on its own accord. Latency to approach the robot was calculated in seconds for each twin in a pair. Each twin was observed separately during this part of the paradigm.

Postsession Recording.   Following the behavioral observation, heart rate was again recorded while the children watched a segment of "Sesame Street" on the video monitor.

Quantification and Analysis of the EKG Data

The EKG data were quantified off-line on a PDP 11/23 computer. The computer detected the peak of the R-wave of the EKG and timed the interval between successive R-waves to the nearest millisecond. Data files of the R-to-R intervals, or heart periods, were generated for each subject during each of the experimental conditions. Each data file was graphically displayed on the computer and outliers caused by inappropriate detection of the R-wave were manually edited.

The heart period data files were analyzed using a software package developed by Porges (1985) that incorporated a unique signal processing technique. This program calculated the mean heart period, the natural log of the heart period variance, and the vagal tone measure for each sequential 30 second epoch. To calculate vagal tone, the software program (a) sampled heart period in 250 millisecond intervals; (b) subtracted stepwise a 21-point cubic polynomial through the equally spaced intervals to remove aperiodic and slow periodic components; (c) calculated the variance of the residual process within the frequency band of .24 - 1.04 Hz (which is the normal spontaneous breathing frequency for the young children in this experiment; and (d) calculated the natural log of the residual variance. To provide a stable estimate of individual differences, the program calculated the means of each variable across the sequential 30-second epochs.

In this study the data for each subject included between five and ten 30-second epochs for each condition. In order to provide a stable estimate of each autonomic measure, the mean across the three recording conditions (i.e., baseline, "Sesame Street," and the post recording) was computed for each measure (heart period, heart period variance, and vagal tone). Subsequent analyses were conducted on these mean values.

Genetic Analysis of the Physiological Data

Prior to the genetic analyses comparing the MZ and DZ twins, the means and variances were calculated for the physiological variables to determine whether each twin group was sampled from the same population. Table 4.1 displays the means and standard deviations for each autonomic measure by zygosity. As can be seen, there was significantly greater variance in heart period for the MZ group.

The classic method of twin analyses was used for calculating the possible difference in genetic variance attributable to twin status. Intraclass correlations using the analyses of variance method were calculated for each autonomic measure. Prior to the genetic analyses, the effects of age were removed by regressing each variable on age (Plomin & Rowe, 1979). An analysis of variance was then performed on the residual data set to derive the between and within mean square variance that is needed to calculate the intraclass correlation. The statistical difference between the MZ and DZ correlations was determined by applying the Fisher r to z transformation to the square root of the intraclass correlations and by testing the difference between these scores (see Haggard, 1958, and Wilson, 1979, for further elaboration on these methods).

RESULTS

Figure 4.1 displays a graphic representation of the intraclass correlations for the MZ and DZ twins for each autonomic variable. As can be seen, heart period was significantly different between these two groups. Neither heart period variance nor the vagal tone measure showed significant group differences. It should be noted that the large MZ/DZ difference on heart period (i.e., .72 [MZ] vs .06

TABLE 4.1
Means and Standard Deviations for the Physiological Measures

	Mean			Standard Deviation		
	MZ	*DZ*	*p*	*MZ*	*DZ*	*p*
Heart period (ms)	480	468	NS	49.4	32.3	.02
Heart period						
Variance	5.88	5.95	NS	.66	.60	NS
Vagal tone	3.70	3.70	NS	1.00	.79	NS

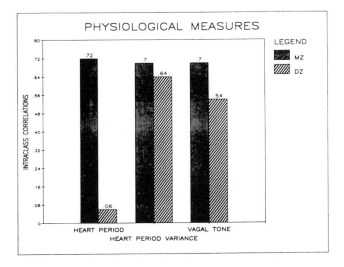

FIG. 4.1. Intraclass correlations for the physiological measures.

[DZ]) is in part due to the significant difference in variance within each group. The smaller between twin variance in the DZ group will tend to deflate the concordance estimate.

The Physiological Measures and Approach/Withdrawal Behavior

The latency to approach the robot (in seconds) correlated positively with all the physiological measures ($r = .33$, $p < .01$ for heart period; $r = .29$, $p < .05$ for heart period variance; and $r = .25$, $p < .05$ for vagal tone). These data indicate that slower tonic heart rate, greater heart period variance, and greater vagal tone were associated with a greater latency to approach this novel object.

CONCLUSION

The results demonstrate a genetic basis for heart rate. As stated earlier, this finding is not surprising given the structural similarity of the cardiovascular system in identical twins. In addition, similar results have been reported in several studies.

Although the intraclass correlations for the identical twins were greater than those of the fraternal twins on measures of heart rate variance and vagal tone, the differences were not significant. This finding suggests that these measures may be influenced more by environmental factors than by genetic factors. Similar to the results found with adult twins in the Shapiro et al. (1968) study, the unfamiliar laboratory environment and the placement of electrodes may be perceived as mildly stressful circumstances and events. However, the catecholamine assays from the identical twins in the Shapiro et al. study were discordant within pairs. It should be noted that these recordings and assays were collected on separate days for each twin. The similar concordance rates for the identical and fraternal pairs in this study probably resulted from: (a) similar levels of anticipatory anxiety in each twin surrounding the recording procedure; and (b) simultaneous recording of heart rate. As an index of stress, the heart period variance and vagal tone may be more influenced by the children's perception of events surrounding the recording procedure than by genetic factors.

Several studies have shown that measures of heart rate variance are sensitive to individual differences in attention and cognitive performance (Fox & Porges, 1985; Porges, 1972; Porges, Arnold, & Forbes, 1973). Higher vagal tone seems to be related to greater attention and better cognitive outcome. The positive correlations between the latency to approach a novel object and heart rate variability in the current study may indicate that children's responses to certain novel situations are mediated by their ability to attend and regulate their affective behavior (cf. Porges, 1976). In addition, Schneiderman and McCabe (1985) have postulated a relationship between emotional stress associated with responses to novelty and a physiological process mediated by both catecholamine and corticosteriod release. As Schneiderman and McCabe state, when confronted with a novel situation "The resulting behavior is characterized by extreme vigilance, inhibition of movement, SNS (sympathetic) activation, but also bradycardia mediated by the parasympathetic nervous system" (p. 19). Individual differences in vagal tone may reflect the subject's ability to attend to and use environmental events to cope with a mildly stressful situation. Also noted, in this context, was that those children who were more latent to approach the robot were rated by their mothers as being more difficult in temperament, more negative in mood, and more distractible. An examination of the videotapes during this approach sequence showed that children who were also smiling and laughing at the presentation of the robot were also hesitant to approach. A distinguishing characteristic among both groups of children (i.e., those who were negative vs. positive in affect during this episode) was that both appeared to spend a period of assimilation of the situational factors prior to approaching the toy. Those children with low heart rate variability were those who approached the toy immediately upon its presentation. A period of attentiveness, or awareness of the situational characteristics, seemed to discriminate the high and low variance groups in this sample.

These data appear to be inconsistent with those reported by Coll et al. (1984), Resnick et al. (1986), and others (Fox & Gelles, 1984; Stifter & Fox, 1990). Kagan, for example, (Coll et al., 1984) reported that children distinguished by their extreme behavioral inhibition (i.e., wariness toward unfamiliar events and unfamiliar adults and peers) displayed a high and stable heart rate, whereas children who were sociable and positive in affect displayed a slow and variable heart rate. These differences may be explained by sampling and methodological differences between studies.

For example, the children in the Coll et al. study were chosen by extreme scores on the approach/withdrawal dimension of the TTS. However, in addition to the approach/withdrawal dimension, the difficult/easy classification is comprised of four other dimensions (rhythmicity, mood, intensity of responsivity, and adaptability). Therefore, in some cases a child could be rated as negative in mood but either less intense in responsivity or less adaptable, for example, and thereby not fit the difficult child classification. In addition, the high and stable heart rate pattern found in the inhibited children in the Coll et al. and Resnick et al. (1986) studies may reflect the inhibited child's ability to sustain attention and to remain vigilant during the presentation of unfamiliar visual and auditory stimuli.

Heart Rate Variability, Temperament and Stress

As several studies have now demonstrated a relation between levels of heart rate variance and temperament, it is interesting to speculate whether certain children (e.g., inhibited children, or temperamentally difficult children) are more reactive to stressful events than more social, approachful, and temperamentally easy children. It seems possible that certain children may display greater reactivity than others in similar situations due to either enhanced vigilance, or a lower sensory threshold. The latter may predispose certain children to an enhanced level of awareness of environmental events. For example, in the Healy (1989) study, those children with higher levels of vagal tone were not only rated as being more reactive to events but also as more distractible. This distractibility may indicate an inability to modulate environmental stimulation. Garmezy (1987) has noted that adaptive temperamental characteristics and their relation to stress have generally gone unexplored; yet he acknowledges that personality dispositions are probably associated with how certain individuals cope with stressful situations. Dunn (1987) has also noted that temperament may be associated with the ability of children to respond in specific ways to environmental change. Further, a study by Wertleib, Weigel, Springer, and Feldstein (1987) reported that temperament was related to socio-emotional functioning, in addition to the ability to cope with stressful situations.

Based on these findings, it appears that temperament may be a useful construct in studying individual differences in children's coping strategies when confronted with stressful circumstances. In addition, the data indicate that certain measures of autonomic nervous system functioning are related to behavioral differences in children during active coping situations. Although measures of heart rate variability and vagal tone appear to be more influenced by situational factors than genetic factors, these measures are undoubtedly useful in understanding the physiological components of temperamental variation in young children.

REFERENCES

Block, J. D. (1967). Monozygotic twin similarity in multiple psychophysiologic parameters and measures. *Recent Advances in Biological Psychiatry, 9,* 105–118.

Boomsma, D. I., & Plomin, R. (1986),. Heart rate and behavior of twins. *Merrill-Palmer Quarterly, 32,* 141–151.

Brazelton, T. B. (1973). *Neonatal behavioral assessment scale.* London: Spastic International Medical Publications.

Campos, J. J. (1976). Heart rate: A sensitive tool for the study of emotional development in the infant. In L. Lipsett (Ed.), *Developmental psychology: The significance of infancy* (pp. 1–31). Hillsdale, NJ: Lawrence Erlbaum Associates.

Cohen, D., Dibble, E. Grawe, J. M. & Pollin, W. (1973). Separating identical from fraternal twins. *Archives of General Psychiatry, 29,* 465–469.

Coll, C. G., Kagan, J., & Resnick, S. J. (1984). Behavioral inhibition in young children. *Child Development, 55,* 1005–1019.

DiPietro, J. A., Larson, S. K., & Porges, S. W. (1987). Behavioral and heart rate pattern differences between breast-fed and bottle-fed neonates. *Developmental Psychology, 23,* 467–474.

Dunn, J. (1986). Stress, development, and family interaction. In M. Rutter, C. Izard, & P. Read (Eds.), *Depression in young people: Developmental and clinical perspectives,* (pp. 479–490). New York: Guilford Press.

Fox, N. A., & Gelles, M. (1984). Face-to-face interaction in term and preterm infants. *Infant Mental Health Journal, 5,* 192–205.

Fox, N. A., & Porges, S. W. (1985). The relation between neonatal heart period patterns and developmental outcome. *Child Development, 56,* 28–37.

Fox, N. A., & Stifter, C. A. (in press). Biological and behavioral differences in infant reactivity. In G. A. Kohnstamm, J. Bates, & M. K. Rothbart (Eds.), *Handbook of temperament in childhood.* Sussex, England: John Wiley & Sons.

Garmezy, N. (1987). Stress, competence, and development: Continuities in the study of schizophrenic adults, children vulnerable to psychopathology, and the search for stress-resistant children. *American Journal of Orthopsychiatry, 57,* 159–174.

Gellhorn, E., & Loofbourrow, G. N. (1963). *Emotions and emotional disorders: A neurophysiological study.* New York: Harper & Row.

Goldsmith, H. H., & Campos, J. J. (1982). Toward a theory of infant temperament. In R. Emde & R. Harmon (Eds.), *The development of attachment and affiliative systems* (pp. 161–193). New York: Plenum.

Grossman, P. (1985). Respiration, stress, and cardiovascular function. *Psychophysiology, 3,* 284–300.

Grossman, P., & Svebak, S. (1987). Respiratory sinus arrhythmia as an index of parasympathetic cardiac control during active coping. *Psychophysiology, 24,* 228–235.

Haggard, E. A. (1958). *The intraclass correlation and the analysis of variance.* New York: Dryden Press.

Healy, B. T. (1989). Autonomic nervous system correlates of temperament. *Infant Behavior and Development. 12,* 289–304.

Kagan, J. (1982). Heart rate and heart rate variability as signs of temperamental dimensions in infants. In C. Izard (Ed.), *Measuring emotions in infants and children* (pp. 38–66). New York: Cambridge University Press.

Katonia, P. G., & Jih, F. (1975). Respiratory sinus arrhythmia: Noninvasive measure of parasympathetic cardiac control. *Journal of Applied Physiology, 39,* 801–805.

Ladar, M. H., & Wing, L. (1966). *Physiological measures, sedative drugs and morbid anxiety.* Oxford: Oxford University Press.

Littmann, B., & Parmalee, A. H. (1978). Medical Correlates of Infant Development. *Pediatrics, 61*, 470–474.

Plomin, R., & Rowe, D. C. (1979). Genetic and environmental etiology of social behavior in infancy. *Developmental Psychology, 15*, 62–72.

Plomin, R., Willerman, L., & Loehlin, J. C. (1976). Resemblance in appearance and equal environments assumption in twins studies of personality traits. *Behavior Genetics, 6*, 43–51.

Porges, S. W. (1972). Heart rate indices of newborn attentional responsivity. *Merrill-Palmer Quarterly, 20*, 231–254.

Porges, S. W. (1974). Heart rate indices of newborn attentional responsivity. *Merrill-Palmer Quarterly, 20*, 231–254.

Porges, S. W. (1976). Peripheral and neurochemical parallels of psychopathology: A physiological model relating autonomic balance to hyperactivity, psychopathy, and autism. In H. W. Reece (Ed.), *Advances in child development and behavior* (Vol. 2, pp. 35–65). New York: Academic Press.

Porges, S. W. (1983). Heart rate patterns in neonates: A potential diagnostic window to the brain. In T. Field & A. Sostek (Eds.), *Infants born at risk: Physiological perceptual and cognitive processes* (pp. 3–22). New York: Grune & Stratton.

Porges, S. W. (1985). Method and apparatus for evaluating rhythmic oscillations in aperiodic response systems. Patent No. 4510944.

Porges, S. W., Arnold, W. R., & Forbes, E. V. (1973). Heart rate variability: An index of attentional responsivity in human newborns. *Developmental Psychology, 8*, 85–92.

Porges, S. W., McCabe, P. M., & Yongue, B. G. (1982). Respiratory-heart rate interactions: Psychophysiological implications for pathophysiology and behavior. In J. T. Cacippo & R. E. Petty (Eds.), *Perspectives in cardiovascular psychophysiology*. New York: The Guilford Press.

Rappaport, J. L., Pandari, C., Renfield, M., Lake, C. R., & Zieglar, M. G. (1977). Newborn dopamine-beta-hydroxlase, minor physical anomolies, and infant temperament. *American Journal of Psychiatry, 134*, 676–679.

Resnick, S. J., Kagan, J., Snidman, N., Gersten, M., Baak, K., & Rosenberg, A. (1986). Inhibited and uninhibited children: A follow-up study. *Child Development, 57*, 660–680.

Richards, J. E. (1987). Infant visual sustained attention and respiratory sinus arrhythmia. *Child Development, 58*, 488–496.

Rothbart, M., & Derryberry, D. (1981). Development of individual differences in temperament. In L. E. Lamb & A. L. Brown (Eds.), *Advances in developmental psychology*, (Vol. 1, pp. 37–86). Hillsdale, NJ: Lawrence Erlbaum Associates.

Schneiderman, N., & McCabe, P. M. (1985). Biobehavioral responses to stressors. In T. Field, N. Schneiderman, & P. McCabe (Eds.), *Stress and coping* (pp. 13–61). Hillsdale, NJ: Lawrence Erlbaum Associates.

Shapiro, A. P., Nicotero, J., Sapira, J., & Scheib, E. T. (1968). Analysis of the variability of blood pressure, pulse rate, and catecholamine responsivity in identical and fraternal twins. *Psychosomatic Medicine, 30*, 506–520.

Sroufe, L. A. (1971). Effects of depth and rate of breathing on heart rate and heart rate variability. *Psychophysiology, 8*, 648–655.

Stifter, C. A., & Fox, N. A. (1990). Infant Reactivity: Physiological Correlates of Newborn and 5-Month Temperament, *Developmental Psychology, 26*, 582–588.

Tennes, K., Downey, K., Vernadakis, A. (1977). Urinary cortisol rates and anxiety in normal one-year-old infants. *Psychosomatic Medicine, 39*, 178–187.

Torgersen, S., & Kringlin, E. (1971). Blood pressure and personality. A study of the relationship between intrapair differences in systolic blood pressure and personality in monozygotic twins. *Journal of Psychosomatic Medicine, 15*, 183–191.

Vandenberg, S. G., Clark, P. J., & Samuels, I. (1965). Psychophysiological reactions of twins:

Hereditary factors in galvanic skin resistance, heartbeat, and breathing rates. *Eugenics Quarterly, 12*, 7–10.

Vanhoutte, P. M., & Levy, N. M. (1979). Cholinergic inhibition of adrenergic neurotransmission in the cardiovascular system. In C. Brooks, K. Koizumi, & A. Sato (Eds.), *Psychophysiology of cardiovascular control* (pp. 27–54). Toyoko: University of Toyoko Press.

Wenger, M. A. (1941). The measurement of individual differences in autonomic balance. *Psychosomatic Medicine, 4*, 427–434.

Wertlieb, D., Weigel, C., Springer, T., & Feldstein, M. (1987). Temperament as a moderator of children's stressful experiences. *American Journal of Orthopsychiatry, 57*, 234–245.

Wilson, R. S. (1979). Analysis of longitudinal twin data. Basic model and applications to physical growth measures. *Acta Genet Med Gemellol, 29*, 93–105.

5

Frontal Brain Asymmetry and Vulnerability to Stress: Individual Differences in Infant Temperament

Nathan A. Fox
University of Maryland

There is a long and interesting history of research on individual differences in brain electrical activity in normal functioning adults. One of the earliest papers is by Travis and Gottlober (1936). In a study reported in *Science* entitled "Do brain waves have individuality?" they recorded EEG from 44 adults while subjects rested with their eyes closed. The researchers cut a two foot strip off the end of each EEG polygraph record. The remaining EEG polygraph record (about 10 feet in length) was then pasted on a wall. Four researchers evaluated the records. Each was given the matching sample (the cut part) and had to find its mate on the wall. Travis and Gottlober report a 94% accuracy in identification of records based upon frequency, amplitude, and form of the waves. Their conclusion was that individuals can be distinguished based upon their pattern of brain electrical activity.

There have been numerous attempts since then to "match" patterns of brain electrical activity (EEG) to individual differences in personality. A comprehensive review of this literature and the methodological issues involved may be found in Gale and Edwards (1986). Interest in this area has also been generated by neuropsychological data from clinical populations. There is a good deal of evidence that injury to the left or right side of the brain differentially affects mood and emotion expression. This is a varied set of data, including the effects of stroke, head injury, or other cerebral vascular accidents. These data present a case for differences in mood and emotion expression based upon the side that is damaged and the proximity of that damage to the frontal pole (e.g., Gainotti, 1972; Robinson, 1985). These data, which have been reviewed in detail elsewhere (Sackeim, Greenberg, Weiman, Gur, Hungerbuhler, & Geschwind, 1982), argue for differences in emotional reaction depending upon which hemisphere is damaged. A good example of this work is from Robert Robinson's laboratory. He has shown that in patients with strokes that were isolated to either the left or right hemisphere, those with left hemisphere stroke showed greater symptoms of depressive affect the closer that damage was to the frontal pole (Robinson, Kubos, Starr, Rao, & Price, 1984; Robinson, 1985).

In a related set of arguments, Fox & Davidson (in press) have reported that individual differences in the arousal level of the cerebral hemispheres may be related to variations in personality and mood state. This argument is similar to that proposed by Levy (1983) in which she presented evidence for the effect of individual differences in hemispheric arousal on cognitive task performance. Levy, Heller, Banisch, & Burton (1983) had found that right-handed subjects with right hemisphere arousal asymmetry (measured via a paper and pencil task) performed poorly on traditional left-hemisphere verbal tasks. On the other hand, right-handed subjects with left hemisphere resting arousal displayed a high level of performance on these same verbal tasks. Levy (1983) argues that there is an interaction between hemispheric specialization for certain competencies (such as left hemisphere specialization for solving a verbal task) and hemispheric arousal. Fox & Davidson (in press) argue that variations in hemispheric arousal may interact with the specialization of the two hemispheres for the experience/expression of different emotions.

This argument is based upon four postulates: First, that certain regions within each of the two hemispheres are differentially lateralized for the experience/expression of emotions; second, that the functional distinction underlying this lateralization involves the continuum of approach and withdrawal (Fox & Davidson, 1984); third, that the region most likely associated with the experience/expression of emotion is the frontal region; and fourth, that hyperactivation of the frontal region of one hemisphere has similar effects as unilateral damage to a hemisphere.

Evidence for the first postulate comes from the work of Fox & Davidson (1986, 1987, 1988), which found differences in the pattern of brain activity to be associated with the expression of different emotions. For example, newborn infants who displayed disgust expressions to novel and sour liquid tastes exhibited greater relative right hemisphere activation. They displayed left hemisphere activation in response to sweet liquid tastes that elicited facial expressions of interest. Infant expressions of joy and anger were found to be coincident with a pattern indicative of greater relative left frontal activation, and the emotions of sadness and disgust were associated with the opposite EEG pattern. Fox & Davidson (1988) also found that different patterns of smiling (smiles involved with orbicularis oculi and those in which this muscle group was absent) were associated with opposite patterns of frontal activation.

Support for the second postulate comes from the model proposed by Kinsbourne (1978) and from the work of Davidson (1984). Kinsbourne discussed the functional significance of asymmetries for language and fine motor control localized to the left hemisphere versus spatial abilities and level of physiological arousal that he said were controlled by the right hemisphere. He argued that the right hemisphere functioned to provide the organism with an orientation in space and an ability to escape quickly if necessary while the left hemisphere provided the competencies for exploration and tool production. These differences could be thought to be associated with the dimensions of approach and withdrawal. Indeed, Schnierla (1957) had written extensively on the ubiquity of the approach withdrawal continuum around which he felt all primitive motivated behavior could be organized. Fox & Davidson (1984) had predicted that infant emotion responses would be associated with different patterns of EEG based upon the emotion's relation to approach or withdrawal. For example, disgust, fear, and distress are withdrawal responses and should be associated with right hemisphere activation whereas interest, joy, and anger may be approach emotions associated with left hemisphere activation. These directional predictions were confirmed.

The third postulate states that the region of the brain within a hemisphere (along the rostral-caudal plane) is of importance in this association between specialization and emotion expression. The best evidence is from the work of Robinson and colleagues (cited earlier) as well as the work of Fox & Davidson (also cited earlier). Robinson found that there was increasing incidence of depressive symptomatology in patients with unilateral cerebral lesions of the left hemisphere the closer these lesions were to the frontal pole. Fox and Davidson, across a number of studies, have found regional specificity for EEG activation associated with infant emotion. In general, differences in EEG were found for the frontal region and not for posterior scalp locations. The fact that the frontal region is implicated in these studies should not be surprising. The frontal region is unique in that it receives input from all the different sensory and association areas (Fuster, 1980; Pribram, 1973). It is seen as an area specialized for the integration of different responses, as well as one primarily involved in the inhibition of motor responses and the development of planful and coping behavior. For example, Diamond (1988; Diamond & Goldman-Rakic, 1983) has implicated dorsolateral frontal cortex as involved in the inhibition of motor responses during the performance of delayed response and Piaget's AB̄ task (Piaget, 1954). These different functions make the frontal region an ideal candidate for the locus of the generation of complex emotional responses. It is important to note that there are primary and direct connections between the amygdala and frontal cortex as well (Fuster, 1980).

Evidence for the fourth and final postulate may be found in the review paper of Sackeim et al. (1982). They found that across multiple case instances, damage to one hemisphere released or was associated with hyperactivation of the opposite hemisphere. Adults with injury to the left hemisphere were more depressed and expressed affects associated with withdrawal, whereas adults with the opposite pattern of injury were more euphoric and indifferent about their medical condition. Davidson (Schaffer, Davidson, & Saron, 1983) has also published data on normal adult subjects that support the relation between hyperactivation of one hemisphere and emotion/mood expression. In a study of undergraduates selected for extreme scores on the Beck Depression Inventory, they (Schaffer et al., 1983) found indirect confirmation of this notion. Subjects with high Beck Depression scores exhibited greater relative right frontal asymmetry recorded at rest compared to those with low Beck scores.

There seems to be evidence, then, that hyperactivation of the frontal region in either the left or right hemisphere, or damage to these areas, is associated with significant changes in mood state. In addition, there is a possibility that individuals with tonic hyperactivation of the frontal region may evidence certain personality characteristics.

The purpose of this chapter is to present evidence from three studies conducted in our lab that examined the relations between individual differences in hemispheric arousal and infant temperament. In particular, we investigated the common tendency of infants to respond with negative affect to maternal separation and the role of hemispheric arousal in separation distress. The choice of separation distress is important. First, it is an occurrence that seems to have wide individual variability in terms of onset, intensity, and duration. Second, distress to separation has been used, in the nonhuman primate literature, as a model for examining the origins of severe psychopathology. In particular, separation responses have been viewed by some as important analogues for studying the etiology of depression (Mineka, 1981).

BASELINE EEG AND DISTRESS TO SEPARATION: A FIRST STUDY

Davidson & Fox (1989) examined the role of hemispheric arousal on expression of affect in 10-month-old infants. EEG was recorded from four scalp locations (F3, F4, P3, P4 referenced to CZ), left and right frontal and parietal leads while the infant sat quietly in a high chair with his or her mother by the side. After three minutes of recording infants were exposed to a series of conditions that included brief separation from mother. Davidson and Fox (1989) divided infants up into those who displayed negative affect and distress during separation versus those who did not, and examined the pattern of EEG in the four scalp leads. As predicted, infants with greater relative right frontal activation at rest were more likely to cry to maternal separation. Those with greater relative left frontal activation were less likely to cry (see Fig. 5.1).

The data presented in Fig. 5.1 represent the relative difference in EEG power between the left and right frontal scalp leads. EEG power is a quantification of the amplitude of the signal at a given frequency or frequency band. Since Berger (1929) first observed changes in EEG amplitude in humans in response to different states of attention electroencephalographers have examined changes in power

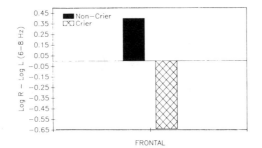

FIG. 5.1. Laterality score (Natural log of right frontal power minus natural log of left frontal power) for infants who cried or did not cry to maternal separation. Positive numbers reflect greater relative left frontal activation while negative numbers reflect greater relative right frontal activation. From Davidson and Fox (1989).

as a function of state or task demands. Lindsley (1936, 1939) described the relation between changes in power and state in terms of the de-synchronization of the alpha waves or alpha blocking. When a hemisphere or region within a hemisphere is engaged in activity the normal state of the EEG is de-synchronized and the alpha rhythm in adults is suppressed. When individuals are at rest and the region or hemisphere is not engaged one can observe synchronous EEG. Thus, decreases in power (reflecting de-synchronous activity or alpha blocking) reflect increases in activity. Researchers who study EEG asymmetry commonly use a ratio of the amount of activity in homologous leads in the two hemispheres to determine the degree of relative activation between two regions and two hemispheres. In Fig. 5.1 the difference score between right minus left natural log transformed power is presented. Numbers above the zero line represent greater relative left hemisphere activity while numbers below the zero line represent greater relative right hemisphere activity (because of the notion of decreases in power reflecting increases in activation). It is important in this type of work to specify the locus of the change in activation. Thus, one should examine not only the pattern of asymmetry but also the individual power in each lead. Inspection of these data can identify the locus of the effects (e.g., is the relative difference between the hemispheres due to increased left or decreased right hemisphere activity).

Figure 5.2 presents the individual power for the Davidson and Fox (1989) study. As can be seen there are differences in both left and right hemispheres between the two groups (criers and noncriers), particularly in the frontal leads. Criers are exhibiting less power in the right frontal lead (greater activation) while noncriers are exhibiting less power in the left frontal lead (greater left frontal activation).

As a check against the possibility that infant EEG activity was a function of their current mood state, Davidson and Fox coded infant facial expressions

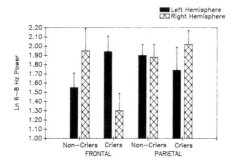

FIG. 5.2.   Individual hemisphere power in the EEG for both criers and non-criers for frontal and parietal scalp leads. Note the opposite pattern of left and right hemisphere power in the frontal leads between those infants who cried to separation and those who did not cry. From Davidson and Fox (1989).

recorded during the baseline EEG session. As can be seen in Table 5.1 there were no differences in affect expression between infants who later would cry to separation and those who later would not cry.

There are three possible interpretations of this finding. The first is in line with the notion that individual differences in hemispheric arousal are related to the heightened experience/expression of emotion. In this case, infant right frontal arousal asymmetry reflects the tendency toward negative emotionality. There are a variety of data that indicate differences early in the first year in infant irritability. Stifter and Fox (1990; Fox & Stifter, 1989), for example, have found that irritability as measured by crying at two days to pacifier withdrawal is a stable

TABLE 5.1
Facial Signs of Emotion During the Baseline Period

Facial Sign	Criers	Noncriers
Interest		
M	9.5	11.3
SD	8.6	7.8
No expression		
M	17.0	15.1
SD	8.2	8.9
Joy/surprise		
M	2.4	3.2
SD	2.9	3.2
Negative affect		
M	0.5	1.4
SD	0.9	1.3

Mean duration of facial expressions observed during the baseline period from infants who eventually cried or did not cry on separation. Expresions were coded from videotape using Izard's MAX system (Izard, 1979). From Davidson and Fox (1989).

individual difference related to crying to arm restraint at five months of age. Thus, infants with greater relative right frontal activation may be those who are in general more irritable and fussy babies. The pattern of hemispheric activation could reflect a lower threshold on the part of a group of infants to display negative affect.

A second alternative is that individuals with greater relative right frontal asymmetry are at the time of recording in a negative mood or emotional state. If an infant is in a negative mood, it is likely that the child will display both greater relative right frontal activation and cry to separation. This alternative is not necessarily exclusive of the first (a temperament explanation). For example, it is quite possible that those infants with a predisposition toward irritability and negative affect are also those infants who would be in a negative mood during the laboratory situation. However, it is also possible that the pattern of frontal asymmetry arousal may not be a marker of some temperamental or personality trait. Rather, it only reflects the emotional state of the individual at that time. To a certain extent, Davidson and Fox (1989) attempted to control for differences in mood by examining facial expressions of infants during the baseline. Their finding of no differences in type of expression lends some support to the notion that the frontal asymmetry is not reflecting current mood state. However, it does not eliminate that possibility. It is certainly the case that negative mood may be present in the absence of certain defined facial expressions of affect.

A third alternative with respect to the infant data is that individual differences in frontal asymmetry activation represent different degrees of maturation. There are data that indicate that the right hemisphere matures earlier than the left (Galaburda, LeMay, Kemper, & Geschwind, 1978). Functions traditionally localized to the left hemisphere such as sequential motor activity and language emerge during the second year of life. Perhaps infants in the Davidson and Fox (1989) study with greater relative right frontal activation were less mature and those with more active left hemispheres were more mature. There are data that separation distress decreases with maturation particularly during the second year of life (Kagan, 1976). Hence the less mature right hemisphere infants would likely display distress, whereas the more mature left hemisphere infants would not display negative responses to separation.

TEMPERAMENT, ATTACHMENT, AND EEG ASYMMETRY

In an attempt to examine these three alternative explanations, we (Fox, Bell, & Aaron, 1991) performed two short-term longitudinal studies. The first study included 33 infants who were part of a research effort to examine the role of infant temperament on social behavior. Infants were seen when they were 14 months of age in the Ainsworth and Wittig Strange Situation (Ainsworth, Blehar,

Waters, & Wall, 1978). This paradigm was developed to assess individual differences in the quality of the attachment bond between mother and infant. It involves a number of brief separations and reunions between mother and infant. Two months later the infants were brought back to the laboratory, at which time EEG was recorded from left and right frontal and parietal scalp locations (F3, F4, P3, P4 referenced to CZ). The EEG was recorded during two conditions. In the first, infants watched an experimenter blow bubbles into the air and in the second condition, infants watched a segment of "Sesame Street." From these two visits we were able to derive the following data: Whether the infant cried to maternal separation (based upon the first maternal separation in the Strange Situation); the degree of distress and resistance displayed by the infant during each of the two reunion episodes of the Strange Situation (based upon a factor analysis of the Ainsworth Scales coded during each reunion); infant affect during the EEG recording (based upon a set of scales that coded posture, vocalization, and facial expression during the EEG recording); and EEG asymmetry (based upon periods of artifact free EEG recorded during both conditions).

As a first step, we examined the relation between EEG asymmetry and infant distress to maternal separation at 14 months of age. Infants were divided into those who cried and those who did not cry to separation, and an analysis was computed to determine if there were differences between the groups. We found a significant group difference in the frontal laterality ratio score (Fig. 5.3). Infants who had cried to maternal separation some two months earlier displayed greater relative right frontal activation whereas infants who did not cry displayed greater relative left frontal activation. We then examined power in the individual hemispheres in order to understand the make-up of the different laterality ratio scores. The results of the analysis examining the contribution of the individual hemispheres revealed a significant group by hemisphere interaction. Infants who cried to separation displayed less power (indicative of greater activation) in the right frontal region compared to infants who did not cry. As can be seen in Fig. 5.4,

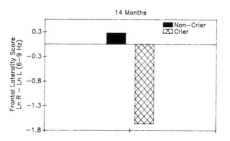

FIG. 5.3.   Laterality score for frontal EEG (Ln R-Ln L 6-9 Hz) from 14-month-old infants. EEG was recorded 6 to 8 weeks after the infants were seen in a brief maternal separation condition. Higher numbers reflect greater relative left frontal activation.

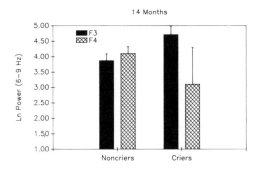

FIG. 5.4. Individual hemisphere power (LN 6-9 Hz) for the two groups of 14 month old infants for the frontal region. The infants who had cried to separation displayed less right frontal power reflecting greater right frontal activation.

there is a clear difference between the two groups of infants in the relative level of power in the right frontal region. There were no differences in parietal activation between the two groups of infants. Note that the EEG was recorded from these infants some two months after they had been seen in the lab for the Strange Situation. This finding replicates the original Davidson and Fox (1989) result in finding differences in EEG asymmetry between those infants who cry or who do not cry to separation. The studies, however, are different in that Davidson and Fox recorded EEG prior to the separation but on the same day while Fox, Bell, & Aaron (1991) recorded EEG some two months after the maternal separation.

Nevertheless, it is possible that infants who displayed the right frontal pattern displayed more negative affect, were in a negative mood during the EEG recording, a finding that could account for their brain pattern. In fact, examination of the relations between EEG and infant affect during recording found just that. There was a relation between EEG and infant affect during the recording. Infants who displayed negative affect in facial, vocal, and body posture behaviors were more likely to exhibit grater relative right frontal activation. It is also interesting to note the strong relation between affect during the EEG recording and affect during the Strange Situation. Infants exhibiting more distress and resistance were also those more likely to exhibit negative affect during the EEG recording. Thus there seems to be modest support for both a concurrent mood/EEG explanation and a stable pattern of behavior that is also associated with the right frontal pattern.

When the infants were 24 months they returned to our laboratory for an assessment of their behavioral reactivity to emotion-eliciting events. Among the events presented to the infants was a novel toy robot, a long tunnel with an attractive toy at its end, an unfamiliar adult who attempted to engage the infant in play, and a clown who attempted to engage the infant in interaction. Two months after this visit, infants returned to our lab for a second EEG visit. At this time EEG was recorded in much the same manner as it had been when the infants were 14 months of age.

From these two assessments we derived the following variables: an index of behavioral inhibition (based upon the infant's response to the novel toy robot, the tunnel, the unfamiliar adult, and the clown). High scores on this index reflected inhibition—a child who would not approach or interact in the various episodes presented and who spent a significant period of time in close proximity to his or her mother. In addition, we computed EEG power in each of the four leads, during the same two recording conditions (bubbles and "Sesame Street").

There was a strong relation between frontal asymmetry and behavioral inhibition. Infants who were uninhibited displayed greater left frontal activation whereas infants who were inhibited displayed greater right frontal activation. An examination of the scatter plot, found in Fig. 5.5, revealed greater consistency among the uninhibited in their pattern of frontal arousal compared to the inhibited infants. Of the 12 uninhibited infants for whom there was clean EEG data available, 10 were left frontal and only 2 were right frontal. On the other hand, among the 12 infants who were inhibited, 7 were right frontal but 5 were left frontal.

Inspection of the relation between affect exhibited during the EEG recording and EEG asymmetry found no significant association. The 24-month data then confirm the relation between certain patterns of infant temperament and frontal EEG asymmetry. They argue that differences in social behaviors that can be grouped under the heading of shyness or behavioral inhibition may in fact be associated with specific patterns of brain electrical activity. It is interesting to note that the strongest associations between social behavior (inhibition/extroversion) and EEG asymmetry were with infants displaying left frontal activation and uninhibited behavior. Kagan and colleagues (Kagan, Reznick, &

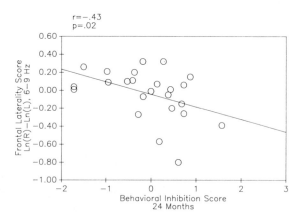

FIG. 5.5. Scatter plot between behavioral inhibition index and frontal EEG asymmetry score for 24-month-old children.

Snidman 1987, 1989) also report that the greatest behavior/physiology relations exist among the uninhibited infants rather than within the inhibited category.

We also investigated the stability between 14- and 24-month measures. These analyses, particularly for the EEG, were complicated by the fact that the number of subjects who had clean artifact-free data at both age points was small. Nevertheless we were interested in investigating the possible stability over this 10 month (14 to 24 month) period of time. We found first that behavior from 14 to 24 months showed clear modest though significant stability. Infants who displayed distress and resistance during the Strange Situation were more likely to display behavioral inhibition at 24 months. The across age correlations between frontal asymmetry at 14 and 24 months wee low and nonsignificant. However, when we examined the cross-age correlation for EEG for those infants who showed stability of behavior pattern (either distressed at 14 and inhibited at 24 or nondistressed at 14 and uninhibited at 24), the 14 to 24 month correlation for frontal asymmetry was now significant.

In summary, the evidence from this study points to the possibility that there is a pattern of EEG which is associated with negative mood or affect. Although the cross-age stability was modest, perhaps due to the number of subjects, there were substantial associations between temperament and EEG. At both 14 and 24 months EEG recorded two months after a laboratory assessment of temperament was associated with behavior in the former lab session. The low degree of stability across the 10-month period was a cause for concern for us. Other researchers (Ehrlichman & Wiener, 1979) had found strong test-re-test correlations for EEG asymmetry. We therefore felt it necessary to examine the stability of EEG asymmetry more carefully, and so we performed a second study with younger infants.

STABILITY OF EEG ASYMMETRY ACROSS A 7-MONTH PERIOD AND ITS RELATION TO AFFECT

There is good reason to believe that specific areas of frontal cortex mature during the second half of the first year of life in the human infant (Fox & Bell, 1991; Diamond, 1988; Diamond, in press) Diamond and Goldman-Rakic (1983) have presented data that dorsolateral frontal cortex is an area necessary for accurate performance on the delayed response task and on the AB̄ object permanence task in nonhuman primates. Indeed, infant monkeys show the same developmental pattern that human infants do on the AB̄ task with delay. And, adult monkeys who could perform either delayed response or AB̄, fail once lesions of dorsolateral frontal cortex are performed. Less is known about the relations between frontal development and affect during the second half of the first year of life. We therefore (Bell & Fox, 1991) performed a study examining maturation of the EEG in frontal cortex and the association between changes in frontal EEG and separation protest.

The study design was quite simple. We saw 13 infants every month in the lab, on their "month" birthday. At their lab visit, we recorded EEG from left and right frontal, parietal, and occipital scalp locations. After the recording was finished, infants were tested on a series of object permanence tasks. Following this testing each infant at each month was presented with brief maternal separation. The infant was at the time seated in an infant seat. The mother stood, said goodbye, and left. We recorded latency to cry to separation at each visit.

The EEG for each infant at each visit was analyzed and the data for each infant coded in terms of the infant's response to separation. We then examined the data in two ways. The first question we asked was: On any given visit if an infant cried, what was the pattern of EEG during that day? The results of that

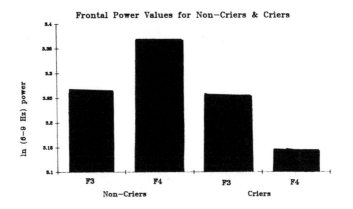

FIG. 5.6. Individual hemisphere power data (natural log of 6-9 Hz band) for frontal scalp leads for infants who cried to separation on the day they came to the lab versus those who did not cry.

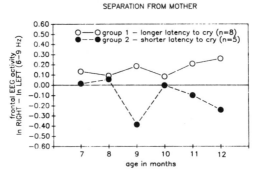

FIG. 5.7. Month-to-month laterality scores for infants who tended to cry at most or few of the lab sessions across the assessment period. Positive numbers reflect greater relative left frontal activation while negative numbers reflect greater relative right frontal activation.

TABLE 5.2
Month to Month correlations for Both Frontal and Parietal Laterality Scores
(Ln R- Ln L, 6-9 Hz Power) for the Thirteen Infants in the Longitudinal Study.

Frontal EEG (n = 13)

	7	8	9	10	11	12
7	–	.26	.33	.13	.13	-.03
8		–	**.73**	.33	.19	-.11
9			–	.45	**.63**	.19
10				–	**.58**	**.49**
11					–	.28
12						–

Parietal EEG (n = 13)

	7	8	9	10	11	12
7	–	**.62**	**.50**	-.24	**.44**	-.10
8		–	**.75**	.16	**.74**	**.47**
9			–	-.11	.39	.34
10				–	**.42**	.37
11					–	**.61**
12						–

Boldface numbers are significant at the .05 level or better.

analysis clearly showed that if the infant cried to separation, the EEG pattern was one of right frontal activation. Conversely, if the infant did not cry to separation on a visit, the EEG pattern was left frontal activation. The mean frontal asymmetry score for the group that cried was $-.11$ while the asymmetry score for those who did not cry was .121 ($t(72) = 2.38$, $p = .02$). Figure 5.6 presents the individual hemisphere data for the frontal leads for the two groups of infants. As can be seen the infants who cried in the lab to maternal separation displayed less right frontal power (more right frontal activation) compared to infants who did not cry. There were no differences between the two groups in left frontal power.

The second question we asked of the data was: Dividing the 13 infants into those who cried on more than two occasions (3 out of the 7 or more) versus those who cried only once or twice, are there group differences in EEG arousal? The answer, graphically depicted in Fig. 5.7 was that there were significant group differences between infants whose predisposition it was to cry to separation versus those who did not cry.

There are a number of points of interest in these data. First, these are among the first data to examine separation responses repeatedly over the first year. The findings from this small sample indicate that there are indeed individual differences in infant response to separation, with some infants consistently displaying distress and other infants either showing sporadic or no distress over the 7-month period. Second, there is a clear pattern of EEG activity associated with the two groups of children. Those infants who are predisposed to cry to separation exhibit greater relative right frontal activation and those who are predisposed not to cry exhibit consistent left frontal activation.

The consistency of the individual difference in frontal activation may be further illustrated by the cross-age correlations of frontal asymmetry presented in Table 5.2. As can be seen, beginning at 8 months of age there is strong within-subject across-age consistency in EEG asymmetry arousal. Subjects seem to maintain the pattern of asymmetry across this 7-month period. Indeed, the stability of parietal asymmetry appears earlier than frontal stability. This is as expected because the parietal area matures earlier than the frontal region.

PREDISPOSITION IS NOT PREDICTION

The data from the three studies presented provide evidence for an underlying predisposition in infants with greater relative right frontal activation to display negative affect in response to mild stress and novelty. What is clear from the data is that there is a subgroup of infants who may be described as having a lower threshold for stress. These infants have the tendency to display distress in response to novel and mildly stressful events. Clearly, however, not all infants with right frontal activation display negative affect and, conversely, not all infants who display negative affect are right frontal. The key, it seems, is in the stability of the behaviors. Those infants who display a high degree of stability in their emotional responses are more likely to exhibit the right frontal pattern compared to other infants. For example, in the 14-24-month study, those infants who showed distress and resistance during the Strange Situation and who were inhibited at 24 months were more likely to be right frontal compared to infants who were either distressed during the Strange Situation or inhibited at 24 months but not both. Similarly, among those infants who cried to maternal separation were those who cried consistently and those who cried only three or fewer times. Among the former there was a greater likelihood of finding the right frontal pattern but among the latter there was not. So the first point regarding these data is that consistency across time in negative affect behavior predicts the right frontal pattern.

The second point to be made is that the opposite is not entirely true. Presence of the right frontal pattern by itself in one sample was insufficient to predict behavioral inhibition or negative affect. This finding is not without precedent. For example, Kagan (Kagan et al., 1987) has argued that the physiological pattern associated with behavioral inhibition (high heart rate, low variability, high cortisol) is only a modest predictor, in the absence of behavior, of future behavioral inhibition. There are two possible reasons why. First, Kagan has written (Kagan et al., 1987) that change in category is most frequent among the inhibited children and rarely among the uninhibited. The environment, family socialization practices, can play a powerful and important role in influencing the child's behavior with adults and peers. Parents can provide a child with the strategies to cope with their low set point by structuring the environment to avoid high levels of stimulation or by providing cognitive strategies to deal with high levels of emotional arousal. It is certainly possible if not probable that these interventions will have physiological consequences, including perhaps reduction of the degree of right hemispheric activation. This in turn would lower the set point for an individual child so that he or she no longer responds as intensively to mild stress or novelty.

These data also address, albeit indirectly, the important issue of the underlying physiological correlates of emotion regulation. Regulation of emotion involves the ability to modulate or reduce the level of distress or negative affect that may be elicited during stressful or novel situations. Often parents will provide their child with strategies by which they can calm themselves down. For example, parents often attempt to distract their distressed and upset infant with a toy or external event. Older children are given verbal strategies for modulating their distress and level of arousal. The data presented here found that infants and young children who exhibited stable left frontal activation were less likely to cry to maternal separation and were less likely to withdraw from novel situations. There may be a link between emotion regulation and the types of strategies that infants and children use to modulate arousal. That link may be through the left hemisphere. Both sustained attention and distractibility, as well as verbal strategies, are left hemisphere competencies (Tucker & Williamson, 1984). Thus, the child with greater left frontal activation may have at his or her disposal the strategies necessary to modulate negative arousal. Certainly, strategies used by children change with age and perhaps with maturation of new and more complex left hemisphere responses. Indirect evidence for the relation between emotion arousal and the left hemisphere may be found in our own 14-24-month study. At 24 months, mothers filled out a questionnaire designed to tap the degree of expressive language facility of their child. When we examined the relation between expressive language facility and behavioral inhibition we found that children with greater expressive language were less likely to be inhibited. And, as one would expect, expressive language facility was related to left frontal activation. Children with greater left frontal arousal were noted to have higher expressive language. Thus, it is possible that language facility, mediated through the left hemisphere, may be an underlying process facilitating young children to cope with mild stress and novelty.

There are two areas of research that must now be undertaken with these data in mind. First, we must understand the interaction of environment and predisposition to finally clarify the different paths that infants with a particular temperament can take in personality development. And, second, we must be aware of certain environments that may for vulnerable infants be ones that might exacerbate their already low threshold for negative affect.

ACKNOWLEDGMENTS

The research presented in this chapter was funded by a grant from the National Institutes of Health (HD #17899).

REFERENCES

Ainsworth, M. D. S., Blehar, M., Waters, E., & Wall, S. (1978). *Patterns of attachment: Psychological behavior in the Strange Situation.* Hillsdale, NJ: Lawrence Erlbaum Associates.

Bell, M. A., & Fox, N. A. (1991). *The relations between frontal brain electrical activity and cognitive development during infancy.* Paper submitted for publication.

Berger, H. (1929). Uber das Elektrenkephalogramm des Menschen. I. *Arch. Psychiatr. Nervenkr, 87,* 527–570.

Davidson, R. J. (1984). Affect, cognition and hemispheric specialization. In C. E. Izard, J. Kagan, & R. Zajonc (Eds.), *Emotion, cognition, & behavior* (pp. 320–365). New York: Cambridge University Press.

Davidson, R. J., & Fox, N. A. (1988). Cerebral asymmetry and emotion: Developmental and individual differences. In S. Segalowitz & D. Molfese (Eds.), *Developmental implications of brain lateralization* (pp. 191–206). New York: Guilford Press.

Davidson, R. J., & Fox, N. A. (1989). The relation between tonic EEG asymmetry and ten month old infant emotional responses to separation. *Journal of Abnormal Psychology, 98,* 127–131.

Diamond, A. (1988). Abilities and neural mechanisms underlying AB performance. *Child Development, 59,* 523–527.

Diamond, A. (in press). The development and neural bases of inhibitory control in reaching. In A. Diamond (Ed.), *The development and neural bases of higher cognitive functions.* New York: New York Academy of Sciences.

Diamond, A., & Goldman-Rakic, P. S. (1983). Comparison of performance on a Piagetian object permanence task in human infants and rhesus monkeys: Evidence for involvement of prefrontal cortex. *Society for Neuroscience Abstracts Part I, 9,* 641.

Ehrlichman, H., & Weiner, W. S. (1979). Consistency of task-related EEG asymmetries. *Psychophysiology, 16,* 247–252.

Fox, N. A., Bell, M. A., & Aaron, N. (1991). The relation of frontal brain asymmetry to attachment behavior and behavioral inhibition in 14 and 24 month old children. Manuscript submitted for publication.

Fox, N. A., & Bell, M. A. (1991). Electrophysiological indices of frontal lobe development: Relations to cognitive and affective behavior in human infants over the first year of life. In A. Diamond (Ed.), *The development and neural bases of higher cognitive functions.* New York: New York Academy of Sciences.

Fox, N. A., & Davidson, R. J. (1984). Hemispheric substrates of affect: A developmental model. In N. A. Fox & R. J. Davidson (Eds.), *The Psychobiology of affective development* (pp. 353–382). Hillsdale, NJ: Lawrence Erlbaum Associates.

Fox, N. A., & Davidson, R. J. (1986). Taste-elicited changes in facial signs of emotion and the asymmetry of brain electrical activity in human newborns. *Neuropsychologia, 24,* 417–422.

Fox, N. A., & Davidson, R. J. (1987). EEG asymmetry in ten month old infants in response to approach of a stranger and maternal separation. *Developmental Psychology, 23,* 233–240.

Fox, N. A., & Davidson, R. J. (1988). Patterns of brain electrical activity during the expression of discrete emotions in ten month old infants. *Developmental Psychology, 24,* 230–236.

Fox, N. A., & Davidson, R. J. (in press). Hemispheric asymmetry and attachment behaviors: Developmental processes and individual differences in separation protest. In J. L. Gewirtz & W. Kurtines (Eds.), *Intersection points in attachment research,* Hillsdale, NJ: Lawrence Erlbaum Associates.

Fox, N. A., & Stifter, C. A. (1989). Biological and behavioral differences in infant reactivity and regulation. In G. A. Kohnstamm, J. E. Bates, & M. K. Rothbart (Eds.), *Temperament in childhood* (pp. 169–183). New York: Wiley.

Fuster, J. M. (1980). *The prefrontal cortex.* New York: Raven Press.

Gainotti, G. (1972). Emotional behavior and hemispheric side of lesion. *Cortex, 8,* 41–55.

Galaburda, A. M., LeMay, M., Kemper, T. L., & Geschwind, N. (1978). Right-left asymmetries in the brain. *Science, 199,* 852–856.

Gale, A., & Edwards, J. A. (1986). Individual differences. In M. G. H. Coles, E. Donchin, & S. W. Porges (Eds.), *Psychophysiology: Systems, processes, and applications* (pp. 431–507). New York: Guilford.

Kagan, J. (1976). Emergent themes in human development. *American Scientist, 64,* 186–196.

Kagan, J., Reznick, J. S., & Snidman, N. (1987). The physiology and psychology of behavioral inhibition in children. *Child Development, 58,* 1459–1473.

Kagan, J., Reznick, J. S., & Snidman, N. (1989). Issues in the study of temperament. In G. A. Kohnstamm, J. E. Bates, & M. K. Rothbart (Eds.), *Temperament in childhood* (pp. 133–144). New York: Wiley.

Kinsbourne, M. (1978). Biological determinants of functional bisymmetry and asymmetry. In M. Kinsbourne (Ed.), *Asymmetrical function of the brain.* (pp. 3–13). New York: Cambridge University Press.

Levy, J. (1983). Individual differences in cerebral hemisphere asymmetry: Theoretical issues and experimental considerations. In J. B. Hellige (Ed.), *Cerebral hemisphere asymmetry: Method, theory, and application* (pp. 465–497). New York: Praeger.

Levy, J., Heller, W., Banich, M. T., & Burton, L. (1983). Are variations among right-handers in perceptual asymmetries caused by characteristic arousal differences in the hemispheres? *Journal of Experimental Psychology: Human Perception and Performance, 9,* 329–359.

Lindsley, D. B. (1936). Brain potentials in children and adults. *Science, 84,* 354.

Lindsley, D. B. (1939). A longitudinal study of the occipital alpha rhythm in normal children: Frequency and amplitude standards. *Journal of Genetic Psychology, 55,* 197–213.

Mineka, S. (1981). Depression and helplessness in primates. In H. Fitzgerald, J. Mullins, & P. Gage (Eds.), *Primate Behavior and Child Nurturance* (Vol. 3, pp. 197–242). New York: Plenum Press.

Piaget, J. (1954). *The construction of reality in the child.* New York: Basic Books.

Pribram, K. H. (1973). The primate frontal cortex—Executive of the brain. In K. H. Pribram & A. R. Luria (Eds.), *Psychophysiology of the frontal lobes* (pp. 293–314). New York: Academic Press.

Robinson, R. G. (1985). Lateralized behavioral and neurochemical consequences of unilateral brain injury in rats. In S. D. Glick (Ed.), *Cerebral lateralization in nonhuman species* (pp. 135–156). New York: Academic Press.

Robinson, R. G., Kubos, K. L., Starr, L. B., Rao, K., & Price, T. R. (1984). Mood disorders in stroke patients. *Brain, 107,* 81–93.

Sackeim, H. A., Greenberg, M., Weiman, A., Gur, R. C., Hungerbuhler, J. P., & Geschwind, N. (1982). Hemispheric asymmetry in the expression of positive and negative emotions: Neurological evidence. *Archives of Neurology, 39,* 210–218.

Schaffer, C. E., Davidson, R. J., & Saron, C. (1983). Frontal and parietal electroencephalogram asymmetries in depressed and nondepressed subjects. *Biological Psychiatry, 18,* 753–762.

Schnierla, T. C. (1957). The concept of development in comparative psychology. In D. B. Harris (Ed.), *The concept of development.* Minneapolis: University of Minnesota Press.

Stifter, C. A., & Fox, N. A. (1990). Infant reactivity: Physiological correlates of newborn and 5-month temperament. *Developmental Psychology, 26,* 582–588.

Travis, L. E., & Gottlober, A. (1936). Do brain waves have individuality? *Science, 84,* 532–533.

Tucker, D. M., & Williamson, P. (1984). Asymmetric neural control systems in human self-regulation. *Psychological Review, 19,* 91–126.

6 Coping and Vicarious Emotional Responding

Nancy Eisenberg
Jane Bernzweig*
Richard A. Fabes
Arizona State University

In recent years, research and theorizing concerning empathy and related vicarious emotional responses have received considerable attention in the psychological literature (e.g., Batson, 1987; Eisenberg & Strayer, 1987; Hoffman, 1984). The topic of affective empathy has been a focus of attention in part because of its hypothesized and empirical relation to a variety of social behaviors, including prosocial behavior and social competence (Eisenberg & Miller, 1987; Hoffman, 1984). Yet despite its apparent role in socially relevant and valued behaviors, there is relatively little research concerning individual differences in empathy and related responses, and the origins of such differences.

In this chapter, we explore the role of coping mechanisms in the way people respond emotionally to others' negative states, especially other individuals' distress or need. At the present time, there is very little research on this topic; thus, we draw on a variety of bodies of work that are tangentially related to our focal issue, and hypothesize regarding the role of individual differences in coping mechanisms in vicarious emotional responding. By doing so, we hope to stimulate further thinking and empirical research on this fascinating topic.

DIFFERENTIATIONS AMONG MODES OF VICARIOUS RESPONSES

The primary purpose of this chapter is to discuss coping-related factors that influence empathy and related emotional responses. In the research on vicarious emotional responding, definitions of empathy and related vicarious responses vary considerably (see Eisenberg & Strayer, 1987), and many investigators have

---

*Jane Bernzweig is currently at Chapman College.

not differentiated among various vicariously induced emotional reactions such as sympathy and personal distress. However, because different vicarious emotional reactions appear to have different motivational bases and relate differently to altruism (e.g., Batson, 1987; Eisenberg, Fabes, Miller, Fultz, Shell, Mathy, & Reno, 1989), it is important to differentiate among them.

In our own work on vicariously induced emotional reactions to other people in distress or need, we have found it useful to differentiate among empathy, sympathy, and personal distress. *Empathy* is defined as an emotional response that stems from another's emotional state or condition and is congruent with the other's emotional state or situation. An empathic response is assumed to be similar in valence and type to the other's emotional state or to the emotional state that is expected to accompany the other's condition. In addition, empathy implies at least a minimal degree of differentiation between one's own emotional states and those of others (i.e., the empathizer is not merely confusing the other person's emotional state with his or her own). Empathy is viewed as often leading to other related emotional responses such as sympathy and personal distress (Eisenberg, Shea, Carlo, & Knight, in press).

Although *sympathy* may often result from empathy, it is defined differently. Sympathy involves "feeling for" someone; it refers to feelings of sorrow and concern for another (Eisenberg & Strayer, 1987). Sympathy involves an other-orientation (Batson, 1987) and may stem from cognitive perspective taking or accessing information stored in memory pertaining to another's situation, as well as empathy (Eisenberg, Shea, Carlo, & Knight, in press).

A third emotional reaction to another's state or condition is *personal distress*. Batson (1987) defines personal distress as an aversive, self-focused state such as anxiety or worry that generally is associated with egoistic concerns (i.e., the alleviation of the aversive reaction). Thus, personal distress is conceptually very different from both empathy (which is, in essence, neither an egoistic nor other-oriented response) and sympathy (which involves a clear other-orientation).

Recent empirical research has confirmed the importance of the differentiation between sympathy and personal distress. In two studies, Eisenberg and her colleagues (Eisenberg, Fabes, et al., 1988; Eisenberg, Schaller et al., 1988) have obtained evidence that emotional reactions akin to personal distress and sympathy responses can be differentiated using not only self-report indexes, but also heart rate or facial reactions. In addition, numerous researchers have found that personal distress and sympathy differ in their relations to prosocial behavior (e.g., Batson, 1987; Eisenberg, Fabes, Miller, Fultz, Shell, Mathy, & Reno, 1989; Schroeder, Dovidio, Sibicky, Matthews, & Allen, 1988). In general, investigators have found that when it is easy to escape cues emanating from another's distressful situation, people experiencing relatively high levels of personal distress escape rather than help a needy or distressed other. In contrast, people experiencing sympathy are more likely to assist. This pattern may be stronger for adults than children (Eisenberg, Fabes, Miller, Fultz, Shell, Mathy,

& Reno, 1989; Eisenberg, Fabes, Miller, Shell, Shea, & May-Plumlee, 1990). However, if it is not easy to escape the cues emanating from the needy or distressed person, people experiencing personal distress tend to help as much as those experiencing sympathy, perhaps to alleviate their own aversive state by terminating the aversive cues stemming from the other person (Batson, 1987).

It is likely that both personal distress and sympathy frequently stem from empathy; which is predominant may depend upon whether the individual focuses on his or her own aversive feelings or on the other's feeling and situation. Moreover, individual differences in what level of emotional response is experienced as aversive, and in how one modulates potentially aversive emotional reactions, may influence whether an observer feels a predominance of sympathy or personal distress. Thus, it is likely that coping processes and capabilities play a role in the experience of sympathy and personal distress.

Investigators seldom have directly considered the role of coping in vicarious emotional responding. However, Hoffman (1984) discussed the possibility of empathic overarousal—when empathy may become overly distressful. He also entertained the possibility that a "self-focused condition arouses more intense empathy because it makes a direct connection between the other's affective state and the observer's own need system. This very connection, however, may also make the self-focused condition more vulnerable to 'egoistic drift' " (p. 119). In egoistic drift, "one becomes lost in one's own egoistic concerns and the image of the other and the other's condition that initiated the process may slip out of focus and fade away" (p. 119).

Thus, although Hoffman did not use the term "personal distress," he seemed to be saying that a self-focused orientation may be especially intense and is likely to lead to egoistic concerns. We would also suggest that individuals who are easily arousable are those who are most likely to become overaroused and therefore focused on their own aversive state. Support for this notion comes from the work of Stotland his colleagues (Stotland, Mathews, Sherman, Hansson, & Richardson, 1978); they found that nursing students who were high on fantasy empathy (i.e., were susceptible to empathizing with story characters and the like) were more likely than other nursing students to avoid contact with dying patients.

In brief, we are suggesting that empathically induced overarousal often results in personal distress whereas sympathy may be associated with more moderate levels of arousal. Whether vicariously induced arousal is experienced as moderate or as overarousal may be a function of many factors, including the constitution of the individual's nervous system, whether individuals typically focus on their own condition or that of others around them, and the ways in which people cope with their own emotional reactions, be they vicariously induced or not. Consequently, it is our view that the concept of coping is relevant to an understanding of vicariously induced emotional responses. In the remainder of this chapter, we review some of the literature relevant to coping with emotions, particularly that relevant to coping in childhood, and then attempt to tie some of this literature to thinking concerning empathy and related vicariously induced responses.

MODES OF COPING

Coping is defined as the constantly changing cognitive and behavioral efforts to manage specific external and or internal demands that are appraised as taxing or exceeding the resources of the person (Lazarus & Folkman, 1984). In both the adult and child literatures, two general modes of coping have been distinguished: problem-focused and emotion-focused. Problem-focused coping strategies are efforts to modify the source of a problem whereas emotion-focused coping strategies are efforts to reduce emotional distress.

Most of the literature on coping in children and adults has focused on the efficacy of either problem-focused or emotion-focused coping strategies for alleviating psychological distress (Aldwin & Revenson, 1987; Compas, 1987; Compas, Malcarne, & Fondacaro, 1988; Hyson, 1983; Lazarus & Folkman, 1984; Miller & Green, 1985). There now exists fairly strong evidence that the efficacy of a coping strategy depends on the source of the problem to be coped with. In adults, problem-focused modes of coping have been found to be most effective in situations that are perceived to be controllable, whereas emotion-focused strategies have been found to be most effective when situations are perceived to be uncontrollable (Band & Weisz, 1988; Compas et al., 1988; Lazarus & Folkman, 1984; Miller & Green, 1985).

Problem-focused coping is perhaps more efficacious when conditions are appraised as amenable to change. Continued unsuccessful efforts to change uncontrollable situations will ultimately lead to lowered motivation, increased passivity, depression, and helplessness (Wortman & Brehm, 1975). Information gathering, for example, which is a form of problem-focused coping, may exacerbate emotional distress and interfere with mechanisms such as avoidance that might reduce distress (Lazarus & Folkman, 1984).

Thus, controlling one's emotions may be more efficacious than problem solving in some circumstances involving an aversive event (e.g., when one lacks control over significant aspects of a situation). Indeed, Lazarus and Folkman (1984) have argued that in most situations people first need to regulate emotional distress in order to facilitate problem-focused coping. Because emotions serve a primary organizing function for behavior (Stroufe & Waters, 1977), the emotion elicited in an aversive context would be expected to influence subsequent action. Thus, the regulation of emotion would be expected to be an important factor in determining how children deal with vicariously induced emotions.

CHILDREN'S REGULATION OF EMOTION

Investigators studying children's coping have found differences in children's use of problem- and emotion-focused coping strategies. One major finding in this literature is that younger children tend to use more problem-focused strategies than older children and it is not until children are older that they begin to use emotion-focused strategies (Cummings & Cummings, 1988; Saarni, 1990; Wertleib, Weigel, & Feldstein, 1987). In addition, younger children report that problem-focused strategies work better than emotion-focused strategies (Band & Weisz, 1988).

Other researchers have also found developmental differences relevant to an understanding of coping with emotion (Compas et al, 1988; Hyson, 1983). For example, Compas et al. (1988) have shown that emotion-focused coping alternatives increase with age and that adaptive problem-focused coping strategies are more fully developed in older children and young adolescents. Similarly, Hyson (1983) found that older children depend more on goal directed behaviors and self-control than younger children in stressful encounters. With regard to coping with others' distresses or needs, Strayer and Schroeder (1989) found that 13-year-olds were more likely than younger children to use proximal, person-centered verbal methods such as reassurance or talking to the person about his or her problem. Five-, 9-, and 13-year-olds all frequently used instrumental methods (defined as acting as an effective agent in helping the other person with respect to achieving goals, alleviating obstacles, or arbitrating differences). However, in considering the results of studies such as these, it should be noted that the obtained age trends in coping behaviors could be due in part to younger children's inability to describe certain types of coping behaviors.

Age differences in children's use of emotion- and problem-focused strategies may be due to differences in the development of emotion-relevant behaviors. Harris and Lipian (1989) found that 6-year olds suggested concrete strategies to make themselves feel better when they felt sad whereas 10-year-olds suggested more mentalistic strategies than instrumental strategies. An interesting result from the same study was that hospitalized children exhibited a regression in maturity when thinking about control of emotions. Fewer 10-year-old hospitalized children than healthy, nonhospitalized children in this study were able to nominate a strategy they used to make themselves feel better when they felt bad. In discussing this study, Saarni (1990) argued that the cognitive sophistication of the 10-year-olds could account for the regression in that they were sophisticated enough to appreciate the threatening aspects of the situation. Specifically, she suggested that the hospitalized children monitored the situation and became more distressed by the information they received, which created a cycle to seek more distressing information, resulting in even more distress.

Consistent with Saarni's hypothesizing, Lazarus and Folkman (1984) claimed that coping behaviors that lead to sustained or increased mobilization are likely to be maladaptive. For example, hypertensive people (as determined by medical procedures) tended to be disposed toward threat appraisals (the belief that something of great importance is at stake in an encounter) and tended to respond to these appraisals with aggressive or angry behavior in social situations; this tendency is hypothesized to eventually lead to a deficit in social competence.

Strayer (1989) demonstrated developmental differences in children's emotional responses to others' negative emotional states. Children under 5 years of age were able to label negative emotions in other children but reported feeling positive emotions themselves when confronted with other persons' distresses. In contrast, older children were able to report negative emotions in themselves as well as others. Strayer argued that children under five may be unable to cope with high levels of another child's distress, may feel engulfed by the child's distress, and therefore blunt their affect and report feeling happy when confronted by another child's trouble. Strayer's assertions are consistent with Glasberg and Aboud's (1982) data indicating that kindergartners are more likely to deny experiencing sadness than are 7-year-olds, and with Carroll and Steward's (1984) finding that 8- to 9-year-olds saw themselves as more able to change their feelings than did 4- to 5-year-olds.

Miller and Green (1985) have discussed blunting and monitoring as two emotion-regulation techniques that children use. They argued that when an aversive event is controllable, monitoring (being alert for and sensitive to the negative aspects of the experience) heightens arousal, and enables the child to execute controlling actions. When an aversive event is uncontrollable, monitoring has little instrumental value; rather, it maximizes one's sense of distress in such a situation. In contrast, blunting (distracting or cognitively shielding oneself from objective sources of danger) can reduce the stressor by tuning it out.

Children's monitoring of uncontrollable situations may lead to greater emotional distress. Miller and Green (1985) found that younger children who had to cope with aversive dental or medical procedures were more overwhelmed than older children with too much information (which forces monitoring) and were more vulnerable to further distress because of the uncontrollable nature of these situations. Exposure to a filmed peer model (of a child who had undergone similar procedures) was stress reducing and appears to have operated through some mechanism other than the provision of increased information or monitoring. Perhaps the peer modeled positive outcomes rather than negative ones, thereby lowering the children's level of arousal.

INDIVIDUAL DIFFERENCES
IN EMOTIONAL REACTIVITY

Individual differences in children's emotional reactivity probably are related to differences in how children cope with negative affect. Children seem to differ in their sensitivity to the environment, with some showing signs of arousal and distress to a much wider array of stimuli than others (Compas, 1987). Ekman (1984) discussed how affective "flooding" occurs for some people in that almost any negative affective experience leads to a consistent negative affective response. For example, for depressed children, negative affect-eliciting situations induce sadness. That sadness is overwhelming because it is hard for the depressed child to regulate the affect once in a depressed state. Thus, the depressed child becomes hypervigilant for cues that may lead to sadness. Consistent with this perspective, there is evidence that suicidal children fail to spontaneously generate cognitive mediational strategies to regulate their affective and behavioral responses to stressful events (Asarnow, Carlson, & Guthrie, 1987).

Individual Differences in Childhood

Individual differences in emotional reactivity and coping abilities are evident in the first years of life. In a study of emotional reactivity in infants, Fox (1989) found that 5-month-olds who were more emotionally reactive to positive and mildly stressful stimuli than were other 5-month olds were more sociable and less distressed by novel situations at 14 months. At 14 months, these infants were highly reactive to their mother's departure, but also spent less time close to their mothers and were likely to approach unfamiliar people. Fox argued that the emotionally reactive infants were not distressed by novelty and were relatively sociable with strangers because they had learned to regulate their emotional responses more effectively than had the less reactive infants. In contrast, the infants who were not emotionally reactive as 5-month-olds and who were less sociable and more wary at 14 months seemed to have already learned a passive mode of responding to novel situations.

Fox and his colleagues (Fox, 1989; Stifter, Fox, & Porges, 1989) also have found that children with low vagal tone (high and stable heart rates) appear to be more anxious and distressed by mildly stressful events and tend not to engage their peers in spontaneous social interaction. Specifically, infants with high vagal tone (more heart rate variability and lower heart rate) were more sociable and approachful at 14 months (Fox, 1989), more reactive to both positive and negative events at 5 months, and more facially expressive at 5 and 14 months of age (Fox, 1989; Stifter et al., in press). Fox (1989) argued that infants with high vagal tone were better able to regulate their own arousal, were more sociable, and responded positively to novel events. Similarly, Kagan (1982) found children with high and stable heart rates were more likely to display shy, fearful, or introverted social behaviors. These children were more anxious and distressed by mildly stressful events and tended not to engage in spontaneous social interaction (Kagan, 1982; Kagan, Reznick, Clarke, Snidman, & Garcia-Coll, 1984).

To summarize, individuals seem to differ in their reactivity to the environment, and this variation in reactivity appears to be correlated with sociability, wariness, and physiological responses. Thus, coping capabilities seem to be related to an individual's reactivity to their environment. Indeed, Fox's (1989) data are consistent with the conclusion that infants that are relatively reactive to the environment may be forced to develop effective coping strategies whereas less reactive infants are not. However, it is possible that the extremely reactive infants would have difficulty developing coping abilities that were sufficient to moderate their sensitivity to the environment.

Socialization and Individual Differences in Emotional Reactivity

One factor that may be especially important in influencing how a person copes with vicarious emotions is his or her socialization experiences. Although the family is considered as a primary agent for socializing empathic-related behavior (Barnett, 1987; Fabes, Eisenberg, & Miller, 1989), few researchers have examined the link between child-rearing experiences and children's coping responses.

Krohne (1979) found that a person's tendency to be either repressive (i.e., to neglect or blunt information) or sensitized (i.e., to attend or monitor information) in aversive situations was positively associated with inconsistent parental reinforcement and restrictiveness, restrictiveness, and failure to provide adequate models of adaptive coping. In his model, individuals in the middle-range of the repressive-sensitization continuum are considered to be adaptive copers; those at the extremes are thought to cope in less adaptive ways. Extrapolating from Krohne's thinking and data, we argue that those children who are likely to be responsive to others' needs and negative affect (i.e., to respond sympathetically and to use more problem-focused coping strategies) are those children who are attentive to the other's condition, but not to the point that they become overly aroused or distressed themselves (i.e., experience high levels of personal distress). These children are likely to come from homes in which parents are consistent and accepting of their children's emotional needs and the expression of such needs, and are adaptive copers themselves.

In our own work (Fabes et al., 1989), we found that mothers' empathic dispositions were related to their children's empathic and prosocial behavior. Although the strength of the associations varied for boys and girls (and was stronger for the latter), in general mothers who were more empathic and other-oriented had children who were more responsive to other persons in need. In contrast, mothers who responded to others' distress with personal distress tended to have children who reported feeling less sympathetic and more positive after being exposed to a needy other (perhaps as a function of masking or denial of negative affect).

The findings from our study suggest that mothers who respond to distressful situations involving their children (as either the distressed individual or as a bystander) with personal distress may be relatively unlikely to focus on their children's negative affective states and likely to focus on their own feelings of distress and anxiety. Such reactions may result in mothers' trying to alleviate their own aversive states (i.e., emotion-focused coping) rather than being sensitive and effective in addressing their children's emotional needs (i.e., problem-focused coping). These mothers also may be relatively unaccepting of their children's negative affective reactions. Thus, those mothers who react with personal distress to others' distresses may hamper the development of empathy-related coping processes in their children because their reactions are oriented more toward buffering their own aversive feelings than towards helping their children develop effective strategies for coping with their own (and others') feelings.

Although our findings are consistent with Krohne's (1979) data and his notion that parental modeling, responsiveness, and restrictiveness are important determinants of children's coping, it is important to note that the maternal data in both Krohne's and our studies were obtained through self-report questionnaires. Because self-report measures may be influenced by social desirability and demand characteristics, interpretation of these data must be made cautiously. However, these data are provocative and do suggest that socialization factors are important correlates of children's vicarious emotional and coping responses.

Social Behavior, Emotional Responding, and Coping

As was just discussed, children's emotional reactivity and coping capabilities (it is difficult to disentangle the two after early infancy) seem to be associated in some way with their sociability. This seems logical; children who are overwhelmed with a negative emotional response in the context of a social interaction would be expected to either withdraw or to exhibit low levels of social competence in the given context. Moreover, children who are less able to cope with negative affect produced in a social interaction may be less inclined to seek out social situations.

Although not plentiful, there is additional evidence indicating a relation between children's ability to regulate affect and children's social behavior. In a study on the effects of marital discord on young children's peer interactions and health, Gottman and Katz (1989) reported that children from unhappy marriage homes who were flooded by anger, fear, and disgust, avoided potentially pleasurable interactions with other children, perhaps out of fear that some interactions might elicit anger. It is reasonable to assume that these children's coping abilities were overtaxed (particularly in the domain of dealing with negative emotions); thus, they simply may have been protecting themselves from the possibility of further distress. In addition, there may be enduring sequelae for these children; by avoiding social encounters, they may fail to learn the social skills necessary for positive social interactions.

Other data also suggest that when children are emotionally distressed and aroused due to exposure to conflict, the quality of their social behavior suffers.

Young children who are exposed to adults' conflicts frequently become more aggressive in their play with peers (Cummings, 1987; Cummings, Iannotti, & Zahn-Waxler, 1985). However, children's style of coping appears to mediate their reactions. Cummings (1987) exposed preschoolers to a simulated angry conflict in an adjacent room, and grouped the preschoolers according to their patterns of coping. His *concerned* group showed negative emotions concurrent with exposure to anger, and later reported that they had felt sad during the fight and wanted to intervene. *Unresponsive* children showed no evidence of emotion, but later reported having been angry. *Ambivalent* responders exhibited high emotional arousal during the conflict, typified by both positive and negative emotions, and reported both feeling happy and admitted to impulses to express arousal and disregulation. Moreover, they were most likely to become physically and verbally aggressive in play with a friend. Perhaps the concerned children were worried about the welfare of the people arguing. However, it also is possible that the children were experiencing moderate levels of personal distress and wanted to end the conflict so that they themselves would feel better. This latter possibility is consistent with Cummings' finding in another study that children classified as concerned exhibited heart rate acceleration (a correlate of personal distress; Eisenberg, Fabes, et al., 1988; Eisenberg, Schaller, et al., 1988) during exposure to conflict (Cummings, personal communication, 1989).

Cummings (1987) suggested that his unresponsive children were exhibiting overcontrol and had inhibited their reactions to the argument. However, the fact that a group of unresponsive children in another study did not exhibit heart rate reactivity to conflict and did not report negative reactions suggests that if these children were overcontrolled, this control was so effective that they had learned to block emotional responding. Perhaps the unresponsive group included children who for various reasons were simply less reactive to others' negative states. Such unresponsiveness could be due to biological factors or might be a product of socialization experiences leading to a lack of interest in, and caring about, other people.

Cummings' (1987) ambivalent group seemed to be relatively arousable and to have the most difficulty dealing with their arousal. Indeed, Cummings described them as *undercontrolled*. Whether these children were particularly arousable or low in coping capabilities (or both) is unclear. In any case, the behavior of this group of arousable children seemed to be the most negatively affected by exposure to conflict.

In some of our own work, we have additional data suggesting that children who experience relatively high levels of personal distress when viewing peers in distress may be less socially competent than peers who experience less personal distress. For example, preschoolers (Eisenberg, Fabes, Miller, Shell, Shea, & May-Plumlee, 1990) and elementary children (Eisenberg, Fabes, Miller, Fultz, Shell, Mathy, & Reno, 1989) who facially display relatively high levels of personal distress when viewing films of distressed and needy peers are relatively unlikely to help the peers when it is easy to escape further contact with them. In addition, among preschoolers, children who exhibit high levels of personal distress in reaction to exposure to needy or injured others appear to be less socially dominant than other children.

Specifically, preschoolers who exhibit personal distress facially are especially likely to comply with peers' requests for toys (Eisenberg, Fabes, Miller, Shell, Shea, & May-Plumlee, 1990; Eisenberg, McCreath, & Ahn, 1988). In contrast, children who exhibit sympathy and concern on their face are especially likely to assist peers without being requested to do so (Eisenberg, McCreath, & Ahn, 1988). In our view, sharing and helping in response to a peer's request are often compliant responses in the preschool classroom; moreover, frequent compliers may acquiesce because it is difficult to escape the peer who is trying to obtain help or an object. Children who are high in personal distress seem to be considered as "easy targets" by their peers; they are asked for help more often than are other children (Eisenberg, McCreath, & Ahn, 1988). Moreover, children who engage in high frequencies of requested sharing (as do children who exhibit high levels of personal distress) are relatively less social, less emotionally reactive to peers, and less assertive than are children who engage in high levels of spontaneously emitted prosocial behaviors (Eisenberg, Cameron, Tryon, & Dodez, 1981; Eisenberg, Pasternack, Cameron, & Tryon, 1984). Furthermore, preschoolers are less likely to respond positively to a peer's compliance with a request if the peer typically engages in relatively high amounts of compliant helping and sharing (i.e., there is a negative correlation between frequency of engaging in requested behaviors and likelihood of a positive reaction from the recipient of the prosocial act.)

Although the aforementioned findings are scattered throughout a number of studies (with social indices, personal distress, and helping often not all being assessed in a single study), we feel that the pattern of findings is suggestive. Children who exhibit high levels of personal distress are not particularly helpful when they can escape from the anxiety-producing context; rather, they exhibit high levels of *compliant* prosocial behavior and low levels of assertiveness, and are the target of frequent requests from peers. Although we have no sociometric data in any of our studies and our indices of social competence are limited, it seems likely that these children are relatively low in social competence and popularity. It also seems reasonable to hypothesize that children who typically experience personal distress in reaction to exposure to needy or distressed persons are not very good at managing their distress in social situations, and that is why they assist primarily when not doing so is likely to result in additional pressure from peers to comply.

Coping and Vicarious Emotional Arousal

In most of the research on vicarious emotional responding, coping strategies or activities have not been directly assessed. Thus, at this point we can only hypothesize about the role of coping in children's vicarious emotional reactions. However, the research that we have reviewed suggests that coping—in social situations and in regard to the regulation of emotion—plays a role in children's vicarious emotional responses and in how children behave once they are vicariously aroused.

It is likely that a variety of factors influence children's coping with vicarious emotion in a given context. Our thinking about this issue generally is consistent with that of Cummings and Cummings (1988), who discussed a process-oriented approach to conceptualizing children's coping with others' anger.

Specifically, how children respond to vicariously induced emotion seems to be a function of multiple factors: (a) the child's characteristics and background, including the children's developmental level, socialization, and previous relevant experiences (see previous sections of this chapter); and (b) characteristics of the context, including who the child is empathizing with, the intensity of the emotion-eliciting cues in the situation, controllability of the situation, and the behavioral affordances in the given context (e.g., whether it is possible for the child to assist the distressed person and whether it is easy for the child to escape from the emotion-eliciting cues). Child/background and situational factors interact in affecting children's level of stress and mode of coping in a given situation. For example, children differing in arousability and in coping styles would be expected to react differently in different situations, depending upon the intensity of cues and the adaptiveness of various coping strategies in the given situation.

Based on this framework, we can offer several specific hypotheses regarding coping with vicariously induced negative emotions such as sadness and distress. In empathy-eliciting situations, children who are easily aroused and less able to modulate their own arousal (i.e., who experience more emotional "flooding" and who are less effective "blunters" in uncontrollable situations) may be particularly likely to focus on their own aversive states when confronted with another person's distress because of the high level of their arousal. These children will display relatively high levels of personal distress, and will be inclined to escape the situation if possible. If they cannot escape from the distressing stimulus, they may attempt to initiate problem-focused coping responses to ameliorate the other person's situation, but primarily as a means of reducing their own distress. However, if their distress is particularly high, they may be unable to initiate problem-focused strategies because of an inability to effectively manage their own affective state and the existing conditions. Moreover, if the situation is particularly evocative, arousable children, especially those low in coping abilities, may be especially likely to try to escape from the situation and may exhibit high levels of undercontrolled behavior.

On the other hand, children who are less easily aroused (but are normative with regard to arousability) or are able to modulate their own arousal (i.e., those who experience less emotional "flooding" and those who are more effective managers of emotion in uncontrollable or highly evocative situations) may be less likely to focus on their own aversive states when confronted with another person's distress. This is because their emotional reaction is likely to be moderate in intensity rather than highly aversive. Such children would be expected to display more sympathy and to be relatively likely to initiate problem-focused coping responses such as helping to ameliorate the other person's situation. However, even these children may not exhibit adaptive behaviors if the characteristics of the situation are such that it is highly distressing or threatening for the child.

A factor that is not emphasized in Cummings' and Cummings' (1988) model is appraisal processes. However, such processes would seem to contribute significantly to how people respond vicariously to others' emotional states or condition. This is because cognitive appraisal is thought to be an important mediator of a person's affective responses to a stressful situation (Folkman & Lazarus, 1988).

Support for the importance of appraisal comes from research demonstrating that attributions about another's condition (e.g., appraisal of the reasons for the other's need or condition) affect a person's affective and behavioral reactions toward another person (see Eisenberg, 1986, for a review). For example, Weiner (1980) found that attributing another's needy situation to internal, controllable factors (e.g., drunkenness) maximized negative affective reactions (e.g., anger, distress) and led to avoidance and low levels of helping the needy other. In contrast, ascription of responsibility of the person's need to uncontrollable factors (feeling ill) was associated with sympathy and concern, and with higher levels of helping. Thus, appraisal of contextual factors (e.g., the needs of the other, controllability, and what is at stake) influences one's vicarious affective and coping responses in that situation.

In thinking about vicarious emotional responding, coping and appraisal are difficult to distinguish, and serve interdependent functions. For example, it has been found that if individuals are unable to assist needy others, they may derogate (i.e., ascribe negative characteristics to) them even if the other people are not responsible for their condition (Lerner & Miller, 1978). Derogating the needy other serves both to shape the meaning of the event (i.e., an appraisal function) and to help regulate distress (i.e., a coping function). Thus, appraisal may determine both the type of vicarious emotional response one has to another's condition and the type of coping strategy employed in that situation (Folkman & Lazarus, 1988).

Consistent with the emotion versus cognitive primacy debate (e.g., Lazarus, 1982; Zajonc, 1980), other researchers maintain that emotions affect coping processes either by motivating or impeding them (e.g., Krohne & Laux, 1982). Thus, it also may be the case that vicarious emotional responses influence one's appraisal and subsequent coping strategies. For example, people who experience personal distress when exposed to a needy other may become more vigilant in their appraisal of aspects of the environment relevant to their own condition and less attuned to the condition of the needy other. When personal distress reactions are relatively intense, other-oriented appraisals may become increasingly aversive because of the distress they evoke. Thus, such appraisals are likely to be curtailed or redirected because they would force the individual's attention back to the condition that induced the aversive state. This avoidance of a focus on the other person would be expected to decrease the likelihood that helping will occur and increase the likelihood of self-oriented, emotion-focused coping. In support of this argument, Mellor-Crummey, Connell, and Trachtenberg (1989) found that children who reported feeling anxious or distressed in conflictual social situations tended to blame others for undesirable social consequences in those situations.

In contrast, a person who responds to another's condition with sympathy or concern is likely to be both more vigilant in their appraisals of the other's needs and more motivated to employ coping strategies that address the needs of the other. Indeed, self-reported empathy and sympathy have been associated with other-oriented moral reasoning (see Eisenberg, 1986), other-oriented attributions for assisting others (Eisenberg & Silbereisen, unpublished data), and other-oriented behavior (Eisenberg & Miller, 1987).

In summary, it is likely that the relation between vicarious emotional responses and appraisal is bidirectional, with each affecting the other and coping strategies. Viewed in this way, empathy-relevant appraisals may be both a cause and an outcome of vicarious emotional responses. Moreover, a given person's appraisals in a specific context would be expected to vary as a function of characteristics of the setting and dispositional characteristics (e.g., dispositional sympathy and the tendency to become overaroused), the latter of which is affected by socialization experiences.

CONCLUSIONS

The hypotheses listed above concerning children's reactions to others in distress or need are tentative and have not, to our knowledge, been tested. However, it is likely that children's coping capabilities and tendencies are highly relevant to how they manage their own vicariously induced emotions and how they react to those who elicit a vicarious response. Thus, research integrating the coping literature with the work concerning empathy and sympathy and prosocial behavior would seem to be a productive endeavor.

REFERENCES

Aldwin, C., & Revenson, T. (1987). Does coping help? A reexamination of the relation between coping and mental health. *Journal of Personality and Social Psychology, 53,* 337–348.

Asarnow, J. R., Carlson, G. A., & Guthrie, D. (1987). Coping strategies, self-perceptions, hopelessness, and perceived family environments in depressed and suicidal children. *Journal of Consulting and Clinical Psychology, 55,* 361–366.

Band, B. E., & Weisz, J. R. (1988). How to feel better when it feels bad: Children's perspectives on coping with everyday stress. *Developmental Psychology, 24,* 247–253.

Barnett, M. A. (1987). Empathy and related responses in children. In N. Eisenberg & J. Strayer (Eds.), *Empathy and its development* (pp. 46–162). Cambridge, UK: Cambridge University Press.

Batson, C. D. (1987). Prosocial motivation: Is it ever truly altruistic? In L. Berkowitz (Ed.), *Advance in experimental social psychology* (Vol. 20, pp. 65–122). New York: Academic Press.

Carroll, J. J., & Steward, M. S. (1984). The role of cognitive development in children's understandings of their own feelings. *Child Development, 55,* 1486–1492.

Compas, B. E. (1987). Coping with stress during childhood and adolescence. *Psychological Bulletin, 101,* 393–403.

Compas, B. E., Malcarne, V. L., & Fondacaro, K. M. (1988). Coping with stressful events in older children and young adolescents. *Journal of Consulting and Clinical Psychology, 56*(3), 405–411.

Cummings, E. M. (1987). Coping with background anger in early childhood. *Child Development, 58,* 976–984.

Cummings, E. M., & Cummings, J. L. (1988). A process-oriented approach to children's coping with adults' angry behavior. *Developmental Review, 8,* 296–321.

Cummings, E. M., Iannotti, R. J., Zahn-Waxler, C. (1985). Influence of conflict between adults on the emotions and aggression of young children. *Developmental Psychology, 21,* 495–507.

Eisenberg, N. (1986). *Altruistic emotion, cognition, and behavior.* Hillsdale, NJ: Lawrence Erlbaum Associates.

Eisenberg, N., Cameron, E., Tryon, K., & Dodez, R. (1981). Socialization of prosocial behavior in the preschool classroom. *Developmental Psychology, 17,* 773–782.

Eisenberg, N., Fabes, R. A., Bustamante, D., Mathy, R. M., Miller, P., Lindholm, E. (1988). Differentiation of vicariously-induced emotional reactions in children. *Developmental Psychology, 24,* 237–246.

Eisenberg, N., Fabes, R. A., Miller, P. A., Fultz, J., Mathy, R. M., & Reno, R. (in press). The relations of sympathy and personal distress to prosocial behavior: A multimethod study. *Journal of Personality and Social Psychology.*

Eisenberg, N., Fabes, R. A., Miller, P. A., Fultz, J., Mathy, R. M., Shell, R., & Reno, R. R. (1989). The relations of sympathy and personal distress to prosocial behavior: A multimethod study. *Journal of Personality and Social Psychology, 57,* 55–66.

Eisenberg, N., Fabes, R. A., Miller, P. A., Shell, C., Shea, R., May-Plumlee, T. (1990). The relation of preschoolers' vicarious emotional responding to situational and dispositional prosocial behavior. *Merrill-Palmer Quarterly, 36,* 507–529.

Eisenberg, N., McCreath, H., & Ahn, R. (1988). Vicarious emotional responsiveness and prosocial behavior: Their interrelations in young children. *Personality and Social Psychology Bulletin, 14,* 298–311.

Eisenberg, N., & Miller, P. (1987). The relation of empathy to prosocial and related behaviors. *Psychological Bulletin, 101,* 91–119.

Eisenberg, N., Pasternack, J. F., Cameron, E., & Tryon, K. (1984). The relation of quality and mode of prosocial behavior to moral cognitions and social style. *Child Development, 155,* 1479–1485.

Eisenberg, N., Schaller, M., Fabes, R. A., Bustamante, D., Mathy, R., Shell, R., & Rhodes, K. (1988). The differentiation of personal distress and sympathy in children and adults. *Developmental Psychology, 24,* 766–775.

Eisenberg, N., Shea, C. L., Carlo, G. & Knight, G. (in press). Empathy-related responding and cognition: A "chicken and the egg" dilemma. In W. Kurtines (Ed.), *Advances in moral development* (Vol. 1). New York: Wiley.

Eisenberg, N., & Strayer, J. (1987). Critical issues in the study of empathy. In N. Eisenberg & J. Strayer (Eds.), *Empathy and its development.* Cambridge, UK: Cambridge University Press.

Ekman, P. (1984). Expression and nature of emotion. In K. P. Scherer & P. Ekman (Eds.), *Approaches to emotion* (pp. 319–343). Hillsdale, NJ: Lawrence Erlbaum Associates.

El-Sheikh, M., Cummings, E. M., & Goetsch, V. L. (1989). Coping with adults' angry behavior: Behavioral, physiological, and verbal responses in preschoolers. *Developmental Psychology, 25,* 490–498.

Fabes, R. A., Eisenberg, N., & Miller, P. (1990). *Maternal correlates of children's emotional responsiveness. Developmental Psychology, 26,* 639–648.

Folkman, S., & Lazarus, R. A. (1988). Coping as a mediator of emotion. *Journal of Personality and Social Psychology, 54,* 466–475.

Fox, N. A. (1989). Psychophysiological correlations of emotional reactivity during the first year of life. *Developmental Psychology, 25,* 364–372.

Glasberg, R., & Aboud, F. (1982). Keeping one's distance from sadness: Children's self-reports of emotional experience. *Developmental Psychology, 18,* 287–293.

Gottman, J. M., & Katz, L. F. (1989). Effects of marital discord on young children's peer interaction and health. *Developmental Psychology, 25,* 373–381.

Harris, P. L., & Lipian, M. (1989). Understanding emotion and experiencing emotion. In C. Saarni & P. L. Harris (Eds.), *Children's understanding of emotion.* New York: Cambridge University Press.

Hoffman, M. L. (1984). Interaction of affect and cognition on empathy. In C. E. Izard, J. Kagan, & R. B. Zajonc (Eds.), *Emotions, cognitions, and behavior* (pp. 103–131). Cambridge, UK: Cambridge University Press.

Hyson, M. C. (1983). Going to the doctor: A developmental study of stress and coping. *Journal of Child Psychology and Psychiatry, 24,* 247–259.

Kagan, J. (1982). Heart rate and heart rate variability as signs of temperamental dimension in infants. In C. E. Izard (Ed.), *Measuring emotions in infants and children* (pp. 38–66). Cambridge, UK: Cambridge University Press.

Kagan, J., Reznick, J. S., Clarke, C., Snidman, N., & Garcia-Coll, C. (1984). Behavioral inhibition to the unfamiliar. *Child Development, 55,* 2212–2225.

Krohne, H. W. (1979). Parental child-rearing and the development of anxiety and coping strategies in children. In I. G. Sarason & C. D. Spielberger (Eds.), *Stress and anxiety* (Vol. 7, pp. 233–245). Washington, DC: Hemisphere.

Krohne, H. W., & Laux, L. (1982). *Achievement, stress, and anxiety.* Washington, DC: Hemisphere.

Lazarus, R. S. (1982). Thoughts on the relations between emotion and cognition. *American Psychologist, 37,* 1019–1024.

Lazarus, R. S., & Folkman, S. (1984). Coping and adaptation. In W. D. Gentry (Ed.) *The handbook of behavioral medicine.* New York: Guilford.

Lerner, M. J., & Miller, D. T. (1978). Just world research and the attribution process: Looking back and looking ahead. *Psychological Bulletin, 85,* 1030–1051.

Mellor-Crummey, C. A., Connell, J. P., & Trachtenberg, S. (1989, April). *Children's coping in social situations.* Paper presented at the biennial meeting of the Society for Research in Child Development, Kansas City, MO.

Miller, S. M., & Green, M. L. (1985). Coping with stress and frustration: Origins, nature, and development. In M. Lewis & C. Saarni (Eds.), *The socialization of emotions* (pp. 263–314). New York: Plenum Press.

Saarni, C. (1990). Emotional competence: How emotions and relationships become integrated. In R. Thompson (Ed.), *Nebraska symposium on motivation* (pp. 115–182). Lincoln, NE: University of Nebraska Press.

Schroeder, D. A., Dovidio, J. F., Sibicky, M. E., Matthews, L. L., & Allen, J. L. (1988). Empathic concern and helping behavior: Egoism or altruism? *Journal of Experimental Social Psychology, 24,* 333–353.

Sroufe, L. A., & Waters, E. (1977). Attachment as an organizational construct. *Child Development, 48*, 1184–1199.

Stifter, C. A., Fox, N. A., & Porges, S. W. (1989). The relation between heart rate variability, facial expressivity, and temperament in five- and ten-month-old infants. *Infant Behavior and Development, 12,* 127–138.

Stotland, E., Mathews, K. E., Jr., Sherman, S. E., Hansson, R. O., & Richardson, B. Z. (1978). *Empathy, fantasy, and helping.* Beverly Hills: Sage.

Strayer, J. (1989). What children know and feel in response to witnessing affective events. In C. Saarni & P. L. Harris (Eds.), *Children's understanding of emotion.* New York: Cambridge University Press.

Strayer, J., & Schroeder, M. (1989). Children's helping strategies: Influences of emotion, empathy, and age. In N. Eisenberg (Ed.), *Empathy and related emotional responses.* New Directions in Child Development. *44,* 85–106.

Weiner, B. (1980). Examination of affect and egocentrism as mediators of bias in causal attribution. *Journal of Personality and Social Psychology, 39,* 186–200.

Wertlieb, D., Weigel, M. A., & Feldstein, M. (1987). Measuring children's coping. *American Journal of Orthopsychiatry, 57*(4), 548–560.

Wortman, C. B., & Brehm, J. W. (1975). Responses to uncontrollable outcomes: An integration of reactance theory and the learned helplessness model. In L. Berkowitz (Ed.), *Advances in experimental social psychology* (Vol. 8). New York: Academic Press.

Zajonc, R. B. (1980). Feeling and thinking: Preferences need no inferences. *American Psychologist, 35,* 151–175.

7 Growing Up Female: Stressful Events and the Transition to Adolescence

Jeanne Brooks-Gunn
Educational Testing Service and Teachers' College, Columbia University

The adolescence period has been characterized as stressful throughout recorded history. Socrates felt that adolescents "are ready to contradict their parents, monopolize the conversation in company, eat gluttonously, and tyrannize their teachers" (Anthony, 1969, p. 77). Psychology continued in a similar vein. G. Stanley Hall, the father of adolescent psychology, characterized adolescence, particularly the first half, as stormy and stressful.

Much of the early research on adolescence focused on testing this widely accepted belief. Two of the most popular topics of study were concerned with whether storm and stress really characterized most young teenagers and whether one's self-image changed dramatically during the transition to adolescence (Nesselroade & Baltes, 1974; Offer, 1987). Somewhat surprisingly, most of this research did not focus on either the biological or social changes that accompany the adolescent transition as possible mediators of tumultuous behavior or on alterations in self-images (Brooks-Gunn, 1989; Brooks-Gunn & Reiter, 1990). Generally, these seminal early studies did not find much evidence for universal storm nor for dramatic, discontinuous changes in self-image (Hamburg, 1974). For example, Offer (1987) found that only about one fifth of white boys in his large sample had "tumultuous growth," characterized by serious parent-child conflict.

Such findings set the backdrop for the last decade of adolescent research on storm and stress in several important ways (Brooks-Gunn, 1989). First, the adolescent life phase became differentiated; the experiences of the child making the transition into adolescence were recognized to be very different from those of the teenager making the transition out of adolescence (Gunnar & Collins, 1988; Lerner & Foch, 1987; Montemayor, Adams, & Gullotta, 1990). Second, this

119

singular differentiation encouraged researchers to consider the types, patterns, and sequencing of different events occurring for younger and older adolescents separately. In the case of the young teenager, both biological and social events became the focus of research (Brooks-Gunn & Petersen, 1983, 1984; Gunnar & Collins, 1988). Regrettably, less work was conducted on possible cognitive and social cognitive changes occurring in the early teenage years (see Collins, 1988; Keating, 1990; Smetana, 1988, as notable exceptions).

Third, older, more crisis-oriented models fell out of favor and were replaced with models focusing on the more normative aspects of young adolescents' experiences. The recognition that early studies did not find universal turmoil or dysfunction (Offer, 1987), and that life span developmental models were easily applied to the adolescent life phase (Brooks-Gunn, Petersen, & Eichorn, 1985; Lerner, 1985; Nesselroade & Baltes, 1974), contributed to conceptual innovations in model development. After all, every child experiences puberty, has stirrings of sexual arousal, and, in Western countries, moves from elementary school to middle or high school, which places new social and cognitive demands on the individual. Could these universal experiences readily be conceptualized as crises? Many researchers, including myself, began to focus on the fact that not all aspects of the transition into adolescence were perceived as a crisis, at least by most adolescents. In the 1970s, Diane Ruble and I began a series of studies on girls' reactions to menarcheal experiences and the factors that influenced their constructions of menarche and menstruation. Perhaps the most widely cited finding has been the lack of an intense, negative response to menarche, as it contradicted prevailing notions about pubertal experiences being traumatic events (Brooks-Gunn, 1984; Brooks-Gunn & Ruble, 1982; Grief & Ulman, 1982; Ruble & Brooks-Gunn, 1982).

Fourth, individual differences in responses and antecedent conditions were highlighted. In the case of the young adolescent, the large interindividual differences in timing of pubertal change could not be ignored (Brooks-Gunn et al., 1985). After all, a 12-year-old girl whose physical development is within normal ranges may look like a child or a fully developed adult or somewhere in between. The timing of social events such as school changes and dating also exhibit variability. As the need to defend the view that many aspects of the adolescent transition were not experienced as a crisis waned, it became possible to study those subgroups for whom certain events were problematic, and the factors that predicted difficulties. In our menarche research, for instance, we found that girls who were early maturers, who did not discuss pubertal events with their mothers, and whose fathers were not told about their daughter's menarche immediately, were more likely to have negative reactions to menarche and to exhibit more long-lasting negative feelings about menstruation (Brooks-Gunn, 1987; Brooks-Gunn & Ruble, 1982).

Today, the question is not whether the transition into adolescence is stressful, but for which girls, in which circumstances, at what ages, and for what outcomes it is stressful. The stress experienced by the young adolescent is defined here in terms of the potentially stressful life events that characterize the transition from childhood to adolescence. These include social and biological events. In this chapter, I examine the evidence for links between the occurrence of potentially stressful life events and adolescent behavior, with a particular focus on the timing of events and the relative effects of biological and social events.

Adolescence has been described as stormy as well as stressful. Storminess refers to moodiness, rapid shifts in moods, and outbursts of often short-lived negative behavior. Pubertal changes, specifically the increase in hormone levels, are frequently mentioned as a prime cause of negative behavior. In this chapter, I focus on how much of this type of behavior can be attributed to pubertal changes. Because these changes occur at precisely the time that multiple social changes are encountered, comparisons of relative effects of biological and social changes on moodiness and affective behaviors need to be considered.[1]

Rather than centering on the less interesting question of whether storm and stress exists during this transition, I consider questions of interindividual variability and the mechanisms underlying such variability. Whenever possible, cognitive, biological, and social mechanisms are mentioned. Regrettably, more work has been done on possible biological and social than cognitive mechanisms underlying changes in adolescent behavior.[2] In addition, longitudinal research focusing on long-lasting effects of experiences during the transition to adolescence is just beginning (see, for example, Baydar, Brooks-Gunn, & Warren, 1990; Block & Gjerde, 1990; Hauser & Bowlds, 1990; Offer, 1987; Paikoff, Brooks-Gunn, & Warren, 1991; Petersen, Sarigiani, & Kennedy, 1991; Stattin & Magnusson, 1990), and opportunities for secondary data analyses are emerging (Brooks-Gunn, Phelps, & Elder, 1991).

Most of the research is based on the premise that negative affect and behavior increase during the first half of adolescence. My research group has focused on several dimensions of affect and behavior—depressive affect and symptoms, aggressive affect and behavior, problem eating attitudes and behavior, and body image (which is highly associated with eating behavior). Generally, the level of

---

[1]The more colloquial use of the storm and stress conceptualization refers to parent-child interactions. The phrase probably arose from adult experiences in the rearing and teaching of young adolescents (Blos, 1979; Hall, 1904), as parental interchanges with young adolescents are almost always portrayed as conflictual. Our research team's work on parent-child relationships is not reviewed in this chapter (see Brooks-Gunn & Zahaykevich, 1989; Paikoff & Brooks-Gunn, 1990a; Paikoff, Carlton-Ford, & Brooks-Gunn, 1990).

[2]Significant exceptions do exist. Research on teenage sexual behavior and contraceptive use focuses on cognitive correlates (Brooks-Gunn & Furstenberg, 1989; Paikoff & Brooks-Gunn, 1990b). Social cognitive explanations for increased parent-child conflict during the early adolescent years is another (Collins, 1988; Smetana, 1988, 1989). And the interesting work on the cognitive underpinnings of depressive affect is yet a third example (Nolen-Hoeksema, Seligman, & Girgus, 1991). Another limitation of the research is that the long-term implications of the biological and social events occurring during adolescence have not been answered satisfactorily.

negative affective expression seems to rise between the childhood and adolescent years (Csikszentmihalyi & Larson, 1984; Larson & Lampman-Petraitis, 1989; Rutter, Graham, Chadwick, & Yule, 1976; Simmons, Rosenberg, & Rosenberg, 1973). Surprisingly few studies actually have charted changes in the prevalence of these three domains from late childhood through late adolescence; either the change from late childhood to early adolescence or the change from early to late adolescence is described. With respect to depression, the incidence of depressive disorders increases dramatically in the first half of adolescence (Rutter et al., 1976), and many but not all studies report higher scores on depressive affect scales in nonclinical samples of girls in the first half of adolescence than earlier (Baydar et al., 1990; Brooks-Gunn & Petersen, in press; Petersen et al., in press; Rutter, Izard, & Read, 1986). Aggressive affect also increases between ages 10 and 15 (Rutter et al., 1976). Eating problem scores rise during the first half of adolescence and in the second half of adolescence (Attie & Brooks-Gunn, 1989; Brooks-Gunn, Rock, & Warren, 1989). Across all studies, large interindividual variation is seen within age periods.

STRESSFUL LIFE EVENTS

Stress is said to occur when an individual is confronted with an event that is perceived as threatening, that requires a novel response, that is seen as important (i.e., needs to be responded to) and for which an individual does not have an appropriate coping response available (Cohen & Wills, 1985; Lazarus, 1966; Lazarus & Launier, 1978). In a vast literature on adults, the occurrence of stressful life events has been associated with physical illness as well as negative emotional states (Broadhead, Kaplan et al., 1983; Kessler, Price, & Wortman, 1985; Thoits, 1983). Most scholars have assumed that events provoking stressful reactions in adults also influence the well-being of adolescents. The measures of well-being in this literature extend past emotional and physical well-being to include school achievement and behavior problems. Like most of the adult literature, little attention is placed on the four criteria just mentioned; it is assumed that particular events are threatening, novel, and important, as well as imbued with uncertainty, vis-à-vis the availability of appropriate responses (see Compas, 1987a, for a discussion of conceptions of stressful events as well as attempts to categorize events along dimensions such as these four).

Is the transition from childhood to adolescence a particularly stressful time in an individual's life? After all, many of the events occurring for most young adolescents are novel, perhaps threatening, and important. Indeed, the concentration of events occurring at this time might be one of two aspects of this transition that marks it as distinct from other life transitions; the other aspect being beginning puberty itself (Brooks-Gunn, 1988a). Almost no research has addressed the issue of distinctiveness in number or type of social events that the young adolescent faces. Also, whether a limited number of coping responses is available is not known. It seems plausible that prepubertal children would have few available coping responses for events such as dating; moving to a large, less personal school; and making decisions about such behaviors as smoking, drinking, and sexual intercourse.

Models are being developed for studying the timing, sequencing, and type of events that young teenagers face. The four models that my research group has developed to study links between stressful life events and adolescent behavior are reviewed here. All but the first make a distinction between biological and social events taking place at this time, because one of the striking features of this transition is puberty and all that it entails. The first model considers the effects of the cumulative number of events occurring during adolescence, testing the premise that negative affect rises because of the number of events with which the young teenager is faced. The second model focuses on the effects of different features of life events (timing, novelty, number of events, number of events relative to one's peers, and type of event). The underlying premise is that the timing and relativity of events experienced is what contributes to changes in negative affect, not just the sheer number of events. A third model explores the possibility that girls are more vulnerable to specific negative events at certain pubertal phases than others, which emphasizes interactions between pubertal and social events. The fourth considers the possibility that stressful life events may alter the course of puberty itself.

Cumulative Effects of Events

At the most simplistic level, adolescents might exhibit negative affect and behavior because of the sheer number of life events that occur during the first half of the teenage years. Simmons and her colleagues (Simmons, Burgeson, & Reef, 1988) have conducted an elegant study demonstrating the effects of the cumulative number of events upon the well-being of youth in middle school. The addition of life events was associated with more school problems and lower self-esteem scores. The associations were primarily linear and were found for both boys and girls. In these analyses, social events as well as one biological event were entered into the equations; separate effects of each were not explored, except to say that all events contributed to the decrements in well-being in an additive sense.

The cumulative number of life events model has been tested in our 4-year longitudinal study of 125 girls seen yearly (Baydar & Brooks-Gunn, 1990; Baydar et al., 1990). Depressive symptoms and aggressive behavior are the outcomes of interest (the data on depressive symptoms are presented here). Our first question was whether depressive symptoms actually increased from age 11 to age 15. As seen in Fig. 7.1, depressive symptoms were highest at ages 13 to 14 than earlier or later, using the Center for Epidemiological Survey Depression

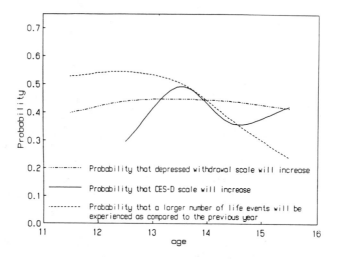

FIG. 7.1. Age dependency of changes in depressive symptoms and life event experiences. From Baydar, Brooks-Gunn, and Warren (1990).

Scale (CES-D; Radloff, 1977, in press), but not using items tapping depression-withdrawal on the Youth Behavior Checklist (Achenbach & Edelbrock, 1987). We then examined whether the number of social life events was associated with age, finding that adolescents experience more life events in the first 3 years than the second 3 years of adolescence (Fig. 7.1). To our knowledge, this is the first study to test directly the underlying premise of most of the research, namely, that girls in the middle of the first half of adolescence experience more events than at other ages.

Modeling changes in negative affect and behavior and changes in life events simultaneously using a differential linear equation regression technique, cumulative number of events was found to be associated with depressive symptoms and aggressive behavior (Baydar & Brooks-Gunn, 1990; Baydar et al., 1990).

Type, Novelty, and Relativity of Events

These cumulative analyses have been extended in several ways. Our earlier work and that of Simmons and her colleagues demonstrated that the number of life events, particularly negative social ones, is linked to decrements in well-being. However, we still do not know what it was about the events that contribute to decrements. Accordingly, we specified five hypotheses to test in our 4-year longitudinal study using depressive symptomatology and aggressive behavior as our outcome measures:

1. The multitude of life experiences during a given time period will increase depressive symptoms due to their cumulative load on resources for coping.

2. The number of experiences in excess of that experienced by an adolescent's peers will increase depressive experiences. Adolescents compare their pubertal and social experience to their peers' experiences, rendering an individual's experience relative to peers salient (Berndt, 1982; Brooks-Gunn, Samelson, Warren, & Fox, 1986; Savin-Williams & Berndt, 1990). This premise has not been tested in previous studies.

3. The novelty of a particular kind of experience will increase depressive symptoms more than subsequent experiences. This premise is particularly important to test in that it is believed that young adolescents experience more novel events than other age groups (Compas, 1986, 1987b), and that in our study, this premise was verified.

4. The occurrence of a novel experience will have an increased impact for young adolescents, due to an increase in emotional vulnerability prior to age 14 (Rutter et al., 1976).

5. Particular types of events will lead to an increase in depressive symptoms. Family and peer events were the most likely candidates (Baydar et al., 1990; Compas, 1987a).

Comparing the number of events experienced in the previous year, more life events occurred in the first 3 than the second 3 years of adolescence (Fig. 7.1). At the same time, when the proportion of girls experiencing certain changes in specific years is examined, the greatest number of girls experienced school or home changes at age 14, the time of the highest mean level of reported depressive symptoms.

We also tested three hypotheses with respect to pubertal events:

1. Pubertal growth will affect depressive symptoms due to the meaning of these changes to the self and to others (Brooks-Gunn, 1984; Brooks-Gunn & Reiter, 1990; Hill, 1988; Koff, Rierdan, & Jacobson, 1981).

2. The timing of maturation will be associated with depressive symptoms, although most research has looked at body image and self-esteem decrements rather than at depressive symptoms (Blyth, Simmons & Zakin, 1985; Brooks-Gunn & Warren, 1985a; Magnusson, Stattin, & Allen, 1985; Petersen & Crockett, 1985). Generally, pubertal timing effects are stronger than pubertal status effects (Brooks-Gunn, 1988b). We expect being an early maturer to have a negative impact and being a late maturer to have a positive impact.

3. Tempo of pubertal development may influence depressive symptoms, although this has been rarely studied (Brooks-Gunn & Warren, 1985b; Eichorn, 1975).

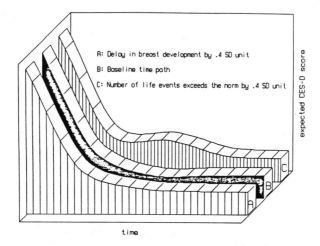

FIG. 7.2. Expected time paths of depressive symptoms based on the dynamic regression model of the CES-D Scale. From Baydar, Brooks-Gunn, and Warren (1990).

As stated earlier, number of life events was associated with an increase in depressive symptoms over the 4 years; these effects were due to the number of events in any year, rather than to an increase in the number of events experienced over time. Importantly, the number of events experienced relative to one's peers was more important than the sheer number of events, although both made significant contributions. Novelty of events was not important, nor was the type of events.

Pubertal changes played a much less significant role than did life events in the developmental course of depressive affect in this sample of girls. Pubertal changes or rate of changes did not contribute to depressive symptoms. However, late maturation acted as a protective factor against depressive symptoms. These findings parallel previous findings for body image (Brooks-Gunn, 1988b; Petersen & Crockett, 1985).

The expected time path of depressive symptoms is illustrated in Fig. 7.2 from Baydar et al. (1990), which shows how the path is altered by experiencing more life events than one's peers and by a delay in breast development.

Interaction of Pubertal and Social Events

Much of my work delves into the interaction of pubertal and social events. The premise is that certain social events are experienced differently as a function of pubertal development. Puberty acts as a social stimulus for others, altering how adults and peers respond to the girl as her body develops. Given the wide variability in physical development in young adolescents of any particular age, studies have been able to tease apart effects of age and pubertal development. Examples include the increased independence given to girls by their parents, interest by boys, and in some cases enhanced same-sex peer relationships, as a function of increases in maturity and controlling for age (Brooks-Gunn et al., 1986; Brooks-Gunn & Warren, 1988a; Magnusson et al., 1985; Simmons & Blyth, 1987). In other cultures and in subgroups of our culture, heightened parental vigilance accompanies pubertal growth as a protection against male interest (Hill & Lynch, 1983).

At the same time, girls' own experiences and interpretations of pubertal events influence how they respond to or interpret social events. As girls mature, they demand more independence from their parents (Simmons & Blyth, 1987). In some cases, they seek out girlfriends who are similar in pubertal maturation (Brooks-Gunn et al., 1986).

More substantive evidence of interactions is found in studies looking at the context in which girls develop physically. David Magnusson and his colleagues (1985) attempted to understand why early maturing girls are likely to engage in smoking and drinking sooner than later maturing girls. They found that the effect was due to many early maturers having older friends who presumably were engaging in such behaviors, which were normative for their age cohort. Roberta Simmons, Dale Blyth, and their colleagues report that early maturing girls have more difficulty moving to middle school in sixth grade than do their peers who are on-time or late maturers and who therefore are not in the midst of puberty during this school transition (Blyth et al., 1985; Simmons, Blyth, & McKinney, 1983).

My research team has reported that timing of maturation is associated with body image and eating behavior differently for dancers and nondancers (Gargiulo, Attie, Brooks-Gunn, & Warren, 1987). We posited that early and on-time maturing dancers, because their bodies do not fit the prevailing standards for elite dancers (we were working with national ballet school companies, which are the training grounds for elite dancers), have more negative body images and problem eating. They do not have the long linear bodies that are valued in the dance world (Hamilton, Brooks-Gunn, Warren, & Hamilton, 1988). Such a mismatch becomes evident at puberty, so that the late maturing dancers are more satisfied with their bodies than are their earlier maturing peers. Timing of maturation has less dramatic effects in girls who, although influenced by the cultural norms stressing thinness, do not have a professional requirement for thinness (Attie & Brooks-Gunn, 1987, in press). This interaction is illustrated in Fig. 7.3, which compares the body images of dancers and nondancers as a function of maturational timing (Brooks-Gunn & Warren, 1985b). Eating problem scores were higher for on-time than late maturing dancers; such differences were not found for nondancers (Brooks-Gunn & Warren, 1985b). Additional support comes from another study in which more mature dancers had more negative body images than less mature dancers (Gargiulo et al., 1987). Comparisons with other

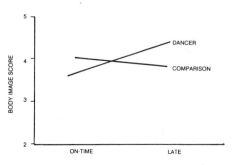

FIG. 7.3. Mean body image score for dancer and comparison students by timing of menarche. From Brooks-Gunn and Warren (1985b).

athletic groups also reinforces our belief that effects such as those discussed here are due to an emphasis on thinness, not on athletics per se (Brooks-Gunn, Attie, Burrow, Rosso, & Warren, 1989; Brooks-Gunn, Burrow, & Warren, 1988).

Another window on possible interactions between pubertal and biological events is provided by a study of fifth to seventh graders where depressive symptomatology was the outcome. Main effects of pubertal events (menarche, breast growth, and timing of maturation) and negative and positive social events (family, peer, school) were examined simultaneously. Negative social events occurring in the past 6 months were associated with more depressive affect, whereas positive events were not (as expected from the adult literature). Somewhat surprisingly, pubertal events were not associated either. However, interactions between pubertal and negative social events were found: For example, premenarcheal girls who experienced negative family events were more depressed than postmenarcheal girls who experienced the same events (Fig. 7.4; Brooks-

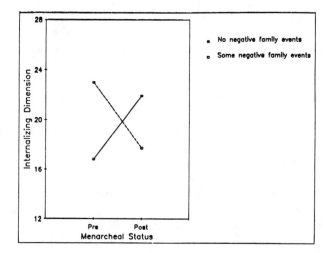

FIG. 7.4. The interaction of menarcheal status and negative family events upon internalizing problem behavior. From Brooks-Gunn, Warren, and Rosso (1991).

Gunn, Warren, & Rosso, 1991). We suggested that the postmenarcheal girls had more opportunity to receive social support from peers than premenarcheal girls, a premise that was partially supported. When negative family life events occurred, premenarcheal girls did not have as much access to another arena of comfort—namely peers—as did their postmenarcheal counterparts. We speculate that parents do not allow their premenarcheal girls as much freedom and that the less physically mature girls demand less autonomy, both of which contribute to their relative isolation from peers (Brooks-Gunn & Zahaykevich, 1989; Hill & Lynch, 1983; Simmons et al., 1988).

Stressful Events Influencing Pubertal Timing

The previous model considered the interaction of social and pubertal events upon adolescent behavior. The underlying premise is that whereas pubertal events may influence social events (i.e., more physically mature or early maturing girls tend to demand more freedom from parents, interact with more mature peers, and engage in so-called adult behaviors earlier; Brooks-Gunn, 1988b), social events are not thought to affect pubertal changes. However, this assumption may be false, as demonstrated by the literature on determinants of pubertal timing. Environmental factors as well as genetic ones play a role, suggesting that reciprocal effects of puberty and social events must be considered. Michelle Warren and I have been exploring the relative effects of genetic factors and certain environmental factors, specifically eating behavior and exercise, upon timing of menarche. To do this, we have compared groups of adolescent girls and young women who vary with respect to menarcheal timing, specifically, different groups of athletes. Menarche, occurring on the average between 12.8 and 13.2 years of age in populations of European and North American girls, may be seen as early as age 10.5 years and as late as 15.5 years, and still fall within normal ranges (Tanner, 1962).

What accounts for the individual variation in menarcheal age? Genetic background has an influence. For example, menarcheal ages of mothers and daughters are associated, with correlations typically ranging from .30 to .45 (Brooks-Gunn & Warren, 1988a; Damon, Damon, Reed, & Valadian, 1969; Zacharias, Rand, & Wurtman, 1976; Zacharias & Wurtman, 1969). However, genetics do not tell the whole story, and environmental factors clearly play a role, which is especially true when environmental conditions are not optimal. Nutrition, leanness, and extensiveness and intensiveness of activity are currently believed to be the most relevant environmental factors (see Brooks-Gunn, 1988b, and Warren, 1983, for a listing of other relevant factors). The secular trend in menarcheal age, which has been documented for Western cultures (Eveleth & Tanner, 1976; Roberts & Dann, 1967; Tanner, 1962, 1972), is typically used as evidence for the role of nutrition. Menarcheal age was higher in times of famine and in poorer segments of earlier societies (Eveleth & Tanner, 1976). Recently, it has been suggested that nutritional conditions early in life (the fetal and infancy periods) may be more potent in influencing menarcheal age than those operating at puberty (using data on the Swedish Gross Domestic Product from 1860 to the present as indicative of the socioeconomic situation and examining its association with infant mortality and menarcheal age, which themselves are highly correlated; Ellison, 1981; Liestol, 1982). However, limits seem to be inherent in the delay of menarche associated with weight. As Garn (1980) has demonstrated, even girls who weigh less than 47 kg do begin to menstruate in the adolescent years, with all of them reaching menarche by age 18 or 19. A critical amount of body weight or fat has been thought to trigger the onset (Frisch, 1984), but much research does not support this hypothesis (Crawford & Osler, 1975; Kulin, Buibo, Mutie, & Sorter, 1982; Sisk & Bronson, 1986). However, it is possible that some alteration of body metabolism, including the ratio of fat to lean body mass may affect CNS restraints on the onset of puberty (Steiner, Cameron, McNeill, Clifton, & Bremner, 1983), rather than menarche, which is a relatively late pubertal event (see Brooks-Gunn & Reiter, 1990, p. 33).

Certain groups are likely to have delayed menarche, specifically elite athletes and young adolescents with anorexia nervosa. In both instances, menarcheal ages are later than population norms would predict. Delayed menarche is a common characteristic of many groups of female athletes, especially those who compete nationally. Delays of one to two years are reported for gymnasts, figure skaters, dancers, volleyball players, and runners (cf. Calabrese et al., 1983; Frisch et al., 1981; Malina, 1983; Warren, Brooks-Gunn, Hamilton, Hamilton, & Warren, 1986). However, other groups, such as swimmers, do not exhibit delays (Brooks-Gunn, Attie, et al., 1989; Malina, 1983).

Both genetic and environmental factors probably account for menarcheal delays seen in athletes. The stringent selection process for elite athletes may make it more likely that late maturers will become athletes: The physical characteristics associated with delayed menarche, specifically relatively narrow hips, long legs, and lower weight for height (McNeill & Livson, 1963; Tanner, 1962) may render an individual girl more suited for most competitive athletics (Brooks-Gunn, Warren, & Hamilton, 1987). Thus, selection, if it does occur, is for physical characteristics associated with delayed menarche, not delayed menarche per se.

At the same time, genetic makeup does not account entirely for differences in menarcheal timing for different groups of athletes or for athletes and nonathletes. For example, in a comparison of girls training at elite national ballet company schools and nondancers of similar socioeconomic status, the mothers' mean age of menarche did not differ for the two groups, even though the adolescent dancers were delayed compared to their nondancer peers (Brooks-Gunn & Warren, 1988a), And, in a comparison of arm lengths of dancers with their sisters and mothers, the dancers had longer arms than their nondancing first-degree relatives, suggesting that the closing of the bony epipheses of the wrist was delayed in the dancers, over and above what would be expected on the basis of familial factors (Warren, 1980).

As found in samples of athletes, environmental factors possibly associated with delayed menarche include weight and body mass, intensity and duration of exercise, and restricted food intake (cf. Brooks-Gunn, 1988b; Brooks-Gunn, Warren, & Hamilton, 1987; Houston, 1980; Malina, 1983). However, it is difficult to assess the relative effects of such factors because they are often interrelated, because large variations in these factors are found in samples of athletes, and because not all studies of athletes report associations between these factors and delayed menarche (Frisch et al., 1981; Malina, 1983; Sidhu & Grewal, 1980). The challenge is to disentangle the contribution of each factor.

Comparing the characteristics of adolescents in different athletic groups may help explain variations in menarcheal age across different sports. At least two dimensions of sports endeavor may be identified that are likely to be associated with variations in menarcheal age. One is the body size and shape preferred by a particular athletic endeavor and the other is the energy expended in training for a sport. Although sports are similar in that high standards of technical proficiency are demanded of all first class athletes (Micheli, 1984; Nicholas, 1975), they may differ in terms of requirements for body shape and size. Low weight is required of gymnasts, figure skaters, and dancers, all of whom are likely to be delayed maturers. In contrast, low weight is not demanded of swimmers, volleyball players, and other athletes. Requirements for thinness sometimes may go beyond what is necessary for the performance of a certain athletic endeavor, becoming an aesthetic preference. The most obvious example is the ballet dancer who, unless she is very thin, may not be accepted into a national company, regardless of talent. The demand for dancers to have very low weights is a fairly recent phenomenon, often attributed to Balanchine's aesthetic preferences (Vincent, 1981). Whereas body size in large part is genetically determined (Stunkard et al., 1986), it is influenced by environmental factors (Garn & Clark, 1976). Diet, exercise, or a combination of the two may affect body size (Stern & Lowney, 1986; Wilmore, 1983).

Another dimension differentiating various athletic endeavors is the amount of energy expended during training. Most elite athletes train 4 or more hours a day; however, sports differ on caloric expenditure. On the average, for example, recreational tennis and cycling are classified as moderate activity, and cross-country skiing, running (7 mph), and swimming (crawl stroke) as hard activity (U.S. Department of Agriculture, 1985). The approximate energy expenditure per hour is estimated to be 25% to 75% higher for activities in the latter than the former category. Estimates of more serious athletic endeavors have been calculated, based on VO^2 maximum estimates. About 200 kilocalories are expended in a typical ballet class (Cohen, Segal, Witriol, & McArdle, 1982), as compared to about 500 kilocalories in swimming (based on a weight of 50 to 53 kg; McArdle, Katch, & Katch, 1986). Such differences may make it more likely that athletes engaged in activities requiring high caloric expenditures will find it easier to maintain a low weight than those in sports using less energy, assuming similar duration of training and levels of cardiovascular fitness. In general, classical ballet does not share the high energy of expenditure of many other athletic endeavors (Calabrese et al., 1983; Schantz & Astrand, 1984).

In one study, adolescents were compared who engaged in three sports that varied on these two dimensions—energy expended and weight demands. Dancing requires low weight and has a low caloric expenditure; figure skating requires low weight but has a higher caloric expenditure; and swimming does not require low weight and has a relatively high caloric expenditure per hour of exercise. The three are similar in that training usually begins in childhood, practice continues year-round, and athletes spend several hours a day in practice. Menarcheal delays were more common and weight for height was lower for figure skaters; one third of the dancers, one half of the skaters, 18% of the swimmers, and 10% of the nonathletes reached menarche after age 15. Dancers and skaters weighed less, relative to their height, than did swimmers, who were similar to nonathletes. In addition, the dancers engaged in more dieting behavior in order to maintain their low weight than did the figure skaters, whereas the swimmers exhibited little if any dieting behavior (see Table 7.1; Brooks-Gunn, Burrow, & Warren, 1988).

Entering athletics prepubertally rather than postpubertally has been associated with menarcheal delays in some but not all studies of athletic groups (Frisch et al., 1981; Sidhu & Grewal, 1980; Stager, Robertshaw, & Miescher, 1984). Duration of current training also may play a factor in menarcheal age. Training and loss of body weight have been shown to suppress the secretion of gonadotropins and cause a secondary hypoestrogenism in postmenarcheal girls and women (Bonen, Belcastro, Ling, & Simpson, 1981; Bonen & Keizer, 1984; Bullen, Skrinar, Beitins, von Mering, Turnbull, & McArthur, 1985; Jurkowski et al., 1978; Warren & Vande Wiele, 1973). Similar processes may occur in the premenarcheal athlete.

Whereas dieting behavior seems to be associated with delayed menarche and secondary amenorrhea (Brooks-Gunn, Warren, & Hamilton, 1987), as well as alterations in metabolic rates (Myerson et al., 1991), less is known about actual nutritional intake and menarcheal delays. In a study of adult dancers, high eating problem scores (indicative of dieting and bulimia) were related to lower levels of protein and fat intake (Hamilton, Brooks-Gunn, & Warren, 1986). In addition, several studies of adult dancers and gymnasts suggest that overall caloric intake and nutrients (e.g., calcium, iron, niacin) are below the MDA even before controlling for energy drain (Calabrese, 1985; Cohen, Potosnak, Frank, & Baker, 1985; Hamilton et al., 1986). In a small study of college athletes, pre-menarcheally-trained women consumed less calories, specifically less fat and protein, than postmenarcheally-trained athletes (Frish et al., 1981). As Malina (1983) has suggested, eating behavior may affect girls differently as a function of body size; if lighter girls are affected more than heavier girls, the effects of

TABLE 7.1
Mean Scores for Physical Characteristics, Eating Behavior, and Self-Image for Dancers, Skaters,
Swimmers, and Nonathletic Adolescent Girls
Means and (Standard Deviations)

| | Group | | | |
	Dancers[a,d,f]	Skaters[b,e]	Swimmers[c]	Nonathletes
Cronological Age	15.63 (1.25)	15.73 (1.18)	15.63 (1.24)	15.66 (1.36)
Physical Characteristics				
Weight (kg)	46.84 (6.33)	48.23 (5.56)	54.91 (6.16)	54.27 (6.92)
Height (Cm)	163.04 (5.31)	160.73 (5.97)	165.84 (5.97)	165.51 (6.93)
Ponderal index	17.45 (1.90)	18.62 (1.28)	20.02 (2.04)	19.93 (2.43)
Menarcheal age	13.29 (1.25)	13.61 (1.50)	12.93 (1.34)	12.72 (1.08)
% Premenarcheal	25% (16)	24% (6)	4% (3)	6% (23)
Eating Behavior				
Diet	3.63 (1.41)	3.34 (1.44)	2.94 (1.23)	3.16 (1.40)
Bulimia	3.26 (1.25)	3.37 (0.52)	2.49 (1.04)	2.43 (1.18)
Oral control	2.97 (1.15)	3.32 (0.48)	2.41 (0.76)	2.18 (0.95)
EAT total	3.19 (1.00)	3.34 (0.34)	2.62 (0.67)	2.59 (0.87)
Self-image				
Perfectionism	3.70 (1.18)	3.41 (0.53)	3.06 (1.29)	3.03 (1.14)
Weight want	43.98 (4.96)	46.24 (4.61)	52.08 (4.70)	50.67 (5.28)

[a]All differences between dancers and nonathletes and dancers and swimmers significant.
[b]All differences between skaters and nonathletes significant except dieting.
[c]No differences between swimmers and nonathletes significant.
[d]All differences between dancers and swimmers significant.
[e]All differences between skaters and swimmers significant.
[f]Differences between dancers and skaters were only significant for diet, oral control and weight want.
From Brooks-Gunn, Burrow, and Warren (1988).

dieting upon reproductive function may be more pronounced in some sports than others, particularly in those with stringent weight requirements.

In brief, antecedents of tempo variations include genetic and environmental components. What is of interest is the fact that a girls' behavior might alter the genetic timetable for maturation.

STORMINESS

Storminess, as evidenced by intense, negative, and labile moods, is believed to characterize the young adolescent's emotional landscape. Hormonal factors have been suggested as a contributor to the expected increases in depressive symptoms and aggressive behavior as hormonal levels rise rapidly during the pubertal years. Since no one-to-one correspondence exists between secondary sexual characteristics and hormonal levels, it is possible to examine the contribution of internal and external pubertal changes on the young adolescent's emotions (Brooks-Gunn & Reiter, 1990, Petersen & Taylor, 1980). Such a separation is critical since we know that the changes in secondary sexual characteristics influence how others treat the developing child and how the child perceives herself (Brooks-Gunn, 1984; Brooks-Gunn & Warren, 1988b).

Several investigative groups are examining hormone-behavior links during the pubertal period (see Paikoff & Brooks-Gunn 1990a, 1990b for a review of pubertal hormone-behavior links across a variety of domains of well-being), focusing on what is called "activational effects of hormonal functioning at puberty." These are possible direct effects of hormonal rises upon emotional states or on arousal levels that in turn might influence emotional states. In contrast, organizational effects involve the effects of prenatal levels of circulating hormones upon brain organization that might influence subsequent pubertal rises or hormones, or, more likely, the brain's responses to the increased levels at puberty. Currently, no study has gathered data on hormonal environment both prenatally and pubertally (Paikoff & Brooks-Gunn, 1990b).

Depressive Symptomatology

Two research groups have examined the links of pubertal hormonal levels and depressive symptoms. Warren and I have seen 100 fifth to seventh grade girls who had hormonal levels assessed (Brooks-Gunn & Warren, 1989; Warren & Brooks-Gunn, 1989). Linear and nonlinear effects of different hormones were examined. Androgens (testosterone and DHEAS) were not associated with reports of depressive symptomatology. A nonlinear effect of estradiol was found (see Table 7.2). Based on this finding, Warren classified hormonal functioning into four categories based on the effects of estradiol on reproductive functioning. These four groupings are:

1. Levels of less than 25 pg/ml of estradiol have little effect.

2. Levels of 25–50 pg/ml have early visible physiological effects such as secondary sexual development, and effects on the vagina estrogens at this level are generally not significant enough to cause proliferation of the endometrium and withdrawal bleeding with a progesterone challenge.

3. Levels of 50–75 pg/ml typically are commensurate with middle or late puberty and early follicular levels in menstruating girls. These levels have significant effects on endometrial growth and other organs such as the breast.

4. Levels greater than 75 pg/ml are associated with cyclicity in women (Gold & Iosimovich, 1980; Grumbach & Sizonenko, 1986; Warren & Brooks-Gunn, 1989).

Although these groupings were based on estradiol levels, they also take into account levels of luteinizing hormone (LH) and follicle stimulating hormone

TABLE 7.2
Possible Linear and Nonlinear Hormonal Relations with Depressive Aggressive Affect

Step	Variable	Depressive Affect			Aggressive Affect		
		Multiple R	R^2 Change	Beta[a]	Multiple R	R^2 Change	Beta
1	Age	.07	.01	.07	.04	.00	-.04
2	Estradiol	.08	.00	.02	.15	.02	-.16
3	Estradiol^2	.22	.04**	-.62	.17	.01	-.27
4	DHEAS	.24	.01	-.09	.26	.04*	-.20
5	DHEAS^2	.24	.00	-.04	.26	.00	.14
6	Testosterone	.26	.01	-.15	.24	.00	-.02
7	Testosterone^2	.27	.00	-.19	.27	.01	.31

*$p < .05$.
**$p < .001$.
From Brooks-Gunn and Warren (1989).

(FSH). Looking at these levels, we found that depressive symptomatology increases from Level 1 to Level 3 and levels off or decreases from Level 3 to Level 4 (Table 7.3; Brooks-Gunn & Warren, 1989). Pubertal stage of development did not influence these findings.

The other research group at the National Institute of Mental Health (NIMH) reports no associations of hormones with depressive symptoms for girls (Inoff-Germain, Arnold, Nottelmann, Susman, Cutler, & Chrousos, 1988; Susman, Inoff-Germain, Nottelmann, Loriaux, Cutler, & Chrousos, 1987). When our data are analyzed in a similar fashion, no effects are found either. Another difference between studies is that our research group used self-reports and maternal reports of depressive symptoms whereas the NIMH group used maternal reports only. The link between depressive symptoms and hormone levels was found for self-reports but not for maternal reports (Warren & Brooks-Gunn, 1989).

Our group also has looked at short-term longitudinal effects of hormonal levels on girls' reports of depressive symptoms and aggressive behavior. Higher levels of estradiol at the initial testing are associated with higher levels of depressive symptoms one year later, even controlling for initial depressive symptoms (Paikoff et al., in press). Pubertal status and age did not influence these results.

What is the relative influence of hormonal levels? We know from the previous discussion that social events are more predictive of depressive symptoms than are pubertal events other than hormone levels. In an analysis entering social events and hormonal events, hormonal levels as characterized by estradiol levels accounted for about 1% of the variance in depressive symptoms and negative life events accounted for 8% of the variance (see Table 7.4). Such findings suggest that hormonal functioning plays a role, albeit a small one, in the young adolescent's report of depressive symptoms.

Aggressive Behavior

Links between hormonal levels and aggressive behaviors or emotions have been found for boys and girls (Brooks-Gunn & Warren, 1989; Olweus, Mattsson, Schalling, & Low, 1980, Susman et al., 1987). Higher levels of testosterone were associated with increases in impatience and irritability, which in turn increased the tendency towards aggressive-destructive behavior in the study by Olweus. In the study by Susman and colleagues, estradiol levels were negatively and androstenedione levels positively associated with parental reports of aggression and delinquency in boys (Inoff-Germain et al., 1988; Susman et al., 1987).

In girls, dehydroepiandosterone (DHEA) and dehydroepiandosterone sulfate (DHEAS) were negatively associated with reports of aggressive behavior in the two studies of girls already discussed (Brooks-Gunn & Warren, 1989; Susman et al., 1987). Also, estradiol category was associated with aggressive symptoms in a similar fashion to the depressive symptom findings (Warren & Brooks-Gunn, 1989). Progesterone and aggression also were associated in the two studies that measured progesterone rather than estradiol (Udry & Talbert, 1988; Eccles et al., 1988).

Putting these findings into a richer context, our research group compared the

TABLE 7.3
Mean Scores for Depressive and Aggressive Affect by Age and Estradiol Level

Estradiol[a]	Depressive Affect[b]		Aggression[c]		
	Mean	S.D.	Mean	S. D.	N
One (2 - 25)	5.88	3.05	10.91	4.62	44
Two (26 - 50)	6.96	3.47	13.00	7.32	24
Three (51 - 74)	8.07	2.84	10.93	4.37	16
Four (75 - 100)	5.94	2.77	9.16	5.92	21
Age	Mean	S.D.	Mean	S. D.	N
10 1/2	6.75	3.89	12.36	8.92	43
11 1/2	6.21	2.90	10.80	5.26	24
12 1/3	6.63	3.19	10.96	5.56	15
13 1/2	6.58	3.29	10.06	4.57	18

[a]Estradiol (pg/ml)
[b]Quadratic trend, $p < .02$.
[c]Quadratic trend, $p < .07$.
From Brooks-Gunn and Warren (1989).

TABLE 7.4
Relation of Hormonal Status and Social Events to Depressive Affect

Step	Domain	Variable	Multiple R	R^2 Change	Beta
1	Age	Age	.10	.01	.10
2	Estradiol^2	Estradiol^2	.12	.01	-.05
3	Negative events	Family	.31	.08*	.20
		Friend			-.12
		School			.18
4	Positive events	Family	.32	.01	.08
		Friend			.06
		School			-.00
5	Negative events	Family	.33	.01	.03
	by Estradiol^2	Friend			-.19
		School			.15

*$p < .05$.
From Brooks-Gunn and Warren (1989).

relative effects of hormonal functioning and social events. We found that DHEAS accounted for 4% of the variance in aggressive symptoms, and negative events accounted for 18% of the variance and an interaction of negative events and DHEAS for an additional 15% of the variance (Brooks-Gunn & Warren, 1989). These findings suggest that hormones may play a larger role in aggressive affect/behavior than in depressive symptomatology.

CONCLUSION

The story about the influence of social and biological events, some of which may be perceived as stressful by young adolescent girls, is unfolding. Although different conceptual models have been proposed to test specific premises, they point to several facts: young adolescents do experience more events than girls do earlier or later; the experience of many events, especially relative to one's peers, is associated with increases in depressive symptoms and aggressive behavior; puberty is not only one of many events, but is a special one, in that it confers some risk of higher depressive symptoms and eating problems if it occurs early (late development acting as a protective factor); and, girls may be vulnerable to the occurrence of social events during the early pubertal changes or in cases of early maturation relative to one's peers. At the same time, adolescent storminess that has been attributed to hormonal changes is multidetermined. Rises in hormonal levels are associated with depressive symptoms, aggressive behavior, body image, and eating problems. However, social events play a much greater role than do hormonal changes in the negative affect reported by young adolescents. Finally, models that assume unidirectional effects between pubertal and social events must be reconsidered. Environmental factors such as eating behavior and exercise influence the timing of puberty as well as the other way around.

Although growing up female is not a crisis, the transition to adolescence does bring with it a concentration of biological and social events not experienced previously by the individual. Depending on the mix of events, their timing and sequencing, and the circumstances in which they occur, certain groups of girls are at increased risk for decrements in well-being, as demonstrated by our results for depressive symptomatology and aggressive behavior.

ACKNOWLEDGMENTS

The research presented in this chapter was supported by the National Institute of Child Health and Human Development and the W. T. Grant Foundation; their support is greatly appreciated. Rosemary Deibler and Florence Kelly are to be thanked for their help in manuscript preparation. The research discussed here could not have been done without the collaboration of Robert Paikoff, Nazli Baydar, Linda Hamilton, Michelle Warren, and our research staff and students; I am pleased to have had the opportunity to work with them.

REFERENCES

Achenbach, T. M., & Edelbrock, C. S. (1987). *Manual for the youth self-report and profile*. Burlington, VT: University for Vermont Department of Psychiatry.

Anthony, J. (1969). The reactions of adults to adolescents and their behavior. In G. Caplan & S. Lebovici (Eds.), *Adolescence: Psychosocial perspectives* (pp. 77). New York: Basic Books.

Attie, I., & Brooks-Gunn, J. (1987). Weight-related concerns in women: A response to or a cause of stress? In R. C. Barnett, L. Biener, & G. K. Baruch (Eds.), *Gender and stress* (pp. 218–254). New York: Free Press.

Attie, I., & Brooks-Gunn, J. (1989). The development of eating problems in adolescent girls: A longitudinal study. *Developmental Psychology, 25*(1), 70–79.

Attie, I., & Brooks-Gunn, J. (in press). Research strategies for studying the emergence of eating problems and disorders. In J. H. Crowther, S. E. Hobfoll, M. A. P. Stephens, & D. L. Tennenbaum (Eds.), *The etiology of bulimia: The individual and familial context*. Washington, D.C.: Hemisphere Publishers.

Baydar, N., & Brooks-Gunn, J. (1990, March). *Determinants of negative emotional expression in adolescent girls: A 4-year longitudinal study*. Paper presented at the Society for Research on Adolescence, Atlanta, GA.

Baydar, N., Brooks-Gunn, J., & Warren, M. P. (1990). *Changes of depressive symptoms in adolescent girls over four years. The effects of pubertal maturation and life events*. Manuscript submitted for publication.

Berndt, T. J. (1982). The features and effects of friendship in early adolescent. *Child Development, 53*, 1147–1460.

Block, J., & Gjerde, P. F. (1990). Depressive symptomatology in late adolescence: A longitudinal perspective on personality antecedents. In J. E. Rolf, A. Master, D. Cicchetti, K. Neuchterlein,

& S. Weintraub (Eds.), *Risk and protective factors in the development of psychopathology* (pp. 334–360). Cambridge, MA: Cambridge University Press.

Blos, P. (1979). *The adolescent passage.* New York: International Universities Press.

Blyth, D. A., Simmons, R. G., & Zakin, D. F. (1985). Satisfaction with body image for early adolescent females: The impact of pubertal timing within different school environments. *Journal of Youth and Adolescence, 14*(3), 207–225.

Bonen, A., Belcastro, A. N., Ling, W. Y., & Simpson, A. A. (1981). Profiles of selected hormones during menstrual cycles of teenage athletes. *The American Physiological Society,* 545–551.

Bonen, A., & Keizer, H. A. (1984). Athletic menstrual cycle irregularity: Endocrine response to exercise and training. *Physician and Sports Medicine, 12*(8), 78–94.

Broadhead, W. E., Kaplan, B. H., James, S. A., Wagner, E. H., Schoenbach, V. J., Grimson, R., Heyden, S., Tibblin, G., & Gehlbach, S. H. (1983). The epidemiologic evidence for a relationship between social support and health. *American Journal of Epidemiology, 117*(5), 521–537.

Brooks-Gunn, J. (1984). The psychological significance of different pubertal events to young girls. *Journal of Early Adolescence, 4*(4), 315–327.

Brooks-Gunn, J. (1987). Pubertal processes and girls' psychological adaptation. In R. Lerner & T. T. Foch (Eds.), *Biological-psychosocial interactions in early adolescence: A life-span perspective* (pp. 123–153). Hillsdale, NJ: Lawrence Erlbaum Associates.

Brooks-Gunn, J. (1988a). Transition to early adolescence. In M. Gunnar & W. A. Collins (Eds.), *Development during transition to adolescence: Minnesota symposia on child psychology, Vol. 21* (pp. 189–208). Hillsdale, NJ: Lawrence Erlbaum Associates.

Brooks-Gunn, J. (1988b). Antecedents and consequences of variations in girls' maturational timing. *Journal of Adolescent Health Care, 9*(5), 365–373.

Brooks-Gunn, J. (1989). Adolescents as children and as parents: A developmental perspective. In I. E. Sigel and G. H. Brody (Eds.), *Methods of family research: Biographies of research projects, Volume I: Normal families* (pp. 213–248). Hillsdale, NJ: Lawrence Erlbaum Associates.

Brooks-Gunn, J., Attie, I., Burrow, C., Rosso, J. T., & Warren, M. P. (1989). The impact of puberty on body and eating concerns in different athletic and nonathletic contexts. *Journal of Early Adolescence, 9*(3), 269–290.

Brooks-Gunn, J., Burrow, C., & Warren, M. P. (1988). Attitudes toward eating and body weight in different groups of female adolescent athletes. *International Journal of Eating Disorders, 7*(6), 749–758.

Brooks-Gunn, J., & Furstenberg, F. F., Jr. (1989). Adolescent sexual behavior. *American Psychologist, 44*(2), 313–320.

Brooks-Gunn, J., & Petersen, A. C. (Eds.). (1983). *Girls at puberty: Biological and psychosocial perspectives.* New York: Plenum Press.

Brooks-Gunn, J., & Petersen, A. C. (1984). Problems in studying and defining pubertal events. *Journal of Youth and Adolescence, 13*(3), 181–196.

Brooks-Gunn, J., & Petersen, A. C. (1991). Studying the emergence of depression and depressive symptoms during adolescence. *Journal of Youth and Adolescence 20*(2).

Brooks-Gunn, J., Petersen, A. C., & Eichorn, D. (Eds.). (1985). Time of maturation and psychosocial functioning in adolescence. *Journal of Youth and Adolescence, 14* (Vols. 3 & 4).

Brooks-Gunn, J., Phelps, E., Elder, G. H. (1991). *Studying lives through time: Secondary data analyses in Developmental Psychology.*

Brooks-Gunn, J., & Reiter, E. O. (1990). The role of pubertal processes in the early adolescent transition. In S. Feldman & G. Elliott (Eds.), *At the threshold: The developing adolescent* (pp. 16–53). Cambridge, MA: Harvard University Press.

Brooks-Gunn, J., Rock, D., & Warren, M. P. (1989). Comparability of constructs across the adolescent years. *Developmental Psychology, 25*(1), 51–60.

Brooks-Gunn, J., & Ruble, D. N. (1982). The development of menstrual-related beliefs and behaviors during early adolescence. *Child Development, 53,* 1567–1577.

Brooks-Gunn, J., Samelson, M., Warren, M. P., & Fox, R. (1986). Physical similarity of and disclosure of menarcheal status to friends: Effects of age and pubertal status. *Journal of Early Adolescence, 6*(1), 3–14.

Brooks-Gunn, J., & Warren, M. P. (1985a). Measuring physical status and timing in early adolescence: A developmental perspective. *Journal of Youth and Adolescence, 14*(3), 163–189.

Brooks-Gunn, J., & Warren, M. P. (1985b). Effects of delayed menarche in different contexts: Dance and nondance students. *Journal of Youth and Adolescence, 14*(4), 285–300.

Brooks-Gunn, J., & Warren, M. P. (1988a). Mother-daughter differences in menarcheal age in adolescent dancers and nondancers. *Annals of Human Biology, 15*(1), 35–43.

Brooks-Gunn, J., & Warren, M. P. (1988b). The psychological significance of secondary sexual characteristics in 9- to 11-year-old girls. *Child Development, 59,* 161–169.

Brooks-Gunn, J., & Warren, M. P. (1989). Biological contributions to affective expression in young adolescent girls. *Child Development, 60,* 372–385.

Brooks-Gunn, J., Warren, M. P., & Hamilton, L. H. (1987). The relationship of eating disorders to amenorrhea in ballet dancers. *Medicine and Science in Sports and Exercise, 19*(1), 41–44.

Brooks-Gunn, J., Warren, M. P., & Rosso, J. T. (1991). *The influence of life events, support and puberty upon girls' internalizing symptoms.* Manuscript submitted for publication.

Brooks-Gunn, J., & Zahaykevich, M. (1989). Parent-child relationships in early adolescence: A developmental perspective. In K. Kreppner & R. M. Lerner (Eds.), *Family systems and life-span development* (pp. 223–246). Hillsdale, NJ: Lawrence Erlbaum Associates.

Bullen, B. A., Skrinar, G. S., Beitins, I. Z., von Mering, G., Turnbull, B. A., & McArthur, J. W. (1985). Induction of menstrual disorders by strenuous exercise in untrained women. *New England Journal of Medicine,* 1349–1353.

Calabrese, L. H. (1985). Nutritional and medical aspects of gymnastics. *Clinical Sports Medicine, 4,* 23–30.

Calabrese, L. H., Kirkendall, D. T., Floyd, M., Rappoport, S., Williams, G. W., Weiker, G. G., & Bergfield, J. A. (1983). Menstrual abnormalities, nutritional patterns, and body composition in female classical ballet dancers. *Physician and Sports Medicine, 11*(2), 86–98.

Cohen, J. L., Potosnak, L., Frank, O., & Baker, M. (1985). A nutritional and hematologic assessment of elite ballet dancers. *The Physician and Sports Medicine, 13*(5), 43–54.

Cohen, J. L., Segal, K. R., Witriol, I., & McArdle, W. D. (1982). Cardiorespiratory responses to ballet exercise and the VO 2max of elite ballet dancers. *Medicine and Science in Sports and Exercise, 14*(3), 212–217.

Cohen, S., & Wills, T. A. (1985). Stress, social support, and the buffering hypothesis. *Psychological Bulletin, 98*(2), 310–357.

Collins, W. A. (1988). Developmental theories in research on the transition to adolescence. In M. R. Gunnar & W. A. Collins (Eds.), *Minnesota symposia on child psychology, Vol. 21* (pp. 1–15). Hillsdale, NJ: Lawrence Erlbaum Associates.

Compas, B. E. (1986). Relationship of life events and social support with psychological dysfunction among adolescents. *Journal of Youth and Adolescence, 15*(3), 205–221.

Compas, B. E. (1987a). Coping with stress during childhood and adolescence. *Psychological Bulletin, 101*(3), 1–11.

Compas, B. E. (1987b). Assessment of major and daily stressful events during adolescence: The Adolescent Perceived Events Scale. *Journal of Consulting and Clinical Psychology, 55*(4), 534–541.

Crawford, J. D., & Osler, D. C. (1975). Body composition at menarche: The Frisch-Revelle hypothesis revisited. *Pediatrics, 56*(3), 449–458.

Csikszentmihalyi, M., & Larson, R. (1984). *Being adolescent: Conflict and growth in the teenage years.* New York: Basic Books.

Damon, A., Damon, S. T., Reed, R. B., & Valadian, I. (1969). Age at menarche of mothers and daughters with a note on accuracy of recall. *Human Biology, 41,* 161–175.

Eccles, J. S., Miller, C., Tucker, M. L., Becker, J., Schramm, W., Midgley, R., Holmes, W., Pasch, L., & Miller, M. (1988, March). *Hormones and affect at early adolescence.* Paper presented at the Biannual Meeting of the Society for Research on Adolescence, Alexandria, VA.

Eichorn, D. H. (1975). Asynchronizations in adolescent development. In S. E. Dragastin & G. H. Elder, Jr. (Eds.), *Adolescence in the life cycle: Psychological change and the social context* (pp. 81–96). Hillsdale, NJ: Halsted Press (Wiley).

Ellison, P. T. (1981). Morbidity, mortality, and menarche. *Human Biology, 53*(4), 635–643.

Eveleth, P. B., & Tanner, J. M. (1976). *Worldwide variation in human growth.* London: Cambridge University Press.

Frisch, R. E. (1984). Body fat, puberty, and fertility. *Biology Review, 59*(2), 161–188.

Frisch, R. E., Gotz-Welbergen, A. V., McArthur, J. W., Albright, T., Witschi, J., Bullen, B., Birnholz, J., Reed, R. B., & Hermann, H. (1981). Delayed menarche and amenorrhea of college athletes in relation to age of onset of training. *Journal of the American Medical Association, 246,* 1559–1563.

Gargiulo, J., Attie, I., Brooks-Gunn, J., & Warren, M. P. (1987). Girls' dating behavior as a function of social context and maturation. *Developmental Psychology, 23*(5), 730–737.

Garn, S. M. (1980). Continuities and change in maturational timing. In O. Brim & J. Kagan (Eds.), *Constancy and change in human development* (pp. 113–162). Cambridge, MA: Harvard University Press.

Garn, S. M., & Clark, D. C. (1976). Trends in fatness and the origins of obesity. *Pediatrics, 57*(4), 443–456.

Gold, J. J., & Iosimovich, J. (1980). *Gynecologic endocrinology.* New York: Harper & Row.

Grief, E. B., & Ulman, K. J. (1982). The psychological impact of menarche on early adolescent females: A review of the literature. *Child Development, 53,* 1413–1430.

Grumbach, M. M., & Sizonenko, P. C. (Eds.). (1986). *Control of the onset of puberty II.* New York: Academic Press.

Gunnar, M. R., & Collins, W. A. (Eds.). (1988). *Transitions in adolescence: Minnesota symposia on child psychology, Vol. 21.* Hillsdale, NJ: Lawrence Erlbaum Associates.

Hall, G. S. (1904). *Adolescence: Its psychology and its relations to physiology, anthropology, sociology, sex, crime, religion and education.* Englewood Cliffs, NJ: Plenum Press.

Hamburg, B. A. (1974). Early adolescence: A specific and stressful stage of the life cycle. In G. V. Coelho, B. A. Hamburg, & J. E. Adams (Eds.), *Coping and adaptation* (pp. 101–124). New York: Basic Books.

Hamilton, L. H., Brooks-Gunn, J., & Warren, M. P. (1986). Nutritional intake of female dancers: A reflection of eating problems. *International Journal of Eating Disorders, 5*(5), 925–934.

Hamilton, L. H., Brooks-Gunn, J., Warren, M. P., & Hamilton, W. G. (1988). The role of selectivity in the pathogenesis of eating disorders. *Medicine and Science in Sports and Exercise, 20*(6), 560–565.

Hauser, S. T., & Bowlds, M. K. (1990). Stress, coping, and adaptation within adolescence: Diversity and resilience. In S. Feldman & G. Elliott (Eds.), *At the threshold: The developing adolescent.* (pp. 388–413). Cambridge, MA: Harvard University Press.

Hill, J. P. (1988). Adapting to menarche: Familial control and conflict. In M. R. Gunnar & W. A. Collins (Eds.), *Development during the transition to adolescence.* (Vol. 21, pp. 43–77). Hillsdale, NJ: Lawrence Erlbaum Associates.

Hill, J. P., & Lynch, M. E. (1983). The intensification of gender-related role expectations during early adolescence. In J. Brooks-Gunn & A. C. Petersen (Eds.), *Girls at puberty: Biological and psychosocial perspectives* (pp. 201–228). New York: Plenum.

Houston, M. E. (1980). Diet, training and sleep: A survey study of elite Canadian swimmers. *Canadian Journal of Applied Sport Sciences, 5,* 161–163.

Inoff-Germain, G., Arnold, G. S., Nottelmann, E. D., Susman, E. J., Cutler, G. B., & Chrousos, G.

P. (1988). Relations between hormone levels and observational measures of aggressive behavior of young adolescents in family interactions. *Developmental Psychology, 24*(1), 129–139.

Jurkowski, J. E., Jones, N. L., Walker, W. C., Younglai, E. V., & Sutton, J. R. (1978). Ovarian hormonal responses to exercise. *Journal of Applied Physiology, 44*, 109–114.

Keating, D. P. (1990). Adolescent thinking. In S. Feldman & G. Elliott (Eds.), *At the threshold: The developing adolescent.* (pp. 54–89). Cambridge, MA: Harvard University Press.

Kessler, R. C., Price, R. H., & Wortman, C. B. (1985). Social factors in psychopathology: Stress, social support, and coping processes. *Annual Review of Psychology, 36*, 531–572.

Koff, E., Rierdan, J., & Jacobson, S. (1981). The personal and interpersonal significance of menarche. *Journal of the American Academy of Child Psychiatry, 20*, 148–158.

Kulin, H. E., Buibo, N., Mutie, D., & Sorter, S. (1982). The effect of chronic childhood malnutrition on pubertal growth and development. *American Journal of Clinical Nutrition, 36*, 527–536.

Larson, R., & Lampman-Petraitis, C. (1989). Daily emotional states as reported by children and adolescents. *Child Development, 60*(5), 1250–1260.

Lazarus, R. S. (1966). *Psychological stress and the coping process.* New York: McGraw-Hill.

Lazarus, R. S., & Launier, R. (1978). Stress-related transactions between person and environment. In L. A. Pervin & M. Lewis (Eds.), *Perspectives in interactional psychology.* New York: Plenum Press.

Lerner, R. M. (1985). Adolescent maturational changes and psychosocial development: A dynamic interactional perspective. *Journal of Youth and Adolescence, 14*(4), 355–371.

Lerner, R. M., & Foch, T. T. (Eds.). (1987). *Biological-psychosocial interactions in early adolescence: A life-span perspective.* Hillsdale, NJ: Lawrence Erlbaum Associates.

Liestol, K. (1982). Social conditions and menarcheal age: The importance of early years of life. *Annals of Human Biology, 9*, 521–536.

Magnusson, D., Stattin, H., & Allen, V. L. (1985). Biological maturation and social development: A longitudinal study of some adjustment processes from mid-adolescence to adulthood. *Journal of Youth and Adolescence, 14*(4), 267–283.

Malina, R. M. (1983). Menarche in athletes: A synthesis and hypothesis. *Annals of Human Biology, 10*(1), 1–24.

McArdle, W. D., Katch, F. I., & Katch, V. L. (1986). *Exercise physiology: Energy, nutrition, and human performance* (2nd ed.). Philadelphia: Lea & Febiger.

McNeill, D., & Livson, N. (1963). Maturation rate and body build in women. *Child Development, 34*, 25–32.

Micheli, L. J. (1984). Physiologic profiling of ballet dancers. *Clinics in Sports Medicine, 3*(1), 199–209.

Montemayor, R., Adams. G. R., & Gullotta, T. P. (1990). *From childhood to adolescence: A transitional period?* Newbury Park, CA: Sage Publications.

Myerson, M., Gutin, B., Warren, M. P., May, M., Contento, I., Lee, M., Pi-Sunyer, F. X., Pierson, R. N., & Brooks-Gunn, J. (1991). Resting metabolic rate and energy balance in amenorrheic and eumenorrheic runners. *Medicine in Science Sports and Exercise, 23*(1), 15–22.

Nesselroade, J. R., & Baltes, P. B. (1974). Adolescent personality development and historical change: 1970–1972. *Monographs of the Society of Research in Child Development, 39*(1, Serial No. 154).

Nicholas, J. A. (1975). Risk factors in sports medicine and the orthopedic system: An overview. *Journal of Sports Medicine, 3*, 243–258.

Nolan-Hoeksema, S., Seligman, M. E. P., & Girgus, J. S. (1991). Sex differences in depression and explanatory style in children. *Journal of Youth and Adolescence. 20*(2).

Offer, D. (1987). In defense of adolescents. *Journal of the American Medical Association, 257*(24), 3407–3408.

Olweus, D., Mattsson, A., Schalling, D., & Low, H. (1980). Testosterone, aggression, physical, and personality dimensions in normal adolescent males. *Psychosomatic Medicine, 42*(2), 253–269.

Paikoff, R. L., & Brooks-Gunn, J. (1990a). Physiological processes: What role do they play during the transition to adolescence? In R. Montemayor, G. R. Adams, & T. P. Gullotta (Eds.), *From childhood to adolescence: A transitional period?* (pp. 63–81). Newbury Park, CA: Sage Publications.

Paikoff, R., & Brooks-Gunn, J. (1990b). Associations between pubertal hormones and behavioral and affective expression. In C. S. Holmes (Ed.), *Psychoneuroendocrinology: Brain, behavior, and hormonal interactions.* (pp. 205–226). New York, NY: Springer-Verlag.

Paikoff, R., Brooks-Gunn, J., & Warren, M. P. (1991). Effects of girls' hormonal status on depressive and aggressive symptoms over the course of one year. *Journal of Youth and Adolescence, 20*(2).

Paikoff, R., Carlton-Ford, S., & Brooks-Gunn, J. (1990). *Individual differences in parent-adolescent agreement: Effects on adolescent adjustment.* Manuscript in preparation.

Petersen, A. C., & Crockett, L. (1985). Pubertal timing and grade effects on adjustment. *Journal of Youth and Adolescence, 14*(3), 191–206.

Petersen, A. C., Sarigiani, P. A., & Kennedy, R. E. (1991). Adolescent depression: Why more girls? *Journal of Youth and Adolescence 20*(2).

Petersen, A. C., & Taylor, B. (1980). The biological approach to adolescence: Biological change and psychological adaptation. In J. Adelson (Ed.), *Handbook of adolescent psychology,* (pp. 117–155). New York: Wiley.

Radloff, L. S. (1977). The CES-D scale: A self-report depression scale for research in the general population. *Applied Psychological Measurement, 1*(3), 385–401.

Radloff, L. S. (1991). The use of the Center for Epidemiologic Studies Depression (CES-D) Scale in adolescents and young adults. *Journal of Youth and Adolescence 20*(2).

Roberts, D. F., & Dann, T. C. (1967). Influences on menarcheal age in girls in a Welsh college. *British Journal Preventative Social Medicine, 21,* 170.

Ruble, D. N., & Brooks-Gunn, J. (1982). The experience of menarche. *Child Development, 53,* 1557–1566.

Rutter, M., Graham, P., Chadwick, O. F., & Yule, W. (1976). Adolescent turmoil: Fact or fiction. *Journal of Child Psychology and Psychiatry, 17,* 35–56.

Rutter, M., Izard, C. E., & Read, P. B. (Eds.). (1986). *Depression in young people: Developmental and clinical perspectives.* New York: The Guilford Press.

Savin-Williams, R. C., & Berndt, T. J. (1990). Friendship and peer relations. In S. Feldman & G. Elliott (Eds.), *At the threshold: The developing adolescent* (pp. 277–307). Cambridge, MA: Harvard University Press.

Schantz, P. G., & Astrand, P. (1984). Physiological characteristics of classical ballet. *Medicine and Science in Sports and Exercise, 16*(5), 472–476.

Sidhu, S. L., & Grewal, R. (1980). Age of menarche in various categories of Indian sportswomen. *British Journal of Sports Medicine, 14,* 199–203.

Simmons, R. G., & Blyth, D. A. (1987). *Moving into adolescence: The impact of pubertal change and school context.* New York: Aldine De Gruyter.

Simmons, R. G., Blyth, D. A., & McKinney, K. L. (1983). The social and psychological effects of puberty on white females. In J. Brooks-Gunn & A. C. Petersen (Eds.), *Girls at puberty: Biological and psychosocial perspectives* (pp. 229–272). New York: Plenum Press.

Simmons, R. G., Burgeson, R., & Reef, M. J. (1988). Cumulative change at entry to adolescence. In M. Gunnar and W. A. Collins (Eds.), *Development during transition to adolescence: Minnesota symposia on child psychology, Vol. 21* (pp. 123–150). Hillsdale, NJ: Erlbaum.

Simmons, R. G., Rosenberg, F., & Rosenberg, M. (1973). Disturbance in the self-image at adolescence. *American Sociological Review, 38,* 553–568.

Sisk, C. L., & Bronson, F. H. (1986). Effects of food restriction and restoration on gonadotropin and growth hormone secretion in immature female rats. *Biological Reproduction, 35*, 554–561.

Smetana, J. G. (1988). Concepts of self and social convention: Adolescents' and parents' reasoning about hypothetical and actual family conflicts. In M. Gunnar & W. A. Collins (Eds.), Development during transition to adolescence. *Minnesota Symposia on Child Psychology, Vol. 21* (pp. 79–122). Hillsdale, NJ: Lawrence Erlbaum Associates.

Smetana, J. G. (1989). Adolescents' and parents' conceptions of parental authority. *Child Development, 59*(2), 321–335.

Stager, J. M., Robertshaw, D., & Miescher, E. (1984). Menarche in swimmers in relation to age of onset of training and athletic performance. *Medicine and Science in Sports and Exercise, 16*(6), 550–555.

Stattin, H., & Magnusson, D. (1990). *Pubertal maturation in female development.* Hillsdale, NJ: Lawrence Erlbaum Associates.

Steiner, R. A., Cameron, J. L., McNeill, T. H., Clifton, R. K., & Bremner, W. J. (1983). Metabolic signals for the onset of puberty. In R. L. Norman (Ed.), *Neuroendocrine aspects of reproduction* (pp. 183–227). New York: Academic Press.

Stern, J. S., & Lowney, P. (1986). Obesity: The role of physical activity. In K. D. Brownell & J. P. Foreyt, (Eds.), *Handbook of eating disorders: Physiology, psychology, and treatment of obesity, anorexia, and bulimia* (pp. 145–158). New York: Basic Books.

Stunkard, A. J., Sorensen, T. I. A., Hanis, D., Teasdale, T. W., Chakraborty, R., Schull, W. J., & Schulsinger, F. (1986). An adoption study of obesity. *New England Journal of Medicine, 314*, 193–198.

Susman, E. J., Inoff-Germain, G., Nottelmann, E. D., Loriaux, D. L., Cutler, G. B., & Chrousos, G. P. (1987). Hormones, emotional dispositions, and aggressive attributes in young adolescents. *Child Development, 58*, 1114–1134.

Tanner, J. M. (1962). *Growth at adolescence* (2nd ed.). New York: Lippincott.

Tanner, J. M. (1972). Sequence, tempo, and individual variation in growth and development of boys and girls aged twelve to sixteen. In J. Kagan & R. Coles (Eds.), *Twelve to sixteen: Early adolescence.* New York: Norton.

Thoits, P. A. (1983). Dimensions of life events that influence psychological distress: An evaluation and synthesis of the literature. In H. P. Kaplan (Ed.), *Psychosocial stress; Trends in theory and research* (pp. 33–103). New York: Academic Press.

Udry, J. R., & Talbert, L. M. (1988). Sex hormone effects on personality at puberty. *Journal of Personality and Social Psychology, 54*(2), 291–295.

U.S. Department of Agriculture. (1985). Dietary guidelines for Americans. *Home and Garden Bulletin* (2nd ed.), *232*, U.S. Department of Health and Humans Services.

Vincent, L. M. (1981). *Competing with the Sylph: Dancers and the pursuit of the ideal body.* Kansas City, KS: Andrews & McMeel.

Warren, M. P. (1980). The effects of exercise on pubertal progression and reproductive function in girls. *Journal of Clinical Endocrinology and Metabolism, 51*(5), 1150–1157.

Warren, M. P. (1983). Physical and biological aspects of puberty. In J. Brook-Gunn and A. C. Petersen (Eds.) *Girls at puberty: Biological and psychosocial perspectives* (pp. 3–28). New York: Plenum Press.

Warren, M. P., & Brooks-Gunn, J. (1989). Mood and behavior at adolescence: Evidence for hormonal factors. *Journal of Clinical Endocrinology and Metabolism, 69*(1), 77–83.

Warren, M. P., Brooks-Gunn, J., Hamilton, L. H., Hamilton, W. G., & Warren, L. F. (1986). Scoliosis and fractures in young ballet dancers: Relationship to delayed menarcheal age and secondary amenorrhea. *New England Journal of Medicine, 314*(21), 1348–1353.

Warren, M. P., & Vande Wiele, R. L. (1973). Clinical and metabolic features of anorexia nervosa. *American Journal of Obstetrics and Gynecology, 117*, 435–449.

Wilmore, J. H. (1983). Body composition in sport and exercise: Directions for future research. *Medicine and Science in Sports and Exercise, 15*, 21–31.

Zacharias, L., Rand, W. M., & Wurtman, R. J. (1976). A prospective study of sexual development and growth in American girls: The statistics of menarche. *Obstetrical and Gynecological Survey, 31*(4), 325–337.

Zacharias, L., & Wurtman, R. (1969). Age at menarche, genetic and environmental influences. *New England Journal of Medicine, 280*(16), 868–875.

II CLINICAL STRESSORS

8

Transcutaneous Oxygen Tension in Preterm Neonates During Tactile/Kinesthetic Stimulation, Behavioral Assessments, and Invasive Medical Procedures

Connie J. Morrow
Tiffany M. Field
University of Miami School of Medicine

Medical care for the preterm neonate has undergone dramatic technological advances in the past decade. Consequently, mortality rates have declined (Stahlman, 1984), and survival rates for preterm infants are now in the 50–70% range (Bennet, Robinson, & Sells, 1983). Improvements in the quality of medical care have not been introduced without adverse effects. Preterm infants suffer not only from the inherent medical complications of their underdeveloped systems, but are also at risk for potential iatrogenic complications resulting from extended hospitalizations and advanced Neonatal Intensive Care Unit (NICU) technology.

Many routine hospital procedures employed in the care of the preterm infant can result in additional medical complications, yet, such procedures are often necessary for treatment of life-threatening conditions. The issue, then, has become one of balancing the benefits of various procedures with their adverse sequelae. Consideration of the benefits and risks of any procedure, ranging from the use of sophisticated ventilators to the simple handling of an infant during a diaper change, is imperative to creating an optimal healthcare environment for the preterm infant.

Of prime concern in this regard has been maintenance of appropriate blood oxygen levels in the infant. Even routine handling of the preterm infant for medical procedures has been observed to cause significant decreases in blood oxygen levels (Long, Alistair, Philip, & Lucey, 1980). Such declines can result in hypoxemia (inadequate oxygen in the blood), which in turn can lead to disturbances in autoregulation of cerebral blood flow, intracranial pressure, cerebral oxygen, and carbon dioxide tension (Gorski, Huntington, & Lewkowicz, 1986). Hypoxia can also result, predisposing infants to other severe medical complications. Infants suffering from hypoxia are at greater risk for postnatal intraventricular hemorrhage or infarction, patent ductus arteriosus, necrotizing enterocolitis, atelectasis, and hypoglycemia (Gorski et al., 1986; Norris, Campbell, & Brenkert, 1982). It is therefore important to understand the effects of handling procedures on oxygen levels in the preterm neonate. In this chapter we evaluate the effects of various types of procedural handling upon regulation of blood oxygen levels in the preterm infant.

ARTERIAL OXYGEN TENSION IN THE SICK INFANT

Prior to the late 1970s, blood oxygen levels were measured through arterial oxygen tension (PaO_2) sampling. Because this method required blood sampling, continuous monitoring of arterial oxygen in sick infants was not possible. The introduction of the transcutaneous oxygen tension ($TcPO_2$) monitor, a noninvasive device that provides a continuous measure of estimated blood oxygen levels, revealed substantial variability in the sick infant's arterial oxygen tension (Lucey, 1981). Horbar et al. (Horbar, Soll, McAuliffe, Clark, & Lucey, 1985) monitored $TcPO_2$ in 25 very low birth weight infants (1500 grams or less) during their first 3 days of life. They found frequent episodes of hyperoxemic (>100 mmHg) and hypoxemic (<40 mmHg) $TcPO_2$ levels, varying dramatically in number and duration across infants. Other studies have found noise levels in the NICU, and infant squirming and breathing patterns to be associated with hypoxemic events (Abu-Osba, Brouillette, Wilson, & Thach, 1982; Long, Philip, & Lucey, 1980).

Subsequent documentation has indicated that numerous routine nursing procedures involving handling, once considered benign, can result in drops of oxygen tension to clinically unsafe levels (Horbar et al. 1985; Lucey, Peabody, & Philip, 1977; Lucey, 1981). For example, Long and colleagues (Long, Alistair, Philip & Lucey, 1980) monitored $TcPO_2$ in 30 low birth weight infants, and found that 75% of "undesirable time" (i.e., when $TcPO_2$ levels were <40 or >100 mmHg) was directly associated with nursery staff handling. Such "undesirable time" was significantly reduced when nursery staff monitored $TcPO_2$ levels during nursing procedures.

Several case studies have also noted drops in blood oxygen levels during medical procedures. Observing three infants, Speidel (1978) reported average PaO_2 drops of 30 mmHg in 75% of all handling procedures. Consistent declines occurred during heelsticks, x-rays, urine bagging, insertion of intravenous needles, and undersheet changes. Murdoch and Darlow (1984) observed five low birth weight infants. They reported suctioning, peripheral and arterial venous sampling, capillary blood sampling, intubation, chest radiographs, position changes, blood pressure cuff placement, and axillary temperature measurement resulted in undesirable TcPO$_2$ readings (<40 and >100 mmHg). These studies, however, are clearly limited by their small sample size.

Other studies have reported somewhat mixed findings. Danford and colleagues (Danford, Miske, Headley, & Nelson, 1983) found significant drops in TcPO$_2$ during chest x-rays, phototherapy, heelsticks, weighing, vital signs, and gavage feeding. Actual values for TcPO$_2$ drops were not reported, however, leaving it unclear whether TcPO$_2$ levels declined to clinically unsafe levels. Norris et al. (1982) evaluated TcPO$_2$ in 25 preterm infants with Respiratory Distress Syndrome. They documented significant changes in TcPO$_2$ during suctioning and repositioning, but not during heelsticks. Despite the occurrence of significant decreases in TcPO$_2$ (10–15 mmHg) during the procedures studied, 76% of these declines did not result in what would be considered clinical unsafe levels of TcPO$_2$. (<40 mmHg).

THE MINIMAL TOUCH POLICY

The medical implications of substantive fluctuations in blood oxygen levels remain unclear, consequently, it has been suggested by several authors that procedures potentially resulting in hypoxemia should be kept to a minimum (Long, Alistair, Philip & Lucey, 1980; Murdoch & Darlow, 1984; Norris et al., 1982; Speidel, 1978). Since medical procedures involving handling have consistently been documented to cause declines in TcPO$_2$, a minimal touch policy has become standard protocol in many Neonatal Intensive Care Units across the nation. This policy dictates infants in the intensive care unit be handled only when necessary medical and caretaking procedures must be performed.

The minimal touch policy is based upon research oriented specifically toward medical and nursing procedures, but its implementation has also been generalized to social forms of touch. Unlike the full-term infant who receives considerable social stimulation and parental contact, the preterm infant's interactions occur primarily during necessary invasive medical or nursing procedures (Gaiter, Avery, Temple, Johnson, & White, 1981). Parental touching and holding is discouraged while the infant is in intensive care. Once an infant is stabilized, however, this pattern of minimal interaction tends to continue. Parents may still be hesitant to touch, hold, or interact with their infant, and nurses are frequently too busy to provide more than essential care.

Research clearly suggests that a minimal touch policy for medical and routine nursing procedures is essential in maximizing health care and prognosis for the very sick preterm infant. It is not nearly as evident that generalization of this policy to social stimulation, especially when dealing with more stabilized infants, is an equally necessary or beneficial practice. The effects of social forms of stimulation upon TcPO$_2$ have not been adequately addressed in the literature.

SOCIAL STIMULATION AND DEVELOPMENT

Despite the minimal touch policy, a growing body of literature suggests social stimulation programs may be quite advantageous to the growth and development of the stabilized preterm infant. Tactile-kinesthetic massage is one type of social stimulation that has been studied. Massage programs usually involve some type of tactile touch and kinesthetic movement of various body parts. Researchers have documented significant weight gains, superior neurological and mental development, improved functioning on various indices of the Bayley and Brazelton scales, shorter hospital stays, and increased alertness and activity in response to tactile and kinesthetic stimulation (Barnard & Bee, 1983; Field, Schanberg, Scafidi, Bauer, Vega-Lahr, Garcia, Nystrom, & Kuhn, 1986; Leib, Benfield, & Guidubaldi, 1980; Rice, 1977; White & Labarba, 1976). It has also been hypothesized that regular, predictable stimulation may enable the infant to develop better self-regulating systems at a more rapid rate (Barnard & Bee, 1983).

Given the documented benefits of social stimulation on the growth and development of preterm infants, minimizing social touch may be an unnecessary and potentially detrimental practice. Although incidences of hypoxemia can be reduced by limiting medical and nursing procedures (Long, Alistair, Philip, & Lucey, 1980), the effects of social stimulation (e.g., tactile and kinesthetic stimulation) upon $TcPO_2$ have never been examined. We attempted to determine the effects of social stimulation on $TcPO_2$ levels in stabilized preterm infants, and assessed whether a reconsideration of handling policies for the more stabilized neonate is in order.

This question is also relevant when considering the normal types of parent-infant social interactions that are not part of a preterm infant's early hospital life. Parents of preterm infants often remain hesitant to touch and hold their infants even after they become stabilized in the hospital. If tactile-kinesthetic stimulation can be substantiated as noncompromising to an infant's blood oxygen stability, then perhaps it can be utilized as a parent training tool to facilitate development of parent-child interactions.

INFANT BEHAVIORAL ASSESSMENT AND BLOOD OXYGEN LEVELS

Another area of handling that has not been adequately evaluated is the relationship between $TcPO_2$ and infant behavioral assessments. Behavioral assessments are typically conducted for developmental/neurological screening and research. Because behavioral assessment scales often involve substantial amounts of handling, their impact on $TcPO_2$ in the preterm infant is an important question. One of the most widely used scales is the Brazelton Neonatal Behavioral Assessment Scale (BNBAS; Brazelton, 1973). Because this scale was devised for full-term infants, there is some question as to the aversive nature of this assessment for the less developed, easily taxed preterm. This concern has been further substantiated by findings indicating the BNBAS may be physiologically stressful for infants. For example, cortisol levels have been found to increase (Gunnar, Isensee, & Fust, 1987) and growth hormone levels decrease (Field, 1987) following administration of the Brazelton.

Results such as these suggest the need for assessment instruments that are less stressful for preterm infants. A second scale, the Neurobehavioral Assessment for Preterm Infants (NAPI; Korner, Thom, & Forrest, 1990), has been devised specifically for the preterm neonate's more fragile response system and involves less handling of the infant during the procedure. We also evaluated $TcPO_2$ levels in the preterm neonate during administration of the BNBAS and NB-MAP assessment instruments.

HYPOTHESES

The present study was designed to evaluate $TcPO_2$ in preterm infants during tactile/kinesthetic stimulation, invasive medical procedures (heelsticks and gavage feedings), and infant behavioral assessments. Although heelsticks and gavage feedings have been previously evaluated in the literature, they were included in this study for a benchmark comparison. The specific questions examined include: a) the immediate effect of tactile/kinesthetic stimulation, invasive procedures, and behavioral exams on $TcPO_2$ as compared to baseline; b) a comparison of the BNBAS and the NAPI scales for differences in aversive effects on $TcPO_2$; and c) the differential effects, if any, of stimulation, invasive procedures, and assessments on $TcPO_2$.

It was hypothesized that $TcPO_2$ would be most compromised during invasive procedures such as heelsticks and gavage feeds, followed by procedures requiring sustained handling and maneuvering, such as the BNBAS and the NAPI. Of these two procedures, it was hypothesized that the BNBAS would have a greater impact on $TcPO_2$ than the NAPI. The stimulation was hypothesized to have a noncompromising effect upon $TcPO_2$.

METHODS

Subjects

The total sample consisted of 37 preterm infants who were participating in a larger study evaluating the effects of tactile-kinesthetic stimulation on growth and development (Scafidi et al., 1989). Neonates were selected for this Infant

Stimulation Project (ISP) from the Intermediate Care Nursery at the University of Miami/Jackson Memorial Hospital. Sample selection was based on the following criteria: (1) gestational age <36 weeks as determined by the Dubowitz Scale (Dubowitz, Dubowitz, & Goldberg, 1970), (2) birth weight <1500 grams, (3) the absence of genetic anomalies, congenital heart malformations, gastrointestinal disturbances, central nervous system dysfunctions, and history of maternal drug abuse, (4) duration of intensive care <45 days, and, (5) an entry weight into the study between 1000 and 1450 grams. The sample was comprised of 28 females and 19 males. Average gestational age was 30 weeks, and average birthweight was 1172 grams. Ethnic composition was as follows: 32 Black, 8 Hispanic, and 7 Caucasian infants. The average hospital stay prior to beginning the study was 26 days.

Infants were enrolled in the study following informed parental consent. All subjects were medically stable, free from ventilatory assistance, and were no longer receiving medications or fluids intravenously. As part of the ISP study, infants were randomly assigned to control and massage treatment groups. For the purpose of the present study sub-samples of the total 37 infants were evaluated for each set of analyses. This was because not all of the total sample received the stimulation protocol. Data collection of $TcPO_2$ also varied across the procedures, depending on the availability of the $TcPO_2$ monitor and staffing. Accordingly, the sample size for each individual hypothesis being tested varied, and included only those infants that had repeated measures for the procedure being evaluated.

Materials

The Corometrics 515A Transcutaneous Oxygen Monitor was used to record trends in $TcPO_2$. A heated electrode, attached to the infant's calf, was used to measure oxygen tension as it diffuses from the arterial capillary bed to the skin surface. At least one-half hour prior to each procedure, the $TcPO_2$ monitor was attached to the infant. A time period of at least 20 minutes was necessary for the equipment to stabilize and provide accurate $TcPO_2$ levels. Baseline $TcPO_2$ was monitored for 5 minutes prior to and following the completion of each procedure. The lag time, determined by skin thickness, was estimated to be 10 seconds. This value is typical of neonates (Lucey, 1981).

Procedures

Tactile/kinesthetic Stimulation.   Stimulation sessions were conducted over a 10-day period. For the purposes of this study, $TcPO_2$ was monitored during stimulation on Days 2 and 9 of that period. The stimulation protocol involved three 15-minute sessions, at the beginning of each of 3 consecutive hours, and starting approximately 60 minutes prior to the noon feeding. Each 15-minute session was divided into three standardized 5-minute intervals of stimulation in the following order: a) tactile, b) kinesthetic, and c) tactile.

During the tactile sessions the infant was placed in a prone position. The stimulation was administered with the flat sides of the fingers of both hands. Each region of the body received six 10-second strokes in the following manner and order: a) progressing from the infant's head, down the side of the face to the neck, and back up to the top of the head; b) beginning at the back of the neck, across the shoulders and back to the neck; c) moving from the upper back, down to the waist, and returning to the upper back, (note: for this segment the stimulator's fingertips were placed on either side of the spine and the flats of the fingers were on the back; d) progressing from the thigh to the foot to the thigh on both legs simultaneously; and e) from the shoulder to the wrist to the shoulder on both arms simultaneously. During the stroking intervals, the stimulator's fingers remained in continuous contact with the infant's skin.

For the kinesthetic phase the infant was placed in a supine position, and the limbs were moved in six passive flexion/extension motions lasting approximately 10 seconds each and occurring in the following order: a) right arm, b) left arm, c) right leg, d) left leg, and e) both legs simultaneously. During each segment, the long bones of the infant's limbs were gently grasped, avoiding the palms of the hands and the soles of the feet so as not to elicit a reflex response. Upon completion of this phase, the infant was returned to a prone position for the final phase of tactile stimulation as previously described.

All stimulation sessions were conducted by trained examiners. During the procedure the infant remained in a temperature controlled isolette, and the stimulation was conducted through the open portholes located on the sides of the isolette. Examiners warmed their hands prior to each session, and remained silent throughout the procedure.

Neonatal Behavioral Assessment Scale.   Administration of the BNBAS occurred on Day 1 and Day 10 of the ISP. However, for the purposes of this study only Day 1 BNBAS administrations were evaluated. The scale consists of 27 behavioral items and 20 elicited reflexes. The infant's state organization, motor behavior, affect, responsiveness, and reflexes were assessed. Administration time was approximately 30 minutes. The major portion of the exam was conducted within the protection of the heated isolette; however, the infant was swaddled and removed from the incubator during the orientation items and several of the reflex assessments. Order of item administration was varied on occasion, depending upon the responsiveness and state of the individual infant.

Neurobehavioral Assessment for Preterm Infants (NAPI).   (Korner, Thom, & Forrest, 1990). The NAPI was conducted on Day 2 of the stimulation study. This exam evaluated the following domains: a) active tone and motor vigor; b) resistance to passive movement; c) maturity of vestibular response; d) alertness and orientation; e) excitability in response to stimulation; f) inhibition in response to stimulation; and g) crying and sleeping behavior. Approximately half of the exam items were observational in nature. Administration time was comparable to the BNBAS, as was the proportion of the time the infants spent swaddled and out of the isolette. Order of item presentation was standardized and did not vary.

Invasive Medical Procedures. Heelsticks and gavage feeds were conducted according to nursery protocol by registered nurses. $TcPO_2$ was randomly monitored for both of these procedures, on either one of the first two or last two days of the stimulation period. The heelstick procedure involved warming the infant's heel with a chemically activated warmer, cleaning the heel with alcohol, making a small puncture with a microlancet, and gently squeezing until 0.5 cc's of blood was obtained. Occasionally, it was necessary to make more than one puncture. The entire procedure was completed in approximately 10–15 minutes. Gavage feedings included monitoring of temperature, pulse, and respirations, followed by insertion of a small nasogastric tube from the mouth to the infant's stomach. The formula, contained in a syringe, was then allowed to flow through the tube into the infant's stomach. Upon completion the tube was immediately removed. The procedure took approximately 5–10 minutes to complete.

DATA REDUCTION

The data were recorded in trends on Corometrics recording paper, scaled in 10 second epochs across time on the horizontal axis, and incremented by increases of 10 mmHg on the vertical axis. Data was coordinated with events by use of a manual marker, signaling onset and completion of procedures on the tape.

For each procedure, three summary scores were calculated during a 5 minute baseline period, the procedure period, and a 5 minute postprocedure period. These scores included a mean, a range score (the high $TcPO_2$ value—the low $TcPO_2$ value for a given period), and a percentage score reflecting the amount of time an infant's $TcPO_2$ declined below 40 mmHg. The range score was added because $TcPO_2$ can be quite variable during a given procedure, and this itself may be clinically important. Mean $TcPO_2$ levels were obtained by determining the average $TcPO_2$ level per minute (by averaging each 10 second mean), and then calculating the average of the averages for each period. For all means calculated, the initial 10 seconds of the procedure was not included in order to account for lag time in $TcPO_2$. Percentage of time spent below 40 mmHg was determined by counting the elapsed time during a given period (baseline, procedure and post) that an infant's $TcPO_2$ dropped below 40 mmHg, and dividing that by the total time period. Fourty was chosen as our cutoff because it is the most frequently cited cutoff value for clinical hypoxemia in the literature (Horbar et al., 1985; Long, Alistair, Philip, & Lucey, 1980; Murdoch & Darlow, 1984). When such drops occurred, the stimuli with which they were associated were also recorded. Procedure length was somewhat varied. The stimulation session was 15 minutes and the behavioral assessments averaged 30 minutes. Feedings and heelsticks averaged from 5 to 10 minutes. Reliability between coders was assessed by dividing number of agreements (+ or–3 mmHg) by total number of required calculations for each procedure. Two coders were initially trained to 94% reliability on the NAPI tracings. Reliability checks were conducted randomly during the coding of the other procedures, and were always above 84%. Additionally, disagreements were rarely of greater magnitude than 8 mmHg. Approximately halfway through the coding process, two additional coders were employed. Their reliability was assessed in the same manner as above, using one of the original coders as a standard for comparison. Their reliabilities were 89% and 91% respectively.

RESULTS

Effects of Individual Procedures on TcPO$_2$

All data analyses were performed using the SPSSX computer program package. To evaluate hypotheses concerning the overall effect of individual procedures upon TcPO$_2$ homeostasis, a Repeated Measures Analysis of Variance (ANOVA) was conducted on baseline, preparation procedure (gavage feeds only), procedure, and postprocedure mean TcPO$_2$ levels. This analysis was run individually for each procedure. The same analysis was also conducted on range scores (high minus low TcPO$_2$ values). Percent time spent below 40 mmHg during any given procedure was reported descriptively in text. In order to evaluate the different phases of the stimulation, a Repeated Measures ANOVA was conducted on pre, tactile, kinesthetic, tactile and post sessions for mean TcPO$_2$ and range scores.

On all Repeated Measures runs, two additional tests were also conducted to ensure that assumptions for ANOVA were not violated. Tukey's Test for Nonadditivity[1] (TTN) and Mauchley's Test for Sphericity[2] (MST) as described in Kirk (1982), were conducted in conjunction with all Repeated Measures Analyses.

Tukey's Honestly Significant Difference (HSD) test was used for post hoc analysis, unless the Mauchley test statistic was also significant. A significant Mauchley test indicates unequal variance/covariances. In such instances it is not appropriate to use the combined error variance (Mean Square Residual) required to compute the Tukey's HSD test. Instead, paired t-tests were employed. A Bonferroni correction to control for Type 1 errors was used in conjunction with the paired t-tests.

Heelstick Repeated Measures Comparisons

Average differences in $TcPO_2$ were evaluated for the heelstick procedure 5 minutes pre, during, and 5 minutes post, using a Repeated Measures ANOVA. As hypothesized the overall F test was significant, $F(2,42) = 21.97$, $p < .0000$, and remained significant when adjusted for a significant MST using the conservative F test. Post hoc paired t-tests were conducted to determine which means differed significantly. All pairwise comparisons between pre, during, and post periods were significant. The average mean for the heelstick period was significantly lower than both the pre and post period means, and there was a significant increase in $TcPO_2$ from the preheelstick period to the postheelstick period. These results are summarized in Table 8.1.

To assess $TcPO_2$ variability during the heelstick procedure, range scores were also analyzed across the three periods using a Repeated Measures ANOVA. This analysis yielded a significant overall F test ($F[2,42] = 5.31$, $p < .009$). Tukey's HSD test was conducted for post hoc analysis of mean differences. In accord with the previous findings, the range of $TcPO_2$ fluctuation was found to be significantly greater during the heelstick period when compared to the preheelstick period.

Further examination of the data revealed that 10 of the 22 infants (45%) dropped below a 40 mmHg level during the procedure, and 2 remained below this level for a portion of the 5 minute postheelstick period. For the group who dropped below 40 mmHg during the heelstick procedure, they remained below 40 mmHg for an average of 52% of the procedure period, or 3 minutes 40 seconds.

Gavage Feed Repeated Measures Comparisons

Mean $TcPO_2$ levels were recorded for a 5-minute baseline period, a preparatory period that usually involved monitoring of vital signs and temperature, the gavage feed period (measured from tube insertion to tube withdrawal), and a 5-minute post baseline period. A Repeated Measures ANOVA was conducted, yielding a significant overall effect, $F(3,63) = 4.46$, $p < .007$. Post hoc analyses were conducted using Tukey's HSD test; however, none of the comparisons between the different periods were significant (HSD $= 3.89$, $p < .05$). A Repeated Measures ANOVA was also conducted on range scores in order to assess variability of $TcPO_2$ during the four periods specified above. This analysis was also not significant. Means and standard deviations for these analyses are reported in Table 8.2.

In contrast to the heelstick procedure, only 2 infants of the 20 (10%) had $TcPO_2$ values that dropped below 40 mmHg for a period of time during the feeding period. These two infants spent, on the average, 15% of the feeding period below 40 mmHg. The feeding period was much shorter than some of the

TABLE 8.1
Heelstick Post Hoc Results: Mean TcPO2 and Range Scores

Mean TcPO2	M	SD
pre	65.7	11.9
during	51.3	20.0
post	72.3	11.6

Paired T-Test Results

	M-DIF	(SD)	T	DF	P
pre-during	14.4	(17.9)	3.79	21	.000*
pre-post	6.5	(7.0)	4.35	21	.000*
during-post	20.9	(17.9)	5.48	21	.000*

Range Scores	M	SD
pre	14.2	14.1
during	28.0	17.6
post	22.0	11.4

Tukey's Post Hoc Results
(Absolute Value Mean Differences)

	pre	during	post
pre	—	13.72**	7.77
during		—	5.95
post			—

Notes. N = 22.
Significance level for paired t-test results based on a Bonferroni correction of .05/3 = *$p < .017$.
For Tukey's HSD results: **$p < .01$, HSD = 13.02.
                            *$p < .05$, HSD = 11.32.

other procedures, however, and the average duration of time spent below 40 mmHg was 24 seconds.

An additional analysis was conducted to determine whether $TcPO_2$ changed dramatically during gavage tube insertion. Because each feeding period was coded from tube insertion to tube withdrawal, an initial drop in $TcPO_2$ due to the tube insertion may have lost its significance when averaged together with the actual feeding period. An additional analysis was conducted to further investigate this concern. A Repeated Measures ANOVA was conducted on the average low value recorded during each of the four periods. The overall test was signifi-

TABLE 8.2
Gavage Feeds: Mean TcPO^2 and Range Scores

Mean TcPO^2	M	SD
pre	75.3	11.4
prep	73.3	12.4
during	74.8	12.5
post	78.5	12.1

Range Scores	M	SD
pre	15.5	14.1
prep	18.9	11.9
during	22.4	10.5
post	16.5	10.6

Note. N = 22

TABLE 8.3
Summary of Repeated Measure and Post Hoc Analyses:
Gavage Feed Low Values

Variable	M	SD
GF Low Values		
pre	65.7	12.2
prep	63.7	15.9
during	62.4	15.2
post	69.2	14.9

Tukey's HSD Results
(Absolute Values of Differences Among Means)

	Pre	Prep	During	Post
pre	—	1.95	3.32	3.50
prep		—	1.37	5.45
during			—	6.82*
post				—

Note. N = 22.
For Tukey's HSD results: **$p < .01$, HSD = 7.68.
*$p < .05$, HSD = 6.26.

cant, $F(3,63) = 3.13$, $p < .03$. Post hoc follow-ups using Tukey's HSD test revealed a significant increase in $TcPO_2$ low scores from the gavage feeding period to the post feeding period, but no significant declines in low scores were noted from baseline or prep periods to the feeding period. These results are summarized in Table 8.3.

BNBAS Repeated Measures Comparisons

Mean $TcPO_2$ levels pre, during, and post BNBAS administration were evaluated using a Repeated Measures ANOVA. The overall test was significant, $F(2,74) = 9.91$, $p < .000$. Tukey's HSD test was conducted for follow-up analysis of mean differences (Table 8.4). A significant increase in $TcPO_2$ was found from baseline to the post period, and from the procedure period to the post period. There were no significant changes in $TcPO_2$ from the baseline period to the BNBAS procedure period.

Overall results for range scores were significant, $(F(2,74) = 52.07$, $p < .000$, and remained significance when corrected for a positively biased test using the conservative F test. For post hoc analysis, paired t-tests were conducted on all pairwise comparisons. Variability of $TcPO_2$ was found to be significantly greater during the BNBAS procedure than during both baseline and post periods (see Table 8.4).

Additionally, 8 of the 38 infants, or 21% dropped below 40 mmHg during the BNBAS procedure, whereas no infants exhibited such a pattern during baseline and post periods. The average period of time spent below 40 mmHg during the BNBAS was 4 minutes, 5 seconds. Items on the BNBAS that were more likely to result in significant $TcPO_2$ drops were those that required handling outside the isolette, including the orientation items and occasional reflexes (tonic deviation of the eyes, glabella, rooting, sucking, and nystagmus).

NAPI Repeated Measure Comparisons

Mean $TcPO_2$ levels differed significantly over baseline, NAPI periods and post-NAPI $(F(2,70) = 9.91$; $p < .000)$. Post-hoc analysis revealed differences between mean $TcPO_2$ during baseline and NAPI administration periods, and also between the NAPI period and the post period. In both instances mean $TcPO_2$ levels were significantly lower during the NAPI procedure (see Table 8.5). The overall F test for range scores was also significant $(F(2,70) = 85.95$, $p < .000)$, and remained so when adjusted for a significant MST. As in the previous analysis, the average range score was significantly greater during the NAPI than during the pre or post procedure periods. Evaluation of drops in $TcPO_2$ during the procedure revealed that 10 of the 36 infants (28%) dropped below a $TcPO_2$ level of 40 mmHg. These 10 infants spent an average of 8% of the assessment time, or 1 minute and 55 seconds below 40 mmHg. Similar to the BNBAS, a

TABLE 8.4
BNBAS Post Hoc Results: Mean $TcPO_2$ and Range Scores

Mean $TcPO_2$	M	SD
pre	71.2	11.4
during	71.9	11.0
post	76.9	11.8

Tukey's HSD Results
(Absolute Value of Differences Among Means)

	Pre	During	Post
pre	—	.77	5.69**
during		—	4.92**
post			—

Range Scores	M	SD
pre	13.2	7.9
during	38.2	20.2
post	15.3	8.5

Paired T-Test Results

	M-DIF	(SD)	T	DF	P
pre-during	25.0	(18.9)	8.16	37	.000*
pre-post	2.1	(8.1)	1.60	37	.118
during-post	22.3	(20.5)	6.89	37	.000*

Note. N = 38
For Tukey's HSD results: **$p < .01$ HSD = 4.36.
*$p < .05$ HSD = 3.46.
Significant level for paired t-test results based on a Bonferroni correction of $.05/3 = p < .017$.

very consistent pattern of $TcPO_2$ declines was observed during the orientation items that were conducted outside of the isolette.

Stimulation Session Repeated Measures Comparisons

Mean $TcPO_2$ Comparisons. $TcPO_2$ was examined during four separate stimulation periods of the massage study. These included stimulation Sessions 1 and 2 on Day 2 and Day 9 of the massage study. The four periods were initially evaluated to determine if $TcPO_2$ changed across the various periods of the stimulation as the infant became more accustomed to the stimulation procedure.

Means and standard deviations for the four stimulation sessions are reported in Table 8.6. The overall test for mean TcPO$_2$ during stimulation on Day 2, Session 1 was significant, $F(4,72) = 10.57$, $p < .000$. Post hoc analysis was conducted using Tukey's HSD test. Mean TcPO$_2$ levels significantly declined from the baseline period to the first tactile period, and from the baseline period to the kinesthetic period. There was a significant increase in mean TcPO$_2$ levels from all three of the stimulation periods to the post period, indicating a recovery to baseline levels. Additionally, TcPO$_2$ during the post period approached significance when compared to the baseline period, suggesting a slight increase in overall TcPO$_2$ following the stimulation period (see Table 8.7).

TABLE 8.5
Post Hoc Results for the NB-MAP: Mean TcPO^2 and Range Scores

Mean TcPO^2	M	SD
pre	72.6	10.7
during	69.6	10.1
post	74.7	12.1

Tukey's HSD Results
(Absolute Value of Differences Among Means)

	Pre	During	Post
pre	—	3.0*	2.11
during		—	4.92**
post			—

Range Scores	M	SD
pre	13.2	7.4
during	43.6	16.2
post	16.1	8.5

Paired T-Test Results

	M-DIF	(SD)	T	DF	P
pre-during	30.4	(18.3)	9.96	35	.000*
pre-post	2.8	(9.9)	1.73	35	.092
during-post	27.5	(16.6)	9.96	35	.000*

Note. N = 36
For Tukey's HSD results: **$p < .01$, HSD = 3.48.
*$p < .05$, HSD = 2.77
Significance level for paired t-test results based on a Bonferroni correction to .05/3 = *$p < .017$.

TABLE 8.6
Descriptive Statistics for Repeated Measure Analysis of the Stimulation Sessions: Mean TcPO^2

Stimulation	M	SD	N
	Day 2, Stim 1		
pre	72.1	10.8	19
tactile	67.8	14.1	
kinesthetic	67.5	13.5	
tactile	69.3	12.6	
post	75.6	11.7	
	Day 2, Stim 2		
pre	73.3	8.5	13
tactile	69.9	10.2	
kinesthetic	67.4	9.0	
tactile	72.1	10.3	
post	76.9	12.6	
	Day 9, Stim 1		
pre	66.3	15.3	13
tactile	64.7	12.9	
kinesthetic	64.0	12.9	
tactile	67.8	13.4	
post	69.6	13.5	
	Day 9, Stim 2		
pre	68.6	13.6	10
tactile	68.4	12.9	
kinesthetic	69.4	14.1	
tactile	70.6	11.4	
post	73.3	9.8	

The overall test comparing mean TcPO$_2$ levels on Day 2, Session 2 was also significant, $F(4,48) = 8.34$, $p < .000$. Tukey's HSD test was used for post hoc analysis. TcPO$_2$ did not differ significantly from the baseline period to the first or second tactile period, but did decrease significantly from the baseline period to the kinesthetic period. Additionally, TcPO$_2$ levels increased significantly from the first tactile and the kinesthetic periods to the post period, and the post period approached significance when compared to the baseline period (Table 8.7).

Overall analysis of the first session on Day 9 was significant, $F(4,48) = 3.74$, $p < .000$., and remained significant when adjusted for a positively biased test. Paired t-tests, using a Bonferroni correction, were conducted for post hoc comparisons. $TcPO_2$ was found to increase significantly from the kinesthetic period to the post period. Several other comparisons were also significant, but when evaluated with the more rigorous Bonferroni corrected probability level, did not remain significant. Included in these was a trend toward significant increases in $TcPO_2$ from the first tactile to the second tactile period, from the first tactile to the post period, and from the kinesthetic to the second tactile period (see Table 8.7). The Repeated Measures analysis of the second stimulation session on Day 9 was not significant. Tukey's Test for Nonadditivity was significant, however, so it is unclear whether the lack of significant findings was due to a negatively biased test, insufficient power, or a true null hypothesis.

TABLE 8.7
Post Hoc Results for the Stimulation Sessions: Mean $TcPO_2$ Levels

Tukey's HSD Results
(Absolute Value of Differences Among Means)

Comparison	Day 2, Stim 1	Day 2, Stim 2
pre-1st tactile	4.21* (D)	3.46
pre-kinesthetic	4.52* (D)	5.93* (D)
pre-2nd tactile	2.75	1.23
1st tactile-kinesthetic	.31	2.47
1st tactile-2nd tactile	1.46	2.23
kinesthetic-2nd tactile	1.80	4.70
kinesthetic-post	8.10** (I)	9.47** (I)
1st tactile-post	8.05** (I)	7.00** (I)
2nd tactile-post	6.28** (I)	4.77
pre-post	3.53	3.54
	HSD = 4.12, *p < .05	HSD = 4.96, *p < .05
	HSD = 4.98, **p < .01	HSD = 6.03, **p < .01

Paired T-Test Results

Day 9, Stim 1	M-DIF	(SD)	T	DF	P
pre-1st tactile	1.62	(6.0)	.98	12	.348
pre-kinesthetic	2.31	(8.3)	1.00	12	.335
pre-2nd tactile	1.46	(6.9)	.77	12	.457
1st tactile-kinesthetic	.69	(5.9)	.43	12	.103
1st tactile-2nd tactile	3.08	(4.4)	2.55	12	.025
kinesthetic-2nd tactile	3.77	(4.7)	2.90	12	.013
kinesthetic-post .000* (I)	5.62	(3.3)	6.13	12	.000* (I)
1st tactile-post	4.93	(6.8)	2.63	12	.022
2nd tactile-post	1.85	(4.0)	1.66	12	.123
pre-post	3.73	(8.3)	1.75	12	.103

Note. Direction of significant $TcPO_2$ changes indicated according to the order of the stimulation period specified in the comparison column: (I) = Increase, (D) = Decrease.
Significance level for paired t-test results based on a Bonferroni correction of .05/10 = p < .0005.

Range Score Comparisons.   Fluctuation in $TcPO_2$ levels, measured by range scores, were assessed across baseline, tactile, kinesthetic, tactile and post periods for each of the four stimulation sessions. For each of these Repeated Measures analyses, means and standard deviations are reported in Table 8.8. The overall test for the first stimulation session on Day 2 was significant, $F(4,72) = 5.59$, $p < .001$. Tukey's HSD test was conducted for post hoc analysis (see Table 8.9). Average $TcPO_2$ range scores were significantly greater during the kinesthetic phase of the stimulation session than during the baseline, first tactile, or post stimulation periods. Neither of the tactile periods exhibited range scores that

TABLE 8.8
Descriptive Statistics for Stimulation Session Repeated Measures: Range Scores

Stimulation	M	SD	N
Day 2, Stim 1			
pre	16.8	9.3	19
tactile	17.1	11.6	
kinesthetic	29.8	15.9	
tactile	21.7	15.9	
post	17.4	9.5	
Day 2, Stim 2			
pre	14.1	7.0	13
tactile	17.7	6.5	
kinesthetic	29.8	15.9	
tactile	22.8	21.1	
post	17.4	9.8	
Day 9, Stim 1			
pre	11.4	5.7	13
tactile	14.5	7.2	
kinesthetic	28.2	11.6	
tactile	14.7	7.7	
post	13.4	6.4	
Day 9, Stim 2			
pre	13.3	6.1	10
tactile	14.3	8.4	
kinesthetic	31.7	20.9	
tactile	16.8	9.9	
post	15.5	7.5	

TABLE 8.9
Post Hoc Results for the Stimulation Sessions: Range Scores

Tukey's HSD Results
(Absolute Value of Differences Among Means)

Comparison	Day 1, Stim 1	Day 2, Stim 2
pre-1st tactile	.26	3.64
pre-kinesthetic	13.00**	16.43**
pre-2nd tactile	4.95	8.86
1st tactile-kinesthetic	12.74**	12.79**
1st tactile-2nd tactile	4.69	5.22
kinesthetic-2nd tactile	8.05	7.57
1st tactile-post	.37	.35
kinesthetic-post	12.37**	13.14**
2nd tactile-post	4.32	5.57
pre-post	.63	3.29

$**p < .01$, HSD = 11.28 $**p < .01$, HSD = 11.53
$*p < .05$, HSD = 9.31 $*p < .05$, HSD = 9.43

Paired T-Test Results

Day 1, Stim 9	M-DIF	(SD)	T	DF	P	
pre-1st tactile	3.13	(5.3)	2.29	14	.038	
pre-kinesthetic	16.80	(9.4)	6.91	14	.000*	(I)
pre-2nd tactile	3.33	(9.3)	1.39	14	.187	
1st tactile-kinesthetic	13.67	(12.8)	4.13	14	.001*	(I)
1st tactile-2nd tactile	.20	(9.6)	.08	14	.937	
kinesthetic-2nd tactile	13.47	(15.2)	3.43	14	.004*	(D)
1st tactile-post	1.13	(10.7)	.41	14	.690	
kinesthetic-post	14.80	(11.5)	4.99	14	.000*	(D)
2nd tactile-post	1.33	(7.7)	.67	14	.513	
pre-post	2.00	(7.4)	1.04	14	.314	

Day 9, Stim 2

	M-DIF	(SD)	T	DF	P
pre-1st tactile	1.00	(4.8)	.69	10	.505
pre-kinesthetic	17.83	(20.2)	3.05	10	.011
pre-2nd tactile	5.33	(10.9)	1.69	10	.119
1st tactile-kinesthetic	17.46	(21.9)	2.64	10	.025
1st tactile-2nd tactile	2.55	(10.4)	.81	10	.434
kinesthetic-2nd tactile	12.50	(22.0)	1.97	10	.075
1st tactile-post	1.18	(9.23)	.42	10	.680
kinesthetic-post	14.67	(20.7)	2.45	10	.032
2nd tactile-post	2.17	(8.4)	.89	10	.390
pre-post	3.17	(8.3)	1.33	10	.210

Note. Direction of significant $TcPO_2$ changes indicated according to the order of the stimulation period specified in the comparison column: (I) = Increase, (D) = Decrease.
Significant level for paired t-test results based on a Bonferroni correction of .05/10 = $p < .005$.

were significantly different from baseline or post stimulation periods. The overall test for the second stimulation session on Day 2 was also significant, $F(4,52) = 7.45$, $p < .000$. Tukey's HSD test was again conducted for post hoc comparisons, and results were identical to those found in the first stimulation session (Table 8.9).

TcPO$_2$ range scores also differed significantly during the first stimulation session on Day 9, $F(4,56) = 12.81$, $p < .000$, after adjustment of the critical F value due to a positively biased test the overall test remained significant. Paired t-tests were conducted for follow-up comparisons of mean differences. Similar to the post hoc results from the stimulation session on Day 1, TcPO$_2$ range scores were found to be significantly greater for the kinesthetic period of the stimulation than for baseline, first tactile, second tactile, and post stimulation periods. An overall Repeated Measures analysis of range scores during the second stimulation session on Day 9 was also significant, $F(4,40) = 5.66$, and remained significant when corrected for a positive bias. Paired t-tests were conducted to assess which means were significantly different. Although trends similar to the previous stimulation sessions were noted, none of the t-tests were significant when evaluated using the Bonferroni correction (see Table 8.9).

Percent Time Below 40 mmHg.   The number of infants dropping below 40 mmHg during any given stimulation period are summarized in Table 8.10. Of note, the majority of the drops below 40 mmHg occurred during the kinesthetic period. The single drop below 40 mmHg during the two tactile periods on Day 2, Session 1 occurred in the same infant. This infant tended to run low across the three stimulation periods. Additionally, the single drop below 40 mmHg during the second tactile period on Day 9, Session 1 occurred in an infant who began dropping below 40 mmHg during the kinesthetic period. This infant did not begin recovery from the kinesthetic drop until 1 minute into the tactile period. Further inspection of the TcPO$_2$ tracings during the kinesthetic phase revealed that in all instances, TcPO$_2$ did not begin to drop noticeably from a stable pattern until the leg segment of the kinesthetic sequence. Drops typically became observable during either the right or left leg movement, but occasionally evidence of a drop did not occur until both legs were moved. A second pattern was also observable in many of the tracings. Typically, if a drop was first evident on the right leg (the first leg moved), there would be a brief recovery during the left leg movement, and then a second drop off during movement of both legs. If TcPO$_2$ did not begin to drop until the left leg, it often remained compromised during part or all of the both leg movement period.

Because of the systematic trend of this observation, the concern was raised that a potential confound might be affecting the data. Several authors have commented that pressure placed on the TcPO$_2$ electrode can cause artifactual declines in TcPO$_2$ (Horbar et al., 1985; Lucey, 1981). Because the electrode was always located on one of the calves, it is possible that inadvertent pressure was

TABLE 8.10
Infants Dropping Below 40 mmHg During Stimulation Sessions

Stimulation	Number of Infants	% of Infants	Mean Time* Below 40 mmHg (Range)	Mean % Time Below 40 mmHg (Range)
		Day 2, Stim 1		
pre	0	.00	—	—
tactile	1	.05	20	.06
kinesthetic (.29)	5	.26	34 (20-120)	.14 (.07-)
tactile	1	.05	20	.07
post	0	.00	—	—
		Day 2, Stim 2		
pre	0	.00	—	—
tactile	0	.00	—	—
kinesthetic (.21)	2	.14	49 (22-75)	.15 (.08-)
tactile	0	.00	—	—
post	0	.00	—	—
		Day 9, Stim 1		
pre	0	.00	—	—
tactile	0	.00	—	—
kinesthetic (.30)	4	.27	73 (45-130)	.20 (.15-)
tactile	1	.07	55	.18
post	0	.00	—	—
		Day 9, Stim 2		
pre	0	.00	—	—
tactile	0	.00	—	—
kinesthetic (.33)	3	.25	81 (40-140)	.23 (.15-)
tactile	0	.00	—	—
post	0	.00	—	—

*Time spent below 40 mmHg expressed in seconds.

occasionally placed upon the $TcPO_2$ electrode during the kinesthetic movement of the legs. This segment of the kinesthetic stimulation requires the examiner to grasp the leg in the calf/ankle area in order to initiate the infant's leg movement. Because interpretation of the kinesthetic data has direct bearing on interpretation of the stimulation procedure overall, it was considered necessary to investigate the possibility that the data had been confounded by accidental pressure placed on the $TcPO_2$ electrode. This was done by evaluating $TcPO_2$ in four additional infants during manipulated periods of applied pressure and kinesthetic leg move-

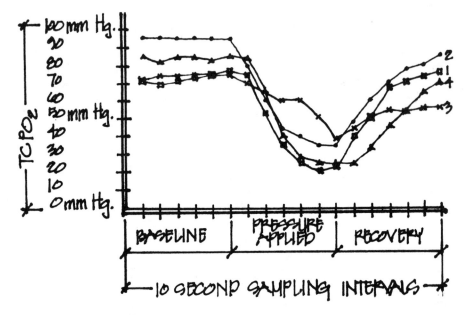

FIG. 8.1. TcPO₂ during purposefully applied pressure on four pre-term infants in the Neonatal Intensive Care Unit.

ment. The infants had either recently completed the ISP protocol, or had been a potential candidate for that study. Thus they were considered to be similar in nature to the current study's sample.

Each infant's TcPO₂ was observed for a 1-minute baseline period, followed by a 1 minute period of leg movement similar to that conducted during kinesthetic stimulation, but involving only the leg on which the electrode had been placed. This leg movement was accompanied by gentle but purposeful pressure applied to the TcPO₂ electrode. Postintervention TcPO₂ was then monitored for a 1-minute period. As is illustrated in Fig. 8.1, the pressure resulted in immediate and dramatic declines in TcPO₂ in all of the four infants. Recovery following pressure release tended to be equally rapid, but varied across the infants.

Additionally, TcPO₂ was monitored in each of the four infants during a regular stimulation period. The person performing the stimulation was instructed to be very careful not to place any pressure on the TcPO₂ electrode, and leg placement of the electrode was noted. Because care was taken not to pressurize the electrode, great variability during the kinesthetic phase was not generally observed in the four infants, although slight trends were still noted. Two of the infants were also observed on a second day in a counterbalanced observation, with the TcPO₂ electrode placed on the opposite leg. One of these infants showed a notable trend, similar to the pattern that had been described during the kinesthetic TcPO₂ declines observed in the original sample. When the $TcPO_2$ electrode was placed on this infant's right leg (the first leg to be moved during the kinesthetic phase), $TcPO_2$ immediately declined 35 mmHg when that leg was moved, and then recovered approximately 25 mmHg during the left leg movement, declining again during the movement of both legs. Conversely, when the electrode was placed on the same infant's left leg, $TcPO_2$ remained highly stable during the initial right leg movement, but then declined 30 mmHg during the left leg movement and remained compromised during movement of both legs. Table 8.11 summarizes the mean and range $TcPO_2$ values for each 1-minute period of the stimulation in each of the four infants, including the two counterbalanced sessions.

These findings indicate quite clearly that $TcPO_2$ can be affected by pressure placed on the $TcPO_2$ electrode, and also suggest that movement of the leg where the electrode is placed may cause artifactual $TcPO_2$ declines. Based upon these findings, the first tactile period of the stimulation was felt to be the most representative of accurate $TcPO_2$ levels, and was consequently used in the remaining analyses.

TABLE 8.11

Means and Ranges of $TcPO^2$ Values During Kinesthetic Stimulation When Avoiding Placing Pressure on the $TcPO^2$ Electrode

	Infant 1A	Infant 1B	Infant 2A	Infant 2B	Infant 3	Infant 4
Electrode Placement	Left	Right	Left	Right	Left	Right
Baseline	96	82	77	86	68	65
	92-97	75-86	75-79	83-89	62-75	55-73
Kinesthetic						
Right arm	100	70	82	77	73	70
	95-102	68-78	79-83	75-79	70-74	66-71
Left arm	100	75	86	78	60	70
	98-102	74-79	85-87	75-79	58-64	68-73
Right leg	98	58	82	75	61	72
	95-99	42-75	78-85	70-79	58-63	70-75
Left leg	78	58	77	72	59	58
	60-97	45-65	75-81	71-74	55-60	52-70
Both legs	75	43	75	75	56	55
	56-85	38-72	71-81	74-77	54-64	52-56
Post	96	90	80	75	70	78
	88-99	80-100	75-85	72-82	60-78	68-82

Comparisons Between Stimulation Sessions

In order to assess directly whether $TcPO_2$ changes differed significantly across stimulation sessions, the stimulation periods were compared to each other using a paired t-test. Baseline $TcPO_2$ levels across the four sessions were first compared, to ensure that initial differences in $TcPO_2$ were not present prior to the stimulation sessions. There were no significant differences in baseline $TcPO_2$. The stimulation periods were analyzed in the same manner, and no differences in $TcPO_2$ were found across the four stimulation periods. Because mean $TcPO_2$ and range scores during the four stimulation sessions did not differ significantly, the first stimulation session on Day 2 was chosen as the comparison session for follow-up analyses with the other procedures. This session was chosen because it had the largest sample size of the four stimulation periods.

DIFFERENTIAL EFFECTS ON $TcPO_2$
BETWEEN PROCEDURES

$TcPO_2$ was also evaluated between procedures, in order to determine if some procedures were more costly to $TcPO_2$ homeostasis than others.

BNBAS versus NAPI

First, the NAPI and BNBAS assessments were compared. Baseline comparisons revealed no differences. Comparison of mean $TcPO_2$ levels and range scores during the two behavioral assessments also revealed no significant differences.

Procedural Comparisons

To evaluate the hypothesis concerning differences in $TcPO_2$ between the stimulation, assessment procedures, and invasive procedures, the following comparisons were made: heelstick versus stimulation, heelstick versus BNBAS, and stimulation versus BNBAS. The heelstick was chosen as the invasive procedure for comparison because of the clearly documented changes in $TcPO_2$ that occurred during the heelstick procedure and the minimal reactivity of $TcPO_2$ during the gavage feedings. Since the BNBAS and NAPI were not significantly different, only one of the assessments was chosen for the procedural comparisons in order to limit the overall number of statistical tests.

Comparisons of baseline $TcPO_2$ levels yielded no significant differences. Paired t-tests were conducted on mean $TcPO_2$ levels for the three specified comparisons, using a Bonferroni correction of $p < .05/3 = .02$. Accordingly, means differed across analyses, depending on which cases were available for matched comparisons. Mean $TcPO_2$ differed significantly between the BNBAS ($M = 75$) and the heelstick ($M = 58$) procedures, $t(16) = 3.51, p < .003, n =$

17. The heelstick (M = 39.8) also differed significantly in the second comparison, with lower mean $TcPO_2$ levels than the stimulation (M = 73), $t(7)$ = 4.70, p < .002, n = 8. There were no significant differences, however, between mean $TcPO_2$ during the stimulation (M = 69) when compared to the BNBAS (M = 71).

Paired t-tests were also conducted on range scores for the three comparisons of interest. The heelstick and the BNBAS approached significance when range scores were compared, with the BNBAS (M = 40.6) showing greater variability than the heelstick (M = 24.2), $t(17)$ = 2.34, p < .03, n = 17.

The first tactile period was compared to the heelstick and BNBAS range scores. The BNBAS average range score (M = 40) was found to be significantly greater than the first tactile average range score (M = 17), $t(14)$ = 2.78, p < .02, n = 15. Additionally, the heelstick average range score (M = 28) approached significance when compared to the first tactile average range score (13.9), $t(7)$ = 1.88, p < .103, n = 8.

DISCUSSION

$TcPO_2$ was evaluated in order to provide the most comprehensive picture possible of $TcPO_2$ levels and changes during each procedure. In addition to mean $TcPO_2$, a range score (the high minus the low $TcPO_2$ value for a given period), and the percentage of time spent below 40 mmHg during each procedure were evaluated. Most previous studies have focused only on mean $TcPO_2$ levels as measured by intermittent sampling. Reliance solely upon this measure of $TcPO_2$ for research purposes has several shortcomings. Changes in an infant's $TcPO_2$ can occur quite rapidly, and recovery to the original $TcPO_2$ level may also be rapid. Intermittent sampling may therefore miss the essence of what is actually happening to $TcPO_2$, especially when averaged over a period of time. The mean $TcPO_2$ levels for this study were computed from a continuous sampling of $TcPO_2$. Additionally, $TcPO_2$ variability, assessed in this study by examining range scores and time spent below 40 mmHg has generally not been evaluated in the literature. Range scores reflect the difference between the highest and lowest $TcPO_2$ value for a given period, and thus indicate a picture of overall change, but not directionality. Percent time below 40 mmHg is an index of directional change believed to reflect clinically hypoxemic levels.

Invasive Medical Procedures

As hypothesized, the effect of the heelstick procedure on $TcPO_2$ appeared to be quite dramatic. There was an average drop from the baseline period to the heelstick period of 14 mmHg. Mean $TcPO_2$ was 52 mmHg, a value that is low enough to be of some clinical concern. Additionally, 45% of the infants fell below 40 mmHg for an average period of $3\frac{1}{2}$ minutes. These findings are consistent with general findings in the literature that heelsticks result in lower $TcPO_2$ levels (Danford et al., 1983; Speidel, 1978), although the results from this study are somewhat more dramatic than those recorded in previous studies. It is possible that because the heelstick procedure necessarily involves some manipulation of the leg, it was also affected by artifact declines due to the placement of the $TcPO_2$ electrode on the calf.

Gavage feedings were also hypothesized to cause a destabilization in $TcPO_2$ levels. Contrary to the heelstick procedure, mean $TcPO_2$ and range scores did not differ significantly during the feeding period. Mean $TcPO_2$ across baseline, preparation, feeding, and post periods ranged from 73 to 79 mmHg, with the largest change being a 4 mmHg nonsignificant increase from the feeding to the post period. Additionally, only two infants had $TcPO_2$ levels that fell below 40 mmHg for an average time period of 24 seconds. Compared to the other procedures, this hypoxemic period was relatively short. Observations also indicated very stable and consistent $TcPO_2$ levels during gavage feeds, which were reflected in the lack of significant differences between the range scores across the four periods. Additionally, the notion that tube insertion might be the most aversive phase of the feeding period was also investigated by evaluating only the low $TcPO_2$ values. Again, $TcPO_2$ low values did not significantly decline during the feeding period when compared to baseline, as would be indicated by a drop in $TcPO_2$ following tube insertion. Compared to the heelstick, these findings suggest that gavage feedings are a fairly benign medical procedure.

Although this conclusion is contrary to initial predictions, it can be interpreted in light of several considerations. The literature itself is not entirely decisive about the effects of gavage feeding on $TcPO_2$. Only one investigator separated out the effects of gavage feeding on $TcPO_2$ independently (Danford, et al., 1983). In this study 50% of the infants experienced significant initial decreases in mean $TcPO_2$ (11 mmHg) during gavage feeding, and the same number of infants experienced significant increases in $TcPO_2$ during the 5 minute post period. The sample size for the current study was twice as large, yet such decreases in $TcPO_2$ were not evident. As the Danford et al. study was conducted 6 years ago, it is possible that differences in technology may account for the different findings. The tubes used for gavage feeding have been considerably refined over the years, and are now smaller and easier to insert than those used in the past. Additionally, gavage feeding requires a minimal amount of handling once the tube has been inserted, and insertion usually takes only seconds with the smaller tubes. Thus, it is likely that gavage feeding, as it is currently performed, is not as destabilizing to $TcPO_2$ as once thought.

Behavioral Assessments

Mean $TcPO_2$ did not decline significantly during the BNBAS. Instead, $TcPO_2$ significantly increased by an average of 5–6 mmHg from both the baseline and the assessment periods to the post period. This increase in mean $TcPO_2$ following a handling procedure occurred in most of the procedures in this study, although the increase was not always significant. It is possible that this general trend toward increased post $TcPO_2$ levels was due to a return to quiet sleep following handling, because $TcPO_2$ levels during quiet sleep have been found to be significantly higher than they are during other behavioral states (Hanson & Okken, 1980). This is only speculation, however, as the present study did not record behavioral states. Additionally, mean $TcPO_2$ across the three BNBAS periods remained in the range of 70–79 mmHg, a clinically acceptable $TcPO_2$ level.

When examining variability of $TcPO_2$ during the BNBAS, however, a somewhat different interpretive picture emerged. $TcPO_2$ range scores increased dramatically when compared to the range of $TcPO_2$ change noted during baseline and post BNBAS administration, indicating significant fluctuation in $TcPO_2$ during the BNBAS procedure. Although the range score, by nature of its computation, is reflective of both increases and decreases in an individual infant's $TcPO_2$, these findings still suggest that $TcPO_2$ was much more varied during the BNBAS procedure than was initially indicated by mean $TcPO_2$ values. It was observed on the BNBAS tracings that most $TcPO_2$ variability occurred during the orientation items and during testing for certain reflexes (glabella, rooting, sucking, tonic deviation of the eyes, and nystagmus). Both these sets of items were administered when the infant was swaddled and removed from the isolette. Twenty-one percent of the infants had $TcPO_2$ levels that dropped below 40 mmHg, and almost all such drops occurred while the infants were out of the isolette. Although increases in $TcPO_2$ beyond baseline levels were not uncommon during the BNBAS, in general they were more gradual and less dramatic in nature than the observed declines.

Although mean $TcPO_2$ during NAPI administration was determined to be significantly lower than baseline and post $TcPO_2$, the practical significance of this finding is questionable. Mean $TcPO_2$ declined only 3 mmHg from baseline during the NAPI, and rose 5 mmHg during the 5 minutes following the end of the procedure. In terms of clinical implications, such changes in $TcPO_2$ are marginal despite their statistical significance. This is especially obvious when considering that mean $TcPO_2$ across the three periods remained in the clinically acceptable range of 70–75 mmHg.

Again, however, when range scores were evaluated, a more varied picture of $TcPO_2$ during NAPI administration became evident. Similar to the BNBAS, the range of $TcPO_2$ values during the NAPI was substantially greater than during both baseline and post periods. Additionally, 28% of the infants evaluated had $TcPO_2$ levels that declined below 40 mmHg for an average period of 1 minute, 55 seconds. The topography of $TcPO_2$ increases and decreases during the NB-MAP was very similar to those described during the BNBAS, with the exception of the reflexes identified to be problematic. Most of the reflexes typically conducted outside the isolette during the BNBAS are not part of the NB-MAP procedure.

Taken together, these findings suggest that $TcPO_2$ changes were relatively minor during the assessments, with a small proportion of the infants accounting for most of the changes. The two assessments were also compared for differential effects on $TcPO_2$. Because the NAPI was designed with the more fragile response system of the preterm neonate in mind, we questioned whether it was a more gentle assessment tool. The two instruments appeared, however, to result in similar $TcPO_2$ response patterns. For example, the greatest declines in $TcPO_2$ tended to occur during a similar series of items in both the BNBAS and the NAPI, and included the items typically administered outside the isolette (reflexes such as glabella, rooting, sucking, tonic deviation of the eyes, and Nystagmus during the BNBAS, and the orientation items during both the BNBAS and NAPI). The items of concern occupied only a small segment of the 30–35 minutes typically required for administration of either of the behavioral exams. It appeared that $TcPO_2$ during the remaining exam periods was more stable and similar to baseline $TcPO_2$. This explains why mean $TcPO_2$ during both assessment procedures remained fairly high.

When directly compared, there were no significant differences in mean $TcPO_2$ or range scores between the BNBAS and the NAPI. Of significance, however, was a difference in the average amount of time infants spent below 40 mmHg. The average amount of time a given infant spent below 40 mmHg was substantially longer during the BNBAS procedure. This was probably due to the shorter number of items administered outside the isolette during the NAPI. Additionally, nonresponsive infants are not further stimulated during the NAPI in attempt to elicit an optimal response, as sometimes occurs during the BNBAS. Rather, infants are administered a standardized sequence of items during the NAPI, if the infant is nonresponsive during the procedure, no major attempt is made to arouse him. Because of this procedural difference between the NAPI and the BNBAS, the NAPI may be the more clinically appropriate assessment tool for preterm infants who exhibit greater variability in $TcPO_2$ levels.

Because the NAPI and BNBAS did not differ significantly on the mean $TcPO_2$ and range score variables, the BNBAS was selected to investigate the hypothesis comparing $TcPO_2$ during behavioral assessments and aversive medical procedures. Examination of mean $TcPO_2$ levels clearly suggested that the heelstick resulted in significantly greater compromise to $TcPO_2$. Range scores were somewhat greater during the BNBAS, however, than during the heelstick procedure, although the difference wasn't significant. $TcPO_2$ during the heelstick typically declined from baseline and remained low, whereas $TcPO_2$ during the BNBAS exhibited more increases and decreases, thus resulting in a larger range of $TcPO_2$ values. Importantly mean $TcPO_2$ was not significantly greater during the BNBAS when compared to the stimulation. Overall, the two procedures resulted in comparable levels of stable $TcPO_2$. The range of $TcPO_2$ was significantly greater during the BNBAS, however, again suggesting that certain items resulted in greater $TcPO_2$ fluctuation.

Taken together, these findings suggest the need to more closely evaluate the context of behavioral assessments such as the BNBAS and NAPI when performing them on the more fragile preterm neonate. It is likely that, for some infants, it was the removal from the isolette that triggered a decline in $TcPO_2$, rather than the actual assessment items themselves. The energy that such infants must mobilize when removed from their protective environments, and when stimulated for the purpose of assessing their responsiveness, may be simply too taxing. Interpretation of these findings should clearly be made with the individual infant in mind. Obviously, only a small proportion of the infants assessed with the BNBAS and NAPI appeared to be negatively affected. Additional research should assess whether the decreases in $TcPO_2$ observed while the infants were outside of the isolette were associated with decreased body temperature, increased handling, or artifactual pressurization of the electrode. It is also possible that these decreases could be attenuated by simply monitoring the infants' $TcPO_2$ during the assessment period. Finally, alterations in the assessment procedures themselves might also alleviate this problem. For example, examiners could administer all items inside the isolette and could avoid repeated trials to elicit optimal performance on a given item. Learning to identify the early behavioral distress signs that precede declines in oxygenation will aid in our ability to effectively perform such exams without compromising $TcPO_2$ levels.

This study has clearly documented that preterm infants are a heterogeneous group in terms of $TcPO_2$ responsiveness to certain procedures. Individual variability was evident across both medical and assessment procedures, with some infants exhibiting much less stability in $TcPO_2$ homeostasis. Further research is clearly needed to elucidate the types of factors contributing to decreased $TcPO_2$ levels. It is likely that two sets of variables play a role in individual $TcPO_2$ variability. The first is related to characteristics of the infant, and includes factors such as previous medical complications, prenatal care, gestational age, length of stay in the NICU, overall resiliency, and chronological age. The second set of variables is related to the daily NICU events and their effect on the infant. Included in this category would be characteristics such as time and effectiveness of previous feedings, sleep patterns before and during $TcPO_2$ assessment, and number and timing of procedural interruptions prior to $TcPO_2$ monitoring. Infants who can be identified as being at high risk for $TcPO_2$ instability could then be placed on continuous monitoring and observed more closely. These infants are the types who should be handled with excessive care even when medically stable.

MASSAGE PROCEDURE

Changes in $TcPO_2$ were slight, and of questionable medical significance during the massage procedure. Across the four massage sessions, only the 1st session on day one revealed a significant decrease in mean $TcPO_2$ from baseline to the initial tactile period. Although significant, the decrease in mean $TcPO_2$ was only 4 mmHg, a value that has questionable clinical significance. Additionally, average $TcPO_2$ values across the four sessions, during all phases of the massage, remained in the 65–75 mmHg range.

When evaluating the sessions for differences in mean $TcPO_2$ across the 5 periods (pre, tactile, kinesthetic, tactile, and post), the emergence of significance was almost always associated with the kinesthetic stimulation. As previously documented, this was possibly related to the inadvertent placement of pressure upon the $TcPO_2$ electrode, rather than the kinesthetic movement itself. It is also possible that the differences in oxygenation were related to the position of the infant, rather than the stimulation. The kinesthetic massage is conducted while the infant is in the supine position, while the tactile massage is conducted while the infant is in a prone position. Martin and colleagues (Martin, Herrell, Rubin, & Fanaroff, 1979) found PaO_2 levels rose significantly in preterm infants while they were in the prone, as opposed to supine positions. The authors attributed this finding to enhanced ventilation/perfusion ratios during prone positioning. Although the changes observed in $TcPO_2$ during kinesthetic stimulation for most infants remained within a clinically "safe" level, systematic investigation of the mechanism accountable for increased $TcPO_2$ variability during kinesthetic stimulation is warranted. Tactile and kinesthetic periods should be counterbalanced for study, and the initial infant state evaluated.

$TcPO_2$ range scores during the massage revealed a similar pattern to those observed in mean $TcPO_2$ levels. Consistently, the range of $TcPO_2$ change during the tactile phases of the stimulation was compatible with baseline $TcPO_2$ variability, and emerged as being significantly different only during the kinesthetic phase of the stimulation. Similarly, across all the massage sessions (totaling 55) there was only one brief incident of an infant dropping below 40 mmHg during the first tactile phase, which lasted for 20 seconds. Of note, this incident occurred in an infant who exhibited lower overall $TcPO_2$ levels across the baseline period. The remaining incidents of $TcPO_2$ declining below 40 mmHg occurred during the leg movement of the kinesthetic phase, with two incidents carrying over into the 2nd tactile period, again suggesting placement of the electrode may have affected the results.

Similar findings were reported in a study assessing the effects of a stimulation protocol that included tactile, kinesthetic, vestibular, auditory, and visual stimulation on $TcPO_2$ in 12 low birth weight infants (Eyler, Courtway-Meyers, Edens, Hellrung, Nelson, Eitzman, & Resnick, 1988). No significant change in mean $TcPO_2$ levels were found during this multimodal intervention. Additionally, $TcPO_2$ values did not fall below 40 mmHg and there were no instances of tachycardia recorded in any of these infants during the tactile or kinesthetic stimulation. These findings are particularly significant when considering that the $TcPO_2$ electrode in this study was placed on the chest or abdomen, rather than the leg.

Finally, the comparison between tactile massage and the heelstick procedure supported the prediction that $TcPO_2$ would be more adversely affected by an invasive medical procedure than by social touch. Mean $TcPO_2$ was significantly lower during the heelstick procedure than the massage, and extended declines in $TcPO_2$ below 40 mmHg occurred far more frequently during the heelstick procedure.

CONCLUDING REMARKS

These findings have substantial implications for current NICU handling policies regarding the preterm infant. The effects of massage on $TcPO_2$ had not been thoroughly investigated, resulting in some hesitancy about implementing such stimulation programs in the NICU. Our findings clearly suggest that, at least for the more stabilized preterm neonate, handling policies should not be the same for both social and medical forms of touch.

Similarly, Eyler and colleagues (1988) found a much higher occurrence of $TcPO_2$ declines below 40 mmHg during nursing procedures than when compared to their intervention protocol of tactile, kinesthetic, vestibular, auditory, and visual stimulation. These authors also documented longterm positive developmental outcomes for infants participating in their intervention program, including higher mental and motor developmental indices on the Bayley Scales at 1 and 2 years of age (Resnick, Eyler, F., Nelson, R., Eitzman, D., & Bucciarelli, R., 1987). Other studies have documented favorable developmental outcomes in relation to tactile-kinesthetic massage or vestibular-kinesthetic stimulation including increased alertness, significant weight gains, shorter hospital stays, and superior neurological and mental development (Barnard & Bee, 1983; Field et al., 1986; Leib et al., 1980; Rice, 1977; White & Labarba, 1976).

These findings, taken together with the results of the current study, have important implications for the use of stimulation protocols with preterm neonates. An additional focus should be increasing parental involvement in implementing stimulation protocols. This could have the added benefit of facilitating the parent-infant bond, and could help parents gradually take on increasing responsibility for their preterm infant.

Although $TcPO_2$ levels during kinesthetic stimulation remained in a safe clinical range for most infants, questions regarding placement of the electrode and infant positioning should be addressed as potential explanations for the additional variability observed during the kinesthetic sequences. Additionally, this study has demonstrated that individual infants may exhibit very different physiological response patterns to both medical and social touch. Future research should attempt to delineate potential variables accounting for individual differences. Finally, consideration of the individual infant's needs and $TcPO_2$ response patterns should always be included when evaluating an infant for an early stimulation-intervention program.

ACKNOWLEDGEMENTS

This research was supported in part by an NIMH Research Scientist Aware #MH0031 and NIMH Basic Research Grant #MH40779 to Tiffany Field. The authors would also like to acknowledge Frank A. Scafidi, Jacqueline Roberts, Lisa Eisen, and Sandra K. Larson for their help in data collection and Anne Hogan and Emmalee Bandstra for their comments and review.

REFERENCES

Abu–Osba, Y. K., Brouillette, R. T., Wilson, S. L., & Thach, B. T. (1982). Breathing pattern and transcutaneous oxygen tension during motor activity in preterm infants. *American Review of Respiratory Distress, 125,* 382–387.

Barnard, K. E., & Bee, H. B. (1983). The impact of temporally patterned stimulation on the development of preterm infants. *Child Development, 54,* 1156–1167.

Bennet, F. C., Robinson, N. M., & Sells, C. J. (1983). Growth and development of infants weighing less than 800 grams at birth. *Pediatrics, 71,* 41–45.

Brazelton, T. B. (1973). *Neonatal Behavioral Assessment Scale.* Philadelphia: Lippincott.

Danford, D., Miske, S., Headley, J., & Nelson, R. M. (1983). Effects of routine care procedures on transcutaneous oxygen in neonates: A quantitative approach. *Archives of Disease in Childhood, 58,* 20–23.

Dubowitz, L. M. S., Dubowitz, V., & Goldberg, C. (1970). Clinical assessment of gestational age in the newborn infant. *Journal of Pediatrics, 77,* 1.

Eyler, F. D., Courtway-Meyers, C., Edens, M. J., Hellrung, D. J., Nelson, R. M., Eitzman, D. V., & Resnick, M. B. (1988). *Effects of developmental intervention on heart rate and transcutaneous oxygen in low birth weight infants.* Paper presented at the Society for Pediatric Research.

Field, T. (1987). Alleviating stress in intensive-care unit nurseries. *Journal of AOA, 87*(9), 646–650.

Field, T., Schanberg, S., Scafidi, F., Bauer, C. R., Vega-Lahr, N., Garcia, R., Nystrom, J., & Kuhn, C. (1986). Tactile/kinesthetic stimulation effects on preterm neonates. *Pediatrics, 77,* 654–658.

Gaiter, J., Avery, G., Temple, C., Johnson, A., & White, N. (1981). Stimulation characteristics of nursery environments for critically ill preterm infants and infant behavior. In L. Stern, W. Oh, & Frishanson (Eds.), *Intensive care of the newborn* (pp. 118–132). New York: Mason Publishing.

Gorski, P. A., Huntington, L., & Lewkowicz, D. J. (1986). Handling preterm infants in hospitals: Stimulating controversy about timing stimulation. *Johnson & Johnson Pediatric Round Table,* No. 13.

Gunnar, M. R., Isensee, J., & Fust, S. L. (1987). Adrenocortical activity and the Brazelton Neonatal Assessment Scale: Moderating effects of the newborn's biomedical status. *Child Development, 58,* 1448–1458.

Hanson, H., & Okken, A. (1980). Transcutaneous oxygen tension of newborn infants in different behavioral states. *Pediatric Research, 14,* 911–915.

Horbar, J. D., Soll, R. F., McAuliffe, T. L., Clark, T., & Lucey, J. F. (1985). *Episodic abnor-malities in transcutaneous oxygen recorded during neonatal intensive care.* Paper presented at the Society for Pediatric Research Annual Meeting.

Kirk, R. E. (1982). *Experimental design* (2nd ed.). Belmont, CA: Wadsworth.

Korner, A. F., Thom, V. A., & Forrest, T. (1990). *The Neurobehavioral assessment for preterm infants.* The Psychological Corporation.

Leib, S., Benfield, G., & Guidubaldi, J. (1980). Effects of early intervention and stimulation on the preterm infant. *Pediatrics, 66,* 83–90.

Long, J. G., Philip, A., & Lucey, J. F. (1980). Noise and hypoxemia in the intensive care unit. *Pediatrics, 65,* 143–145.

Long, J. G., Alistair, G. S., Philip, A., & Lucey, J. F. (1980). Excessive handling as a cause of hypoxemia. *Pediatrics, 65,* 203–207.

Lucey, J. F. (1981). Clinical uses of transcutaneous oxygen monitoring. *Advances in Pediatrics, 28,* 27–56.

Lucey, J. F., Peabody, J. L., & Philip, A. (1977). Recurrent undetected hypoxia and hyperoxia: A newly recognized iatrogenic problem of intensive care. *Pediatric Research, 11,* 537.

Martin, R. J., Herell, N., Rubin, D., & Fanaroff, A. (1979). Effect of supine and prone positions on arterial oxygen tension in the preterm infant. *Pediatrics, 63,* 528–531.

Murdoch, D. R., & Darlow, B. A. (1984). Handling during neonatal intensive care. *Archives of Disease in Childhood, 59,* 957–961.

Norris, S., Campbell, L., & Brenkert, S. (1982). Nursing procedures and alterations in trans-cutaneous oxygen tension in premature infants. *Nursing Research, 31*(6), 330–333.

Resnick, M., Eyler, F., Nelson, R., Eitzman, D., & Bucciarelli, R. (1980). Developmental inter-vention for low birth weight infants: Improved early developmental outcome. *Pediatrics, 72,* 198–202.

Rice, D. (1977). Neuropsychological development in premature infants following stimulation. *De-velopmental Psychology, 13,* 69–76.

Sammons, W. A. H., & Lewis, K. (1985). *Premature babies: A different beginning.* St. Louis, MO: Mosby.

Speidel, B. D. (1978, April 22). Adverse effects of routine procedures on preterm infants. *The Lancet,* pp. 864–865.

Stahlman, M. T. (1984). Newborn intensive care: Success or failure? *Journal of Pediatrics, 105,* 162–167.

White, J. L., & Labarba, R. C. (1976). The effect of tactile and kinesthetic stimulation on neonatal development in the premature infant. *Developmental Psychobiology, 9*(6), 569–577.

9 The Stress of Parenting Apneic Infants

Debra Bendell-Estroff
University of California-San Francisco

Rebecca Smith-Sterling
University of Texas at San Antonio

Michael Miller
Marshfield Clinic

The American Academy of Pediatrics Task Force on Prolonged Apnea has defined prolonged apnea as a "cessation of breathing for 20 seconds or longer, or as a briefer episode with associated bradycardia, cyanosis, or pallor" (p. 1). They mandated that "beyond specific treatment of any underlying disorder, 24 hour surveillance is critical to management of the infant." This surveillance most commonly occurs through the use of an electronic home monitor that alerts parents to an apneic episode by an auditory signal so that intervention can occur. The caregiver must respond within 20 seconds and be prepared to initiate cardiorespiratory resuscitation, if necessary. The apneic event has been identified as one of the possible pathways to Sudden Infant Death Syndrome (SIDS) (Anderson & Rosenblith, 1971; Kelly & Shannon, 1981; Meny, Blackmon, Fleischmann, Gutberlet, & Naumberg, 1988; Weissbluth, Brouillette, Liu, & Hunt, 1982).

The identification of an infant with apnea constitutes a crisis for the parents, siblings, and extended family of the infant. In addition to the recommendations already cited, the Task Force reminded pediatricians that these stressors indicate the necessity to evaluate families for strengths, weaknesses, resources, and needs before treatment decisions can be made and implemented. It is important to identify those families who are psychologically at risk for developing conditions that might impair their ability to care for an apneic infant so that preventive measures can be implemented in a timely fashion. Meny and his colleagues (1988) have documented parental noncompliance with home monitoring as contributory and possibly directly causative in the deaths of several infants in their study. Demographic characteristics were associated with noncompliance. These included lack of private medical insurance, unmarried mother, and maternal age of less than 25 years.

ETIOLOGY OF STRESSORS

Most infants with Interrupted Infantile Apnea are discovered by their parent(s) to be limp, pale, or cyanotic, and are revived only after vigorous manual or auditory stimulation and/or mouth-to-mouth resuscitation. The ensuing hospitalization and evaluation of the child with later adjustment to the prescribed treatment is a significant stressor. But, in addition, questions remain regarding the ramifications of apnea; specifically, the effects of possible oxygen desaturation during the episode, as well as concerns regarding the continuing medical problem. Thus, an apneic infant has a significant impact on the personal and social lives of all family members (Black, Hersher, & Steinschneider, 1978).

Home monitoring has changed over the years. In the 1970s monitoring was accomplished by the use of standard impedance respiratory monitors whose alarm was triggered after 20 seconds of apnea. Once triggered, the alarm sounded at 1-second intervals until the infant resumed breathing. During those early years, false alarms were common and were usually caused by broken leads and inappropriate electrode placement. Fortunately, technical aspects of home monitoring are improving. Impedance respiratory monitors continue to be used, but they are accompanied by a cardiac monitor. Often these can be auxiliary powered by a portable yet still cumbersome battery. Not only is this essential for short-term emergencies (power failures), but equally important, it provides caregivers with an escape from being homebound. In addition, electrode belts and recorders are available that are able to differentiate false alarms by recording respiration and heart rate during an alarm. In spite of these technical improvements, the stressors are still great for all family members. For parents of an apneic infant a series of difficult adjustments still must be faced (Black et al., 1978). The parents must learn to cope with the fear of their infant's sudden death. The parents must learn to use, to rely upon, and to live with the monitor, including all the accompanying financial and social restraints that are entailed. The parents must also be prepared to instantly assume the responsibility for resuscitating their infant should breathing cease.

THE FAMILY SYSTEM

Stress in families arise from an actual or perceived imbalance between demands placed on family functioning and the capability of that family to function. This state alters the natural equilibrium of the family system. Its intensity varies depending on the resources available to the family and to the individuals in the family. Slovik & Kelly (1988) note that caring for a child with apnea affects everyone in the immediate and extended family; each member's response has an effect on the child and the child's reaction then affects the other family members in reciprocal fashion. Relationships need to be viewed as feedback systems that either facilitate or frustrate interaction. The intensity of the stress is thus highly dependent on the health of the affected child: The child's health affects its capacity for and quality of interaction behavior.

It is important to understand premorbid histories and familial styles of coping with stress. Although the stressors that are encountered in the monitoring experience are unique, they certainly relate to prior stressors that have affected family functioning. Also, families and individuals are likely to respond to new stressors in the same style as they have to previous stressors, whether adaptive or not, unless new more adaptive styles can be taught and learned.

Abidin (1979) has theorized that parenting stress is related to child and parental characteristics. He has developed the Parenting Stress Index (PSI) (Abidin, 1979), which assesses the magnitude and breadth of stress across multiple domains. Perceived acceptability, demandingness, adaptability, and mood of the child are identified and assessed for their contribution to parental stress. Parental characteristics that affect stress include depression, parental attachment to the child, restriction of role, sense of competence, social isolation, relationship with spouse, appropriateness of expectations for the child, and parental health. Additionally, Abidin factors in and assesses the number of life crises. Research utilizing the PSI has indicated that mothers of apneic infants between the ages of 4 to 8 months of age perceive their infants to be less adaptable, less acceptable, more demanding, and less reinforcing than control infants (Bendell, Culbertson, Shelton, & Carter, 1986). Previous research with the PSI had demonstrated similar findings among other "at risk" populations, including children with physical handicaps and developmental delay (Abidin, 1979).

Theorists have postulated that risk factors are moderated by intrapersonal factors, by social-ecological factors, and by coping abilities (Lazarus & Folkman, 1984; Moos & Schaefer, 1984), all of which constitute a set of resistance factors. These factors are hypothesized to be related to adaptation in both direct and indirect ways. The chronic strain resulting from the apneic infant and the medical apparatus required to monitor this condition thus interacts with these factors in a unique manner for each family, and for each member of the family.

EARLY ADJUSTMENT

The acute episode that identifies the infant as apneic and the circumstances surrounding the discovery of the apneic condition are important for the development of stress. Slovik and Kelly (1988) have observed that "time stops and life changes" (p. 202) following this discovery. The initial affective response to the diagnosis of interrupted Sudden Infant Death Syndrome is often shock mixed with relief. The shock originates from disbelief and difficulty accepting such a grievous and threatening condition in one's baby. Yet this is tinged with the feelings of relief and gratefulness that the child is still alive and the problem is identified. These intensely conflicting emotions are usually complicated by subsequent events. For many families the initial resuscitation, the subsequent emergency room visit, and the follow-up hospitalization culminates in a return home with a confusing amount of new information, new equipment, new instructions, and new worries.

Few studies have examined the impact of the apneic infant; however, there is a relatively large body of literature examining the impact of the monitor on the family. Cain, Kelly, and Shannon (1980) found that although extreme anxiety was prevalent initially in the majority of the 133 parents they studied, only 27% of the parents reported severe anxiety beyond the first month at home. Twice that number of parents (55%) felt that their social life was restricted significantly and that they were socially isolated. However, perhaps most importantly, 79% reported that the presence of the monitor made them feel more comfortable with their baby, and only 14% felt that their marital relationship had deteriorated during the period of home monitoring. Similar findings were reported by Black et al. (1978), who found that the use of the monitor had a significant, but temporary, impact on the personal and social lives of all family members. Specific sources of stress included technical and mechanical problems with the monitoring devices as well as disruptions in daily patterns of living and child care routines. Nonetheless, just as in the Cain et al. study, most parents perceived the monitor to be an anxiety reducer and, in retrospect, not injurious to normal parent–child relations.

Bendell et al. (1986) administered the Neonatal Perception Inventory (Broussard & Sturgeon, 1970) to 25 mothers of apneic infants between 4 and 8 months of age. These results were then compared to the responses of 25 mothers whose infants were matched for gestational age, sex, socioeconomic status of the parents, and educational level of the mothers. Mothers' ratings of their apneic infants did not differ significantly compared to those mothers' ratings of the "average baby." (Bendell et al., 1986). Although results approached significance, mothers of both groups of infants rated their children as slightly less difficult than the average baby; this difference was smaller among mothers of apneic infants than for mothers of comparison infants. When mothers were questioned as to the degree of bother created by such infant behaviors as crying, spitting up, sleeping, feeding, elimination, or the lack of a predictable schedule, mothers of apneic and comparison infants did not differ significantly in their ratings. However, when mothers of apneic infants were asked to rate the degree of bother created by the apnea monitors and their infants' apnea itself on a four-point rating scale ranging from one (not at all) to four (a great deal), the mean rating for the monitor was 2.35 and the mean rating for the apneic episodes was 3.35. This indicates that whereas the monitor was perceived as mildly stressful, the apnea provided the greatest source of stress.

During this early period of adjustment to the infant, the PSI was also administered. As described earlier, this 151-item self-report inventory assesses various dimensions of stress within the mother-child dyadic interaction under three major domains: (a) child characteristics; (b) mother characteristics: and (c) situational/demographic characteristics. Within the three major stressor domains are several subscores that reflect subdivisions of that particular domain. The PSI is designed to identify dyads that are at risk for developing dysfunctional parent and/or child behaviors. Under the child domain, mothers of apneic infants reported significantly more stress on three of the five subscales relative to mothers of comparison infants ($p < .01$). Compared to control infants, apneic infants were reported to have greater difficulty adjusting to changes in the environment and may overreact or be difficult to manage when these changes occur. Apneic infants were perceived as a poor match for the parents' expectations or hopes. In addition, mothers of apneic infants reported their babies to be more demanding—demands that may involve frequent crying, wanting to be held, or frequent minor behavior problems. On the parent domain, mothers of apneic infants also indicated more stress due to a lack of reinforcement they receive from parenting their infants. That is, the interaction between the apneic infant and mother often failed to produce for the mother sufficient positive feelings about her parenting capabilities. And, finally, mothers of apneic infants reported significantly more stress related to social isolation ($p < .001$).

Anecdotal evidence indicates that mothers of apneic infants sometimes impose isolation upon themselves as they express reluctance to trust their infants to the care of even close relatives. Other mothers experience difficulty securing babysitters who they feel are competent to care for an apneic infant. Assisting parents in securing appropriate babysitting services or respite care is a central issue for parents who must otherwise resign themselves to a life of little or no outside social contact. Professional intervention with families of apneic infants needs to focus on counteracting the effects of social isolation. This intervention may include the formation of parent support groups and the provision of trained health-care professionals who can babysit and who are familiar with the use of a home monitor (Bendell, et al., 1986). Encouraging two-parent families to share the responsibility, as well as having other family members or friends trained in infant cardiopulmonary resuscitation, would lessen the burden of care and isolation. There were no other significant differences related to mother characteristics in this sample.

In a companion study, Bendell and her colleagues (Bendell, Goldberg, Urbano, Urbano, & Bauer, 1987) compared mothers of apneic infants to mothers of extremely low birth weight infants and found that the former report significantly more stress, maternal health, isolation, and feelings of restriction. There were significant stressors as revealed in a step-wise multiple discriminant analysis. The families in this study felt that hired babysitters were either unavailable or incompetent. All too often, anger and guilt become the frequent and predictable manifestations of the restricted freedom and fear of death in these families. The reality of being a parent of an apneic infant precludes an easy social life and a normal lifestyle. Even routine activities that mask the sound of the alarm (vacuuming, showering) must be arranged around an infant's sleep schedules and monitoring.

LONGITUDINAL IMPACT OF APNEA

Baroni (1989) analyzed the influence of biological risk on growth and development in apneic infants. Multiple regression analyses indicated that apnea (along with gestational age) was significantly predictive of less optimal mental development and decreased weight, length, and mid-upper arm circumference (when obstetric and postnatal optimality scores were controlled as covariate factors). Apnea also showed significant interaction effects with maternal health and stress. The adverse effect of apnea was most salient for those infants with more frequent episodes and less favorable environmental circumstances as measured by the Home Observation for Measurement of the Environment (Caldwell & Bradley, 1978).

It has been hypothesized that because apneic infants have been hypoxic for various periods of time, or are neurodevelopmentally abnormal, they may have suffered brain damage that may in turn impact upon their intellectual, cognitive, and emotional levels of functioning. Deykin, Bauman, Kelly, Hsieh, and Shannon (1984) documented significant gross motor impairment and mild cognitive deficits in children with histories of apnea when compared with their siblings. Although such differences were not noted in comparisons with their playmates, this may have been due to a bias in the selection of this group. No significant behavioral differences were observed in the apnea group as compared with playmates and siblings, but some trends were noted on a behavioral screen questionnaire. Due to the small sample size, definitive conclusions cannot be drawn without further research.

One primary question relates to differences between mothers and fathers in parenting apneic infants. It is a maxim of child development that both mothers and fathers are important persons in the life of a child. How they are functionally distinguishable has been investigated in multiple studies. Cohen and Campos (1974) reported attachments to both parents, but of a differing nature. Field (1978) noted that fathers engage in more game playing and physical activity with their infants. The literature depicts high-risk infants as less attentive, less responsive, and more irritable than normal infants (Field, 1977; Stern & Kerruker,

1988). Mothers of high-risk infants are described as frequently overstimulating and less sensitive to infant signals of social satiation. Fathers have been found to be less deferential than mothers toward high risk infants (Field, 1978, 1981).

In order to assess the differential effect of an apneic infant on mothers and fathers, we asked families to individually complete a series of questionnaires for formerly apneic three-year-old children and a comparison group. Forty-four children between the ages of 23 and 38 months of age (mean age = 29.5) were evaluated. One half of this group was comprised of children who had experienced apneic episodes and had been placed on home monitors during infancy. The remainder of this group was comprised of age- and sex-matched controls. Twelve males and 10 females comprised each of these groups. The groups were comparable on socioeconomic status and birth order. Children with no history of seizure disorder or gastroesophageal reflux but with an abnormal sleep study pattern were included in the apneic group. The control subjects were obtained by screening medical charts of children seen in a pediatric practice clinic over a period of 2 months. The control subjects showed no history of severe medical disorders or complications of pregnancy, and they were selected by age and sex for matching purposes. Parents were asked to individually complete (without collaboration) a series of questionnaires including:

1. Dimensions of Temperament Survey (DOTS). (Lerner, Palermi, Spiro & Nesselrroade, 1982). This instrument yields five statistically independent factors of temperament: activity, attention span/distractibility, adaptability/approach withdrawal, rhythmicity, and irritability, and is based on the theoretical work of Thomas and Chess (1977).

2. Parenting Stress Inventory (PSI). This questionnaire is designed to assess various dimensions of difficulty and stress within the mother-child interaction (Abidin, 1983). This instrument measures sources of stress within three major areas: child characteristics, parental characteristics, and situational/demographic characteristics.

3. Conners Parent Rating Scales (CPRS). (Conners, 1973). This 48-item instrument assesses parents' perceptions of behavioral problems. Standardized norms for toddlers were utilized.

4. Moos Family Environment Scale (MFES). (Moos & Moos, 1981). This 90-item instrument assesses the social climate of families. Particular focus is placed upon the interpersonal relationships, directions of personal growth, and organizational structure of families. Parents were contacted by phone after selection. Parents agreeing to participate were mailed packets of questionnaires to complete. Follow-up phone calls were made 3 weeks after the packets had been mailed if they had not been returned in order to answer any questions the parents might have regarding the study or the questionnaire. Within the apneic sample, maternal and paternal packets were returned for 95% of the children, and mater-

nal-only packets were returned for the remaining 5% of the children. Within the comparison sample, maternal and paternal packets were returned for 66% of the children, paternal-only packets were returned for 9% of the children, and maternal-only packets were returned for 25% of the children.

Maternal questionnaire data were analyzed using ANOVA with two between-group factors (sex of child and apneic vs. comparison group). The analysis yielded differences on the Family Environment Scale indicating that the apneic children were assessed by their mothers as being less expressive and less independent, ($p < .01$). In addition, the mothers of apneic children tended to report greater family participation in recreation and sporting activities, and greater moral religious emphasis in their family life, ($p < .05$). On the DOTS, mothers of apneic children reported less rhythmicity for their children, ($p < .04$), and less adaptability, ($p < .02$) for themselves.

The final group difference emerged on the PSI on the dimension of maternal health ($p, < .06$). Apneic mothers experienced more illness than comparison mothers, although this result was marginally significant. The only significant results for sex of child indicated that male children were perceived to be less reinforcing ($p < .001$) than female children and male children's mothers had greater health problems ($p < .05$). Father questionnaire data indicated that apneic children were perceived as more active ($p < .05$) and more distractible ($p < .02$) on the DOTS than the comparison group. In addition, the fathers of apneic children viewed parenting as less reinforcing than the comparison fathers ($p < .04$) on the PSI. Also, the fathers of apneic girls tended to report greater stress in the domain of child adaptability ($p < .03$), life stress ($p, < .06$), and relationship with spouse ($p < .03$) than did comparison fathers of girls on the PSI. Significant sex by group interactions were found for two of the parenting stress domains. Inspection of the simple effects revealed that fathers of apneic daughters reported greater stress than fathers of apneic sons on the child characteristics dimension ($p < .03$). In contrast, fathers of comparison children attributed no greater stress to parenting a daughter than a son. Mothers of apneic children reported poorer relationships with their spouses than did their mates ($p < .05$). No patterns of this kind emerged for comparison families.

The anecdotally observed differential impact of parenting a child who has been apneic is underscored by this research. Research by Field (1981) has indicated that fathers appear less disturbed by difficult infants and show more positive affect with their high-risk infants. A portion of this attitude may reflect difficulty reporting emotions, especially of a negative nature. Expression of anger and dissatisfaction may be less socially desirable as viewed by men (Linehan, Paul, & Egan, 1983).

However, fathers of normal infants are notable for their playful approach to early interactions with their infants. (Parke, 1979). Additionally, it has been suggested (Field, 1979) that fathers do not view young infants as being as fragile as the mothers view them to be. Fathers may also expect less of infants than mothers expect. However, fathers who are primary caregivers or those who take care of the infant during the daytime are reported to behave more like mothers who are primary caregivers (Field, 1978). The enormous responsibility involved in the care of an apneic infant may exacerbate these effects. In addition to the care of the baby, the primary parent must have learned to cope with a home monitor, with all the restraints it places on the parent in terms of social and financial restrictions. Additionally, the primary caregiver must assume the responsibility for resuscitating their infant should the baby stop breathing. Recognition of that responsibility entails an essential concomitant fear of sudden death.

MORTALITY AND APNEIC INFANTS

Some infants have died despite evaluation by infant apnea programs and use of home apnea monitoring. (Ward et al., 1985; Oren, Kelly, & Shannon, 1985). Siblings of SIDS victims appear to be at a significantly higher risk of an adverse outcome than nonsiblings, as are infants who develop a seizure disorder during monitoring. One study noted a disturbingly high noncompliance to appropriate monitoring techniques within this population (Meny, et al., 1988). In this study of 221 infants, 10 infants died. The authors report that 90% of the deaths were associated with a SIDS. Characteristics of the infants who died included bronchopulmonary dysplasia, black race, lack of private medical insurance, single status of the mother, maternal age of less than 25 years, cigarette smoking by mother during pregnancy, and low Apgar scores. However, the authors believe that at least 6 to 8 of the 10 families were noncompliant with appropriate monitoring techniques. These conclusions were based on parents' conflicting histories of monitor use or on circumstantial evidence of noncompliance at the time of death, plus a history of previous noncompliance using the monitor. Some of the parents or family members admitted that the monitor was not in use at the time of the death of the infant. Compliance needs to be aided by improving education for families in the proper use of the monitors. Then, in order to assess the effectiveness of such intervention efforts, compliance needs to be assessed, perhaps by utilizing a recorder with a continually updated memory and a data storage system.

Oren et al. (1985) identified a high risk group for SIDS among infants who were resuscitated for sleep apnea. Those infants who had apnea that responded only to resuscitation, who were siblings of SIDS victims, or who developed a seizure disorder during monitoring, were at significantly higher risk for an adverse outcome. In this study there were four cases of delayed caregiver response to an alarm. In one case, the pneumogram recorded during the episode that resulted in the infant's death, had clusters of bradycardia to a low of nine beats per minute and intermittent prolonged apnea to a maximum of 75 seconds before resuscitation was recorded. Fear and immobilization on the part of the caregiver delayed the onset of resuscitation. Parental anxiety regarding the possibility of a SIDS cannot be overestimated, especially in those families who have experienced the death of a previous infant, and who now equate apnea with SIDS. An illustration of the implications of extreme parental anxiety was reported by Bendell, Shelton, Krous and Shirley (1984). A 23-year-old mother with both a previously documented psychiatric history and the loss of two infants to SIDS, presented with extreme anxiety and fear regarding her ability to respond to apneic episodes. The mother was phobic to the point of refusing to practice cardiopulmonary resuscitation because the practice doll's face reminded her of her dead children's faces. Her anxiety was increased further because the responsibility for response to night alarms was hers alone, as her husband worked nights. She was treated with systematic desensitization and response prevention techniques. Following four days of therapy, the mother successfully completed the cardiopulmonary resuscitation course. During the follow-up period, the mother reported the occurrence of three episodes of multiple apneas with accompanying bradycardia alarms. She was able to respond to these incidents successfully.

Home monitoring should be discontinued once medical criteria for termination have been met. Purchit and Saylor (1986) described a population who delayed discontinuing monitoring after termination was advised. In this population, delayed discontinuation of monitoring was related to high maternal anxiety and past experience with a SIDS death.

Legg and Sherick (1976) have observed that parents often attempt to assuage the pain and suffering attendant to the loss of a child by quickly conceiving again. The new infant's entry into the family may interrupt, distort, or delay the mourning process, and the new infant's presence cannot possibly resolve the grief associated with the loss of the SIDS infant. Not only may the birth of an infant disrupt the grieving process, but inadequate time for mourning may interfere with parental attachment to the new infant and impede development of a necessary, realistic view of the subsequent child as an individual.

CONCLUSIONS

This chapter has examined specific aspects of stress in parenting an apneic infant. Having a child with apnea is a highly stressful experience that may contribute to distress and psychopathology in both parents and children. The research reviewed in this chapter provides fairly strong evidence against the notion of inevitable family dysfunction and disruption, delineating instead a broad range of functioning. There are some populations that appear to experience higher levels of distress while parenting an apneic infant. These include parents who have previously lost a child to SIDS, mothers who are socially isolated, and those who have difficulty with monitor compliance. The stress begins with the initial emotional impact of discovering a limp, pale, or cyanotic infant who may be revived only after vigorous stimulation that may include mouth-to-mouth resuscitation. The ensuing disruption of family functioning due to diagnostic testing and hospitalization leads to the necessity of adjusting to a preventive home monitoring regimen. The pressures of such adjustment include initial physical adaptations and restrictions engendered by the apneic infant and the monitoring system. This stress is exacerbated by sleep deprivation, exhaustion, and emotional turmoil. When there is only one primary caregiver for the infant, and that caregiver sees herself as overwhelmed and dominated by the child's needs and demands, the stress becomes significant and perhaps overwhelming. Yet, most families of apneic infants appear to cope adequately.

Mothers of apneic infants report being less healthy than other mothers. It seems reasonable to assume that frequent sleep interruptions, added to ongoing concern regarding the infant's survival and the stress related to its care would contribute to a lessened sense of well-being. Additionally, high life stress has been associated with depressed immunological defenses (Adler & Cohen, 1984). The need for adequate professional support, home monitor training, and frequent review of infant cardiopulmonary resuscitation cannot be overestimated.

This chapter has generated questions that remain to be investigated. As we conclude, let us briefly underscore some of these agenda for future study. Initial research suggests heterogeneous responses to the stress of caring for an apneic infant. In particular, we need research that will allow differentiation of high-risk subgroups. An additional step involves clarifying the relationship between an antecedent loss of a child to SIDS and other risk factors involved for these families who are also parenting apneic infants. Another question deserving further research attention would address the efficacy of different types of support for parents. Parenting support groups and medically based monitor programs are often prescribed without an understanding of specific risks and resources specific to a family. As strategies for coping with stress are developed, families will be aided in parenting their apneic infants.

REFERENCES

Abidin, R. R. (1979). *Parenting stress index.* Charlottesville, VA: Pediatric Psychology Press.

Adler, R., & Cohen, N. (1984). Behavior and the immune system. In W. D. Gentry (Ed.), *Handbook of Behavioral Medicine* (117–173). New York: Guilford Press.

American Academy of Pediatrics Task Force on Prolonged Infantile Apnea. (1985). *PEDIATRICS, 76,* 129–131.

Anderson, R., & Rosenblith, J. (1971). Sudden unexpected death syndrome: Early indicators. *Biology of the Neonate, 18,* 345.

Baroni, M. (1989). *Infants with early pathologic apnea: Influence of biological risk and home environment on growth and development.* Kansas City, MO: Society for Research in Child Development.

Bendell, D., Culbertson, J., Shelton, T., & Carter, B. (1986). Interrupted infantile apnea: Impact on maternal stress, temperament, and early development. *Journal of Clinical Child Psychology, 15*(4), 304–310.

Bendell, D., Goldberg, M., Urbano, M., Urbano, R., & Bauer, C. (1987). Differential impact of parenting sick infants. *Infant Mental Health Journal, 8*(1), 28–36.

Bendell, D., Shelton, T., Krous, H., & Shirley, M. (1984). Behavioral treatment of CPR anxiety: A case study. *Children's Health Care, 13*(2), 77–81.

Black, L., Hersher, L., & Steinschneider, A. (1978). Impact of the apnea monitor on family life. *Pediatrics, 1*(1), 37–40.

Broussard, E. R., & Sturgeon, M. S. (1970). Maternal perception of the neonate as related to development. *Child Psychiatry and Human Development, 1*(1), 16–25.

Cain, L. P., Kelly, D. H., & Shannon, D. C. (1980). Parents' perceptions of the psychological and social impact of home monitoring. *Pediatrics, 66*, 37–41.

Caldwell, B., & Bradley, R. (1978). *Manual for the home observation for measurement of the environment.* Little Rock, AR: University of Arkansas Press.

Cohen, L., & Campos, J. (1974). Father, mother, and stranger as elicitors of attachment behavior in infancy. *Developmental Psychology, 10*, 146–154.

Conners, C. K. (1973). *Parent rating scales:* Instruments for the assessment of childhood psychopathology. Unpublished Manuscript, Children's Hospital National Medical Center, Washington, D.C.

Deykin, E., Bauman, M., Kelly, D., Hsieh, C., & Shannon, D. (1984). Apnea of infancy and subsequent neurologic, cognitive, and behavioral status. *Pediatrics, 73*(5), 638–645.

Field, T. (1977). Effects of early separation, interactive deficits, and experimental manipulations on infant mother face-to-face interaction. *Child Development, 48*, 763–771.

Field, T. (1978). Interaction behaviors of primary versus secondary caretaker fathers. *Developmental Psychology, 10*, 183–184.

Field, T. (1979a). Interaction patterns of high-risk infants and normal infants. In T. Field, A. Sostek, S. Goldberg, & H. Shuman (Eds.), *Infants born at risk.* (pp. 333–356). New York: Spectrum Publications.

Field, T. (1979b). Games parents play with normal and high-risk infants. *Child Psychiatry and Human Development 10*(1), 41–48.

Field, T. (1981). Father's interactions with their high-risk infants. *Infant Mental Health Journal, 7*(4), 249–256.

Kelly, D., & Shannon, D. (1981). Complete airway obstruction in infants. *PEDIATRICS, 67*, 823–827.

Lazarus, R. S., & Folkman, S. (1984). *Stress, appraisal, and coping.* New York: Plenum Press.

Legg, C., & Sherick, I. (1976). The replacement child—A developmental tragedy. *Child Psychiatry and Human Development, 7*(2), 113–126.

Lerner, R., Palermo, M., Spiro, A., III, & Nesselroade J. C. (1982). Assessing the dimensions of tempermental individuality across the life span: The Dimensions of Temperment Survey (DOTS). *Child Development, 53*, 149–159.

Linehan M., Paul, E., & Egan, K. (1983). The parent affect test: Development, validity, and reliability. *Journal of Clinical Child Psychology, 12*(2), 161–166.

Meny, R., Blackmon, L., Fleischmann, D., Gutberlet, R., & Naumburg, E. (1988). Sudden infant death and home monitors. *American Journal of the Diseases of Children, 142*, 1037–1040.

Moos, R., & Moos, B. (1981). *Family Environment Scale Manual.* Palo Alto, CA: Consulting Psychologists Press.

Moos, R. H., & Schaefer, J. A. (1984). The crisis of physical illness: An overview and conceptual approach. In R. H. Moos (Ed.) Coping with physical illness: 2: New perspectives (pp. 3–25). New York: Plenum Press.

Oren, J., Kelly, D., & Shannon, D. (1986). Identification of a high-risk group for sudden infant death syndrome among infants who were resuscitated for sleep apnea. *Pediatrics, 77,* 495–499.

Parke, R. (1979). Perspectives on father-infant interaction. In J. Osofsky (Ed.), *Handbook of infant development.* New York: Wiley & Sons.

Purchit, D., & Saylor, C. (1986). Maternal delay in discontinuation of home monitors. Paper presented at the Fourth Conference on Infantile Apnea and Home Monitoring. Rancho Mirage, CA.

Slovik, L., & Kelly, D. (1988). Family reactions to home monitoring. In J. Culbertson, H. Krous, & D. Bendell (Eds.), *Sudden infant death syndrome: Medical aspects and psychological management* (pp. 198–226). Baltimore: The Johns Hopkins University Press.

Stern, N., & Kerruker, K. (1988). Prematurity stereotyping by mothers of premature infants. *Journal of Pediatric Psychology, 13*(2), 255–264.

Thomas, A., & Chess, S. (1977). *Temperament and development.* New York: Brunner/Mazel.

Weissbluth, M., Brouillette, R., Liu, K., & Hunt, C. (1982). Sleep apnea, sleep duration, and infant temperament. *Journal of Pediatrics, 101,* 164–179.

10 Psychosocial Intervention in Pediatric Cancer: A Strategy for Prevention of Long-Term Problems

F. Daniel Armstrong
University of Miami School of Medicine

Childhood cancer is a rare disease that affects approximately 6000 children in the United States each year. Although still one of the leading causes of death in children, cancer is now in many instances a curable disease, but not without potentially significant short- and long-term toxicity (Young, Ries, Silverberg, Horm, & Miller, 1986). Treatment may involve chemotherapy, radiation, surgery, bone marrow transplantation, or some combination of any or all of these. Families and children are thus exposed to a sequence of aversive events that may lead to survival, or may lead to recurrence of disease and eventual death of the child. It is argued in this chapter that whereas most families of children with cancer are "normal" in their psychological functioning at the time of diagnosis, their attempts to cope with the disease and treatment in a "normal" fashion may lead to ineffective or problematic behavior during and after termination of treatment. The task for the treatment team is to develop a model for understanding how ineffective coping develops and how to prevent problems and/or improve overall functioning of survivors of childhood cancer.

SCOPE OF THE PROBLEM

As recently as 20 years ago, childhood cancer was, in most cases, fatal. In the late 1980s, it was no longer uncommon to hear oncologists talk in terms of "cure" (Hammond, 1986; van Eys, 1987). This change has been brought about through advances in diagnosis and disease categorization; systematic, improved use of multiple chemotherapeutic agents; improved chemotherapeutic and radiation treatment of isolated central nervous system disease; advances in bone

197

marrow transplantation; and recently, technological advances in supportive care (Skelton & Pizzo, 1986). It is now estimated that by the year 2000, 1 in every 1000 adults over age 20 will be a survivor of childhood cancer (Meadows & Hobbie, 1986). The increases in disease-free survival have led health care professionals to include concerns about treatment toxicity and late effects in the total care plan for children with cancer. Among the "toxicities" of concern at this time is the psychological functioning of children, both while on treatment and after treatment is terminated.

Until 1980, the bulk of the psychological literature on childhood cancer focused on helping children and their families cope with issues related to death (Eiser, 1979). Since 1980, a greater focus has been placed on identifying the kinds of problems faced by children and families while on treatment, and recently, on late effects of treatment on the intellectual and psychological functioning of long-term survivors. This focus has led to the development of psychological interventions to reduce or prevent many of the psychological consequences of cancer treatment. As clinicians and researchers become more creative and successful in these intervention efforts, the need for a conceptual model for intervention, and ultimately prevention, has developed.

This chapter approaches this issue in four ways. First, a conceptual model for understanding the factors affecting acute and long-term adjustment in the childhood cancer patient is described. Second, the common problems encountered by the childhood cancer patient and family are outlined, including acute problems resulting from treatment and long-term problems of survivors. Third, the model is expanded to explain not only the problems, but also potential intervention solutions. Finally, the model is applied to the area of prevention, with suggestions of clinical and research efforts for the future.

AVERSIVE NATURE OF CANCER TREATMENT

Before examining the types of problems faced by families of children with cancer, it is important to develop a way of thinking that explains how families and children might be expected to cope with the cancer situation. Two primary factors need to be considered in this model: (a) the nature of the contingent relationship between behavior and environment; and (b) the previous learning history of the child and family. For many types of chronic or severe illnesses in children, the relationship between these factors has been termed the "normal person, abnormal situation" model (Russo & Varni, 1982), and the model has proven effective in describing how and why people respond to the stress of a child's illness. However, the model has more than descriptive utility; it also provides a way to think about intervention and prevention that differs from traditional thinking about psychopathology.

The abnormal situation faced by families and children involves repeated exposure to aversive stimuli on a seemingly noncontingent basis. In most cases, the occurrence of cancer is not related to any behavior or lack of behavior on the part of the child or family, so the diagnosis may be seen as an immediate noncontingent punisher. Following diagnosis, children are faced with a variety of diagnostic procedures that, when viewed from the perspective of the treating medical staff, are contingent upon the behavior of the child's cells; but when viewed from the child's and family's perspective, are again noncontingent aversives. Such procedures include bone marrow aspirations, lumbar punctures, surgeries, magnetic resonance imaging, and gallium scans; all procedures essential to diagnosis, but not related to the behavior of the families. Following diagnosis, children are again faced with a variety of invasive procedures (additional surgeries, radiation, intravenous injections, intrathecal chemotherapy), all of which are not contingent upon the child's behavior and all of which have both immediate aversive consequences (e.g., pain, infections, repeated hospitalization) and delayed aversive consequences (e.g., nausea, alopecia, learning problems) (Stehbens, 1988; Young et al., 1986).

Whereas nursing/medical units often attempt to provide a positive treatment atmosphere for families, the primary positive consequences of treatment follow a negative reinforcement paradigm. If treatment is given, and if it is effective, then the physical effects of the cancer (e.g., tumor size, infections, bleeding) are reduced. Unfortunately, cancer treatment often requires extended chemotherapy after the physical signs of the disease disappear. Thus, although remission induction is a positive consequence of treatment, remission maintenance requiring extended chemotherapy often has no observable benefits, and many aversive consequences.

Classical conditioning theory and research provide a basis for understanding and predicting the types of behavior that might result from a pure aversive conditioning model. The initial response expected is escape, and upon future exposure to the stimuli signaling the onset of an aversive event, avoidance. When escape is not possible, an initial acceleration of behavior that has led to escape in the past often occurs, followed by increases in anxious and possibly aggressive behavior. If these behaviors do not lead to escape from the situation, depression of behavior is likely to occur. Some generalization of escape or avoidance behavior to other stimuli associated with treatment might also be expected (Catania, 1979; Sulzer-Azaroff & Mayer, 1977).

The classical model provides a solid conceptual framework for understanding many of the "problem" behaviors encountered in the oncology clinic. Presentation of a diagnosis and treatment plan is often a powerful noncontingent punisher, and the psychological phenomena of denial, shock, and poor information retention may function as cognitive escape behaviors. Other common parental problems, such as anger at the medical team, increased conflict between parents, sleep disturbances, and some forms of treatment noncompliance, may be the result of blocked attempts to escape from the aversive situation. For children, the aversive conditioning model predicts anxious behavior upon arriving at the clinic, acceleration of distress behavior during invasive procedures, conditioned anticipatory nausea and vomiting, and depression of behavior across time. In all cases, these behaviors may function as escape mechanisms, or as responses to prevented escape from aversives.

In addition to classical conditioning of behavior, other factors such as prior learning history and current contingencies for behavior must be considered in the context of a larger family and community system (Michael & Copeland, 1987; Wahler & Hann, 1986). Behaviors that have previously permitted successful escape or reduced the aversiveness of an unavoidable situation are likely to occur frequently and to be resistant to extinction. At the same time, these behaviors may be noxious to others, and are likely to be concurrently reinforced by other people trying to reduce the aversiveness of the escape behavior for themselves. Thus, a child who has a history of crying or whining when confronted with a difficult or painful task is likely to accelerate whining or crying in the medical treatment situation. Crying reduces the aversiveness of the situation, or delays or avoids the onset of the noxious stimulation. However, although crying is functional for the child, it may simultaneously be noxious for the parent, who may assist the child in avoiding the situation or provide attention and reassurance to child in an attempt to stop the crying. This behavior may or may not reduce the crying across situations, but if it is effective even in a few circumstances, it is likely to continue.

Before jumping to the conclusion that these children and their parents are intentionally sabotaging treatment or have little self-control, it is important to return to the normal person, abnormal situation model. In the normal world, children often cry upon exposure to painful stimuli, and exhibit distress when placed in a situation where those stimuli are present. Likewise, most parents attempt to prevent their children from harm, and actively attempt to remove them from physically threatening situations. Children who are physically ill usually get extra attention, and children in pain are usually provided reassurance and comfort. In most situations with children, pain and illness is short-lived, so providing attention and support during these periods is not only humane, but it is also quite functional in reducing the immediate aversiveness of a time-limited situation.

Unfortunately, cancer treatment does not represent a time-limited or normal situation. Instead, it is a situation where repeated exposures to aversives occur. Normal responses of escape are blocked either by legal mandates to provide appropriate medical care to children, or by parental recognition that the consequence of escape is most likely the death of the child. The only option available to families in this situation is to attempt to cope, or, functionally stated, to try to reduce the aversiveness of the situation. The strategies used to reduce aversiveness will most likely be those that have worked in other difficult situations in the past, but these may be ineffective in the cancer situation. In fact, attempts to cope using accelerated distress behavior (child) and increased comfort giving and protection (parents) may increase stress by positively reinforcing and maintaining ineffective escape behaviors. The aversiveness of treatment may also increase as procedures become more difficult to perform and side effects of chemotherapy become more severe. If these coping attempts are not modified early, a variable schedule of negative reinforcement is likely to develop, making later changes in behavior more difficult (Sulzer-Azaroff & Mayer, 1977).

This conceptual model provides a framework for understanding the kinds of behavior that might be expected in a situation involving noncontingent application of aversive stimuli where escape is limited. It also recognizes the roles of previous learning and current maintaining factors in attempting to predict how problem behaviors develop over time in the cancer treatment situation. Given these pieces of information, it may be possible to predict the way a family or child may cope, and also to develop an intervention plan to prevent, or lessen the intensity, of many psychological and behavioral problems. The task at the intervention stage is to alter one or all of the factors included in the assessment strategy. This may involve altering the way that treatment is administered, teaching strategies to reduce the aversiveness of treatment and its consequences, or teaching families and children to respond to abnormal situations in ways that seem "abnormal" for them, but may be the most effective responses given the situation.

BEHAVIORAL ASPECTS OF CHILDHOOD CANCER

The impact of cancer and cancer treatment is far-reaching, and is felt by all members of a family, and to a lesser degree, by members of the community surrounding the family. The problems faced by these families are numerous. For the purpose of this chapter, I focus on two types of difficulties: (a) acute problems related to treatment and its consequences, and (b) long-term consequences of treatment and treatment-associated behavior. As such, the thrust of this chapter is on preparing for survival, and touches only minimally on issues related to death and its impact on the family.

Acute Treatment-Related Problems

Administration of cancer treatment to children results in four major types of problems: (a) behavioral and cognitive distress related to invasive and sometimes painful diagnostic and treatment procedures; (b) side effects of treatment, including disfigurement, nausea and vomiting, and alopecia (hair loss); (c) compliance with treatment; and (d) generalized emotional responses such as anxiety and depression. However, these problems do not exist exclusively for the child. Family members and community members are also significantly stressed by the responsibility of allowing physicians to perform painful procedures, by the changes in physical appearance produced by the treatment, by administering treatment that makes their child feel worse, and by observing a child who is anxious or depressed (Chesler & Barbarin, 1987). Thus, any consideration of the acute problems faced by the child must also include the impact these problems have on the child's family, and the impact of the family's response on the behavior of the child.

Behavioral Distress.   Treatment of cancer in children involves multiple invasive and sometimes painful procedures, including finger sticks, blood drawing, intravenous injections (or injections into indwelling catheters), lumbar punctures, and bone marrow aspirations. In addition, some children may require naso-gastric tubes for feeding, urinary catheters, and surgeries (Skelton & Pizzo, 1986). Each of these procedures involves a level of discomfort or significant pain, and each is usually a frightening experience for the child and parents. Thus, it is not surprising that children become anxious and display obvious distress when these procedures are scheduled. In fact, procedure-related pain is one reason given for treatment noncompliance (Blotcky, Cohen, Conatser, & Klopovich, 1985).

There are several factors that complicate our understanding of procedure-related pain in childhood cancer patients. First, there appear to be developmental differences in the types of pain behavior displayed by children, with young children displaying more obvious distress (e.g., crying, flailing, verbal expressions of pain) and older children and adolescents displaying more muscle tension and controlled distress (Katz, Kellerman, & Siegel, 1980; LeBaron & Zeltzer, 1984b). Second, there are sex differences, with girls experiencing greater behavioral distress than boys (Katz et al., 1980; Katz, Sharp, Kellerman, Marsten, Hershman, & Siegel, 1982). Third, in contrast to other invasive procedures, such as dental procedures, routine injections, and elective surgeries (Jay, 1988), cancer-related procedures occur repeatedly, and each clinic visit usually involves some element of pain. Whereas some natural habituation and extinction of distress occurs for minor procedures, this does not seem to occur for other procedures, such as lumbar punctures, bone marrow aspirations, and even repeated intravenous injections (Dahlquist, Gil, Armstrong, Ginsberg, & Jones, 1985; Jay, 1988; Katz et al., 1982). In fact, without intervention, children's distress in relation to these procedures may even increase, making it necessary to utilize physical restraint or, in some cases, general anesthesia to provide the treatment. Over time, conditioning of other behavioral responses, such as vomiting during a lumbar puncture or an intramuscular methotrexate injection, may occur. The repeated, aversive nature of these procedures then leads to consequences more severe than those encountered when the procedures are first administered.

Invasive procedures affect the staff and parents in addition to the child. Some parents refuse to observe or support their children while procedures are performed, and others exhibit behaviors that encourage or reinforce anxiety and distress behavior. The normal response of both staff and parents to children's distress is to provide comfort and reassurance, but these behaviors are linked to increased levels of distress rather than increased coping (Blount, Corbin, Sturges, Wolfe, Prater, & James, in press). Research to date has shown limited spontaneous use of encouragement of coping techniques by parents during procedures. Thus, parents respond to the procedure (abnormal situation) using previously effective strategies (normal person), only to find that the outcome of the strategy is worsened rather than improved coping on the part of the child.

Side Effects of Treatment.   Chemotherapeutic agents and radiation cannot tell the difference between good cells and bad cells. For this reason, cancer treatment necessarily destroys functional cells throughout the body of a child, and this often results in recurrent episodes of vomiting, appetite suppression and concurrent weight loss, and hair loss. Although most of these conditions are temporary, some, such as disfigurement due to surgery or hair loss following high doses of cranial radiation, may not be (Skelton & Pizzo, 1986). To complicate matters further, chemotherapy is usually administered when the child is feeling well (i.e., blood counts are up) rather than ill, and the consequence of treatment is not feeling better, but feeling and appearing worse. In fact, some children indicate that the procedures and side effects of treatment are worse than the disease itself (Zeltzer, Kellerman, Ellenberg, Dash, & Rigler, 1980). Unlike antibiotic therapy, which leads to relatively immediate improved health, chemotherapy usually leads to immediate health deterioration.

Acute behavioral side effects of chemotherapy usually fall into two categories: (a) increased nausea/vomiting and food refusal, and (b) social withdrawal and lowered self-esteem due to changes in physical appearance. Many of the chemotherapeutic agents reliably produce symptoms of nausea and vomiting, but over time the intensity and frequency of vomiting may increase without a concurrent increase in medication dose (Burish, Carey, Krozely, & Greco, 1987). Furthermore, anticipatory nausea and vomiting, a condition believed to be classically conditioned, may develop in some children. Repeated exposure to chemotherapy with high emetic potential may cause the nausea/vomiting behavior to generalize to other conditioned stimuli (e.g., nurses in the clinic, smells, thoughts of treatment) and to other chemotherapeutic agents with low emetic potential (Andrykowski & Redd, 1987). It is not uncommon in most childhood cancer clinics to find children who vomit prior to the injection of a chemotherapeutic agent, with current estimates of the incidence of anticipatory nausea ranging from 28–44%, and anticipatory vomiting occurring for about 20% of children on treatment (Dolgin, Katz, McGinty, & Siegel, 1985; Spirito, Hewett, Masek, & Berman, 1987). Associated with nausea/vomiting is a general reduction of appetite, and food refusal and concomitant weight loss is common among children treated with frequent doses of chemotherapy with high emetic potential. These children sometimes develop taste aversions (Bernstein, 1978; Bernstein & Sigmundi, 1980), and indicate that certain previously preferred foods lose all appeal, and may even acquire noxious characteristics. One outcome of the nausea and vomiting and conditioned taste aversion is a child who appears anorectic.

In addition to weight changes, chemotherapy also produces hair loss in some children for some period of time. The extent of hair loss is varied across children, with some children experiencing a thinning of hair and others becoming completely bald. Whereas this change in appearance is disturbing to most children, it is significant for adolescents who are at a time in their lives when physical appearance is critical. It is not uncommon to find children of all ages withdrawing from their friends and limiting social contact outside their families and oncology staff. The implication of hair loss may be even more severe for adolescents, who indicate that physical appearance changes are the single most salient reason for treatment noncompliance and refusal (Blotcky et al., 1985).

The aversive effects of chemotherapy are relatively immediate. Nausea/vomiting may be experienced within hours of chemotherapy administration, and hair loss may occur within 2 weeks of starting treatment. The beneficial effects of the treatment may not be seen until 4–6 weeks after treatment is started, leading to a weak temporal link between the drugs and good outcome, but a strong temporal link between the drugs and aversive consequences. In this situation, parents may question what they have subjected their child to, and may become angry with themselves and the medical team. In an effort to reduce the aversiveness of the treatment, parents may reduce other demands on the child, and increase their "helping" behavior rate (Koocher, 1986; Spinetta & Deasy-Spinetta, 1986). The message given to the child is "You are sick, and it is not fair, and I want to try to make it up to you." The positive consequences of these parental behaviors are powerful for the child. No longer is he/she expected to maintain a level of developmental independence, and concrete rewards are provided somewhat noncontingently. In almost all new cases of childhood cancer, the most overwhelming image is of a child in a hospital bed surrounded by a toy store full of balloons and toys. These noncontingent rewards are provided at precisely the time when the most dramatic effects of chemotherapy are noted (vomiting, hair loss), potentially establishing a reinforcing relationship between treatment side effects and rewards. When this level of attention decreases, extinction theory would predict an extinction burst (Sulzer-Azaroff & Mayer, 1977). In this situation, the extinction burst is an increase in the intensity of the previously reinforced behavior (vomiting, food refusal, and social withdrawal). These behaviors are often aversive for the parents, so the likely response will be unintended increased reinforcement of the illness behavior, further strengthening the behavioral response and the consequences of treatment. Once again, normal behavior (attending to an ill child) in an abnormal situation (repeated chemotherapy administrations) leads to an undesired, and increasingly aversive, outcome.

Emotional Responses to Treatment.   In addition to specific behavioral responses to the aversive aspects of treatment, the aversive conditioning model predicts a generalized emotional response as well. In fact, it has long been assumed that children treated for cancer would necessarily have higher levels of anxiety and depression than their healthy siblings and peers. The explanation for this generalized anxiety and depression is based upon the punishment and learned helplessness literature that suggests that when escape from aversive stimulation is blocked, initial increases in anxious behavior are noted, followed by a general suppression of behavior (depression) (Callahan & Burnette, 1989). Surprisingly, research on children undergoing cancer treatment has not supported this theory. Anxiety, when noted in cancer children, is usually situation specific (i.e., painful procedures and chemotherapy). Formal assessments of depression in children undergoing cancer treatment have also not indicated a generalized depression. In fact, in a study comparing the responses of childhood cancer patients, psychiatric inpatients, and healthy controls, childhood cancer patients scored lower on measures of depression than either of the other groups (Worchel, Nolan, Willson, Purser, Copeland, & Pfefferbaum, 1988).

On the other hand, behavioral measures of emotional distress have yielded different results. Children on treatment have been found to experience more social withdrawal, isolation, and shyness (LeRoy, Noll, & Mondoux, 1988; Noll, LeRoy, Bukowski, Mondoux, Lindauer, & Rogosch, 1988; Sawyer, Crettenden, & Toogood, 1986), and to have a relatively high incidence of aggressiveness and general noncompliance when compared with healthy peers (Sawyer et al., 1986). Once again, these behaviors could be predicted from the system perspective of the aversive conditioning model. Interacting with peers is difficult when there are physical appearance differences, and parents are likely to attempt to protect their children, allowing refuge and failing to reinforce social initiation skills. Likewise, limit setting for normally occurring aggressive, mild norm-violating behaviors is difficult for many parents of healthy children, and the application of restrictions or removal of privileges from an ill child may be too difficult for many parents. In fact, parents are often seen as overprotective, anxious, and lacking in self-control (Schuler, Bakos, Zsambor, Polcz, Koos, Kardos, & Revesz, 1985); behaviors that conceptually and empirically contribute to the development and maintenance of behavior problems in children (Jackson, 1983). Once again, application of normal principles to an abnormal situation leads to unexpected, but predictable undesired outcome.

Long-term Consequences of Treatment

It was once believed that children who survived cancer treatment would be severely scarred for life by their experiences. Fortunately, the data emerging from a host of studies contradict this belief. Although there are clear late effects of cranial-spinal radiation on children's cognitive abilities and growth, serious psychological problems (e.g., depression, suicide, psychosis) in long-term survivors have not emerged (Fritz, Williams, & Amylon, 1988; Holmes & Holmes, 1975; Koocher & O'Malley, 1981; Kupst & Schulman, 1988; Li & Stone, 1976; Teta, Del Po, Stanislav, Meigs, Myers, & Mulvihill, 1986), except in children with brain tumors (Kun, Mulhern, & Crisco, 1983). However, there have been some less severe behavioral problems, particularly social adjustment and difficulty with noncompliance and aggressiveness, that have been reported. Fortunately, whereas psychosis and severe depression are difficult to prevent and treat, behavioral adjustment problems are both treatable and potentially preventable.

Behavioral Problems and Emotional Adjustment.   Although few serious psychological problems have been identified in childhood cancer survivors, a significant number have been found to experience mild to moderate adjustment problems. It is estimated that 22% (Fritz et al., 1988) to 59% (Koocher & O'Malley, 1981; O'Malley, Koocher, Foster, & Slavin, 1979) of long-term survivors experience mild to moderate adjustment problems. A number of factors are linked to the emergence of these problems. Physical impairment or disease severity has not been linked to adjustment outcome (Fritz et al., 1988; O'Malley, Foster, Koocher, & Slavin, 1980; Tebbi & Mallon, 1987), but openness of communication between the medical team and the patient and within the child's family has. In general, the more open the communication, the better the adjustment (Fritz et al., 1988; Koocher & O'Malley, 1981; Kupst & Schulman, 1988). Koocher & O'Malley (1981) found that whether and when children learned their diagnosis was a strong predictor of whether they adjusted well or poorly; although multiple factors (e.g., family structure, age of the child, parent religious or philosophical orientation) affect how children are told (Chesler, Paris, & Barbarin, 1986). Another predictor of adjustment is the child's age at diagnosis. Unfortunately, the data related to this factor are contradictory. In some cases, older age at diagnosis is related to poor adjustment (Koocher & O'Malley, 1981), and in others younger age is related to greater maladjustment (Cella, Tan, Sullivan, Weinstock, Alter, & Jow, 1987). It is clear that much information is needed to understand the relationship between child and family factors and psychological adjustment of survivors.

One of the real difficulties in interpreting much of the data on long-term survivors is the construct of adjustment. In some studies, adjustment is based upon employment, school attendance, or psychiatric interviews; but little information about the specific factors used in making adjustment decisions is provided in these studies. However, as the body of literature grows, and more specific questions are asked, there appear to be patterns of problems that may be sensitive to intervention and prevention efforts.

Long-term survivors of childhood cancer have a much higher incidence of both internalizing (anxiety, worries, withdrawal) and externalizing (aggressiveness, poor impulse control) behavior problems than healthy children

(Mulhern, Wasserman, Friedman, & Fairclough, 1989; Olson, Boyle, & White, 1987; Sawyer et al., 1986), although the severity of these problems seems tied to the severity of other physical late effects (Greenberg, Kazak, & Meadows, 1989). In addition, they report many more somatic complaints (Mulhern et al., 1989). These findings are not surprising when considered in the context of the aversive conditioning model. Repeated exposure to noncontingent punishment usually results in a generalized anxiety, even when the specific stimuli for punishment are removed (Kratochwill, Accardi, & Morris, 1988). The high rate of internalizing behavior problems in long-term survivors may be the result of repeated exposures to painful procedures and noxious chemotherapy, leading to a sense of generalized loss of control. In fact, survivors report a greater external locus of control than peers and somewhat lower self-esteem (Greenberg et al., 1989; Olson et al., 1987). Functionally, this sense of external control and generalized anxiety may interfere with normal developmental tasks, as long-term survivors sometimes have difficulty meeting socioeconomic goals (Teta et al., 1986) and disengaging from their parents during early adulthood (Cella et al., 1987).

The identification of externalizing behavior problems and a high rate of somatic complaints in long-term survivors also has implications for the aversive conditioning model. Although there are few controlled studies substantiating the fact, a number of clinical observations suggest that parents of childhood cancer patients are often overprotective and have difficulty in limit setting (Schuler et al., 1985). It is precisely these parental behaviors that are related to externalizing behavior problems in normal children, and treatment of these problems usually targets parenting style (Wells, 1988). Likewise, children with cancer have multiple opportunities to receive positive social reinforcement for illness behavior, so the occurrence of frequent somatic complaints in survivors is not surprising. These findings provide support for the conceptualization that the normal responses of families and children to the abnormal situation of cancer treatment may produce abnormal responses in a predictable fashion, and that these abnormal behaviors may maintain over time.

Social Adjustment.   Until recently, very little attention has been paid to the impact of cancer treatment on children's social functioning. However, evidence that disruptions in social functioning and poor psychosocial adjustment in long-term survivors are related has been available for some time (Koocher & O'Malley, 1981; Koocher, O'Malley, Gogan, & Foster, 1980; O'Malley et al., 1979). Recent research examining social skills in cancer patients and long-term survivors has further indicated that these children are at significant risk for social difficulties. School-aged cancer survivors report feelings of loneliness (LeRoy et al., 1988), feel they receive less help from their friends than others (Kazak & Meadows, 1989), see themselves as less socially competent than their peers (Olson et al., 1987; Spirito, Stark, Cobiella, Drigan, Androkites, & Hewett,

1990), and are seen by their peers as being left out, shy, and socially withdrawn (Noll et al., 1988).

There are several possible explanations for these findings. First, hospitalizations and frequent clinic visits may limit the opportunities of these children for interaction at school with their peers, perhaps interfering with their acquisition of age-appropriate social skills (Michael & Copeland, 1987). Second, the physical impact of treatment may lead to feelings of embarrassment, further resulting in avoidance of situations where this feeling might occur. Third, because of the difficult nature of cancer treatment, staff and parents may inadvertently reinforce behaviors that facilitate interactions with adults and medical staff, while failing to teach and reinforce age-appropriate social skills. In fact, there is clinical speculation that children are rewarded for dependency behaviors (which may in turn be reinforcing for staff and parents), and protected from situations where social assertiveness can be learned and practiced (Spinetta & Deasy-Spinetta, 1986). Once again, a normal response (protection) to an abnormal situation (potential social embarrassment) may result in long-term abnormal implications for the child.

Cognitive Difficulties.   One of the most significant strides in treatment of childhood cancer was the initiation of prophylactic treatment of the central nervous system (CNS) using chemotherapy and/or radiation. Although this approach resulted in a substantial jump in survival statistics, it was not without costs. Numerous studies have looked at the cognitive functioning of children who receive CNS treatment. In general, children treated with cranial radiation fairly consistently experience problems in learning 1 to 3 years after CNS treatment, with many qualifying for learning disability services. The degree of learning impairment is, however, related to a number of factors, including age at the time of radiation, and dose of radiation. Because radiation has been so consistently linked to later learning problems, most nonbrain tumor CNS protocols now use only intrathecal chemotherapy (injected into the spinal fluid surrounding the brain). Whereas some studies report learning impairments resulting from this treatment, the severity does not approach that obtained with cranial radiation, and there are studies finding no impairment (Fletcher & Copeland, 1988; Stehbens, 1988).

IMPLICATIONS FOR INTERVENTION

There are a variety of intervention strategies that are available for use with childhood cancer patients and their families. Some, such as reciprocal inhibition/systematic desensitization, are effective in treating problems believed to result from an aversive conditioning model, namely fears and phobias (Kratochwill et al., 1988). Others, such as supportive counseling and insight-oriented psychotherapy, may momentarily reduce stress and improve the perspective of families on the issues they are facing and help them to feel less isolated (Adams-Greenly, 1986). However, the critical issue in pediatric psychosocial oncology is not what specific intervention approach should be used, instead, the question centers around what the focus of intervention should be, and what intervention technique should be used to accomplish the goals deemed appropriate by physicians, families, and the community.

The appropriate focus of intervention/prevention activities is difficult to determine, and is affected by both short-term and long-term consequences. Short-term problems, such as acute distress over hearing a diagnosis or dealing with side effects of treatment, are significant stressors, and interventions that offer even momentary relief from stress will be valued. Long-term problems, such as social competence and self-esteem difficulties, are also significant stressors when treatment is completed, but their temporal removal from immediate stressors may lessen their importance as a target for intervention during cancer treatment. It has been argued that psychosocial interventions should be administered in stages according to the demands faced by the families (Adams-Greenly, 1986), but more than reactive intervention is needed. If the focus of psychosocial efforts in pediatric oncology is to parallel that of medical oncology, intervention, and ultimately prevention efforts, must look to the future of the child who lives, rather than exclusively to the distress of the current situation. Interventions that ignore the long-term implications of treatment may ultimately prove to be part of the problem rather than a solution to it.

This is not to advocate that short-term problems be ignored or that efforts to alleviate situational stress be abandoned. Instead, it is to suggest that a more comprehensive intervention and prevention plan be developed that effectively deals with short-term problems in ways that contribute to long-term adjustment. In order to accomplish this task, levels of intervention need to be identified, and each level should include intervention components that reduce the immediate stress of the situation and teach coping skills that prevent problems and improve life functioning in the future.

STRATEGIES FOR INTERVENTION AND PREVENTION

Although there are major gaps in our knowledge of the effects of cancer treatment on children, several specific areas of concern can be identified. First, there is an almost universal problem with invasive procedures necessary for diagnosis and treatment. Second, acute side effects of chemotherapy such as nausea, vomiting, and physical appearance changes are disturbing for most children and families. Third, many cancer patients appear at risk for the development of social and behavioral problems during and upon completion of treatment. Finally, late effects of CNS treatment place these children at risk for learning problems and possible school failure. Just as the aversive conditioning model, viewed from a system perspective, could be used to describe and predict most of these problems, it may also provide a structure for designing intervention and prevention plans.

Based on this comprehensive behavioral model, at least three levels of intervention efforts (child, family, community) are needed (Michael & Copeland, 1987). First, because so much of the cancer treatment process is aversive, treatments need to be developed that extinguish or reduce the intensity of the aversiveness of treatment for both parents and children. Second, the potential for problems to result from normal attempts to manage an abnormal situation needs to be addressed. At this point a new perspective on coping needs to be developed (Spinetta & Deasy-Spinetta, 1986). In the days when children were expected to die from cancer, coping could be seen as daily or hourly attempts to reduce immediate distress. However, as more children survive, coping takes on a different perspective. In this situation, coping involves not only managing the daily stresses in an effective manner, but also anticipating problems and developing "abnormal" rather than "normal" responses to the abnormal situation in an effort to prevent long-term maladjustment. Based on the model presented in this chapter, effective intervention should involve education about the development of problems and how they can potentially be prevented, reduction of stress associated with confronting aversive situations using an approach rather than escape focus, and teaching skills for coping with the abnormal situation in an abnormal manner. Third, such an approach is needed not only with the parents and families of the children, but also with the greater medical, school, and social community of the child.

Studies of the effectiveness of psychosocial interventions in pediatric oncology have multiplied since 1980. The majority of these interventions have involved behavioral management of pain and chemotherapy-related problems. Other interventions, such as providing information to children and families (Chesler & Barbarin, 1987; Chesler, Paris, & Barbarin, 1986; Koocher, 1986), insight-oriented psychotherapy (Adams-Greenly, 1986) and providing social support to children and parents (Chesler & Barbarin, 1987; Morrow, Carpenter, & Hoagland, 1984) have been suggested, but the effectiveness of these intervention components has not been empirically investigated. There are, however, theoretical and empirical reasons for selecting strategies that rely heavily upon behaviorally based rather than insight based conceptual models. First, control over the behavioral aspects of treatment (e.g., daily routines, treatment regimens, procedures) have been linked to better adjustment outcomes for childhood cancer patients and their families (Nannis, Susman, Strope, Woodruff, Hersh, Levine, & Pizzo, 1982; Worchel, Copeland, & Barker, 1987). Second, behavioral approaches are usually both theoretically and empirically based, and are clearly defined in terms of the type of impact they are likely to have. This clarity permits careful planning, process monitoring, and outcome evaluation. Third, the problems that result from cancer treatment, according to the model presented in this chapter, may require the development of new skills and strategies, a task usually involving education, behavioral rehearsal, and strategies for reinforcement and maintenance. Finally, there are no empirical studies to suggest that interventions using nonbehavioral approaches are as successful at alleviating short-term problems in children treated for cancer. Therefore, until such empirical support is provided, it seems appropriate to utilize interventions and strategies that have proven clinically and statistically effective.

Interventions for Acute Aspects of Treatment

The immediate problems faced in psychosocial pediatric oncology are those related to cancer treatment, most notably painful procedures and nausea/vomiting. It is not, therefore, surprising that the primary focus of intervention research has been in these areas, with a number of successful results. Although multiple treatment components have been tried, most involve education, teaching arousal reducing skills, and then providing gradual exposure to the painful event, with gradual shaping of more active coping skills. This approach is quite consistent with the tenets of reciprocal inhibition/systematic desensitization, a standard behavioral treatment of behaviors resulting from aversive conditioning.

Systematic desensitization involves teaching a response incompatible with arousal, and then gradually exposing the patient to the stimuli associated with arousal in a systematic fashion while coaching them in the use of the arousal-incompatible response. Effective use of systematic desensitization depends upon breaking the association between stimuli associated with an aversive event and anxiety responses (Kratochwill et al., 1988). Unfortunately, the feared stimuli in cancer treatment are unavoidable, and each time they are presented a negative consequence (e.g., pain, vomiting) is highly probable. This situation necessitates the inclusion of an additional intervention strategy with cancer patients and their families, namely skills training. Not only is there a need to reduce conditioned responses to the aversive situation, but there is also a need to actively manage the situation as well. In this sense, the approaches to managing the aversive aspects of cancer treatment not only focus on reducing distress, but also focus on providing the child with a level of control that may contribute to increased self-competence. This situation may lead to potentially positive long-term consequences.

Painful Procedures.   Over the past 10 years, attempts to help children with painful procedures have involved the use of either sedative medication (Jay, Elliott, Katz, & Siegel, 1987; Miser, Ayesh, Broad, McCalla, Steinberg, Wall, Jelenich, Lees, Wilkinson, & Miser, 1988) or some combination of relaxation, distraction, attention focusing, visual imagery, information provision, and positive reinforcement for coping (Jay, 1988). Although the two intervention strategies are quite different in their focus, both are conceptually linked to the aversive conditioning model. On the one hand, medications are used to physiologically and biochemically block the connections between the invasive procedure and the sensation of pain. If this connection is successfully blocked, then children should theoretically not experience pain, and the conditioning of anxiety responses should not occur. On the other hand, behavioral interventions usually include the principal components of a desensitization model, namely information provision, the use of some arousal reducing skill, and reinforcement for coping with repeated exposures to the stimulus.

Attempts to medically manage pain are grounded in the anesthesia literature, and in parts of Europe general anesthesia is often used in reducing pain and distress during painful procedures. In the United States, however, general anesthesia is avoided due to consideration of medical risk to the child, expense (Jay, 1988), or risk to staff, even though it is effective in reducing children's distress (Miser et al., 1988). Instead, medical treatment in this country has involved the use of analgesic medications (e.g., demerol, nitrous oxide, versed) in combination with psychotropic medications (e.g., benzodiazapines, thorazine) and antimetics (e.g., phenergan, nembutal, lorazapan). Whereas clinical observations of the use of these drugs suggest that they are effective in accomplishing the purpose of pain reduction in some children, they are not without problems. First, most of these drugs require administration by intravenous or intramuscular injections, a procedure that may increase the child's distress beyond that experienced during a nonmedicated procedure. Second, to achieve complete sedation, significant doses of drugs must be administered, resulting in a prolonged period (sometimes hours) of sedation following the procedure (Jay, 1988). Third, when sedation is not complete, for reasons of convenience or concern for potential harmful side effects, blocking of pain may not occur. In this case, sedation may interfere with the child's normal methods for coping, leaving him/her aware of the pain but limited in ability to deal with the situation. Early research suggests that when the pharmacological approach is incomplete, other behavioral approaches may be more effective (Jay et al., 1987).

Most behavioral attempts to reduce pain and distress behavior involve (a) information about the procedure, and (b) some type of arousal reducing skill such as visual imagery, deep breathing, hypnosis, or progressive muscle relaxation (Hilgard & LeBaron, 1982; Jay, 1988; Jay & Elliott, 1983; Kellerman, Zeltzer, Ellenberg, & Dash, 1983; Zeltzer & LeBaron, 1982). In some cases, behavioral rehearsal or imaginal rehearsal and positive reinforcement are included as treatment components (Jay, Elliott, Ozolins, Olson, & Pruitt, 1985; Dahlquist et al., 1985). Although it is unclear which of these components are most responsible for alleviation of pain and distress in children, approaches including combinations of these techniques have consistently proven to be effective in this task (Jay, Elliott, & Varni, 1986).

Side Effects of Chemotherapy.   Treatment of chemotherapy-related problems has typically involved approaches similar to those used for alleviating procedure-related pain. Although some have cautioned against providing information to children about the possibility of nausea and vomiting (Jay, 1988), strategies that theoretically block association of sensation with neutral stimuli (e.g., distraction) or that produce responses that are incompatible with nausea and vomiting (e.g., hypnosis) have been successfully attempted. Utilization of videogames (Kolko & Rickard-Figueroa, 1985) and hypnosis (LeBaron & Zeltzer, 1984a; Zeltzer, LeBaron, & Zeltzer, 1984) has resulted in reduction in treatment associated nausea, vomiting, and bother. In the opposite direction, utilization of reinforcement and shaping led to increases in weight gain and decreases in anorexia symptoms in a pediatric cancer patient (Cairns & Altman, 1979).

The interventions for pain and chemotherapy-related problems represent successful approaches to specific aversive situations based upon an aversive conditioning model. In each case, some information was provided, some arousal reducing skill was taught, and some level of behavioral rehearsal (exposure to the stimulus) was included. In addition, a focus on shaping new skills for coping in each situation was included. Although much more research is needed on the effectiveness of different components in reducing distress and improving coping, these studies provide a first step in understanding ways to reduce aversiveness while simultaneously improving active coping.

Interventions for Non-Acute Problems

Although there have been numerous studies evaluating the effectiveness of interventions for acute aspects of treatment, the literature on interventions to improve behavioral and social functioning of children on treatment and long-term survivors is essentially nonexistent. Despite the growing literature suggesting that these children are at risk for behavior problems, social skills deficits, and learning problems, there is only one published report identified by this author that details and evaluates an intervention targeted to these problems. In this study, a summer camp experience was found to increase physical activity, social activity, and decrease solitary activities in childhood cancer patients (Smith, Gotlieb, Gurwitch, & Blotcky, 1987). Unfortunately, camp experiences are short and not readily available to all families, thus limiting the practical use of this strategy in most settings.

Clearly, the next phase of intervention research needs to focus on strategies for alleviating and preventing the problems not specific to acute treatment. Suggestions for intervention include teaching parents to reduce stress associated with parenting an ill child in a healthy manner. This may involve teaching parenting skills, providing support for parents as they provide appropriate consequences, and intervening in the community to maintain normal psychosocial development. It may also involve teaching children assertiveness and stress reduction skills for dealing with difficult social situations, rather than reinforcing their social withdrawal because they appear different. Finally, intervention strategies are needed to help children left with learning problems after CNS treatment function better in school. It is hoped that the next 10 years will see an increase in research evaluating the effectiveness of studies focusing on these long-term outcomes as well as acute aspects of treatment.

SUMMARY

The medical treatment of pediatric cancer has improved steadily over the past 25 years, to the point where long-term survival may mean cure. Whereas attention to the psychological aspects of cancer treatment has increased, it has primarily focused on assessment and treatment of acute treatment-related problems. It has been argued in this chapter that a conceptual model is needed to better understand the problems faced by these children, and to develop intervention and prevention strategies for dealing with these problems. The model presented involves understanding the aversive nature of treatment in light of a family system that functions fairly normally outside the realm of cancer treatment. From this understanding, intervention strategies are suggested that focus on education, stress reduction, and teaching families to cope with abnormal situations in ways that are abnormal for them. At this time, there are numerous studies applying this model to the aversive aspects of acute treatment. Unfortunately, long-term outcomes have been essentially ignored in the intervention literature, but these outcomes are achieving greater importance as more children survive. Clearly, it is time to expand the intervention model to one of prevention, developing intervention strategies that focus not only on the present, but also on the future. After all, the principal reason children are treated for cancer is to help them live, and insuring that the quality of life will be the best possible is now the essential concern facing those working with childhood cancer patients and their families.

REFERENCES

Adams-Greenly, M. (1986). Psychological staging of pediatric cancer patients and their families. *Cancer, 58,* 449–453.

Andrykowski, M. A., & Redd, W. H. (1987). Longitudinal analysis of the development of anticipatory nausea. *Journal of Consulting and Clinical Psychology, 55,* 36–41.

Bernstein, I. L. (1978). Learned taste aversions in children receiving chemotherapy. *Science, 200,* 1302–1303.

Bernstein, I. L., & Sigmundi, R. A. (1980). Tumor anorexia: A learned food aversion? *Science, 209,* 416–418.

Blotcky, A. D., Cohen, D. G., Conatser, C., & Klopovich, P. (1985). Psychosocial characteristics of adolescents who refuse cancer treatment. *Journal of Consulting and Clinical Psychology, 53,* 729–731.

Blount, R. L., Corbin, S. M., Sturges, J. W., Wolfe, V. V., Prater, J. M., & James, L. D. (in press). The relationship between adult's behavior and child coping and distress during BMA/LP procedures: A sequential analysis. *Behavior Therapy.*

Burish, T. G., Carey, M. P., Krozely, M. G., & Greco, F. A. (1987). Conditioned side effects induced by cancer chemotherapy: Prevention through behavioral treatment. *Journal of Consulting and Clinical Psychology, 55,* 42–48.

Cairns, G. F., & Altman, K. (1979). Behavioral treatment of cancer-related anorexia. *Behavior Therapy and Experimental Psychiatry, 10,* 353–356.

Callahan, E. J., & Burnette, M. M. (1989). Intervention for pathological grieving. *The Behavior Therapist, 12,* 153–157.

Catania, A. C. (1979). *Learning.* Englewood Cliffs, NJ: Prentice-Hall.

Cella, D. F., Tan, C., Sullivan, M., Weinstock, L., Alter, R., & Jow, D. (1987). Identifying survivors of pediatric Hodgkin's disease who need psychological interventions. *Journal of Psychosocial Oncology, 5,* 83–96.

Chesler, M. A. & Barbarin, O. A. (1987). *Childhood cancer and the family.* New York: Bruner/Mazel.

Chesler, M. A., Paris, J., & Barbarin, O. A. (1986). "Telling" the child with cancer: Parental choices to share information with ill children. *Journal of Pediatric Psychology, 11,* 407–516.

Dahlquist, L. M., Gil, K. M., Armstrong, F. D., Ginsberg, A., & Jones, B. (1985). Behavioral management of children's distress during chemotherapy. *Journal of Behaviour Therapy and Experimental Psychiatry, 16,* 325–329.

Dolgin, M. J., Katz, E. R., McGinty, K., & Siegel, S. E. (1985). Anticipatory nausea and vomiting in pediatric cancer patients. *Pediatrics, 75,* 547–552.

Eiser, C. (1979). Psychological development of the child with leukemia: A review. *Journal of Behavioral Medicine, 2,* 141–157.

Fletcher, J. M., & Copeland, D. R. (1988). Neurobehavioral effects of central nervous system prophylactic treatment of cancer in children. *Journal of Clinical and Experimental Neuropsychology, 10,* 495–537.

Fritz, G. K., Williams, J. R., & Amylon, M. (1988). After treatment ends: Psychosocial sequelae in pediatric cancer survivors. *American Journal of Orthopsychiatry, 58,* 552–561.

Greenberg, H. S., Kazak, A. E., & Meadows, A. T. (1989). Psychologic functioning in 8- to 16-year-old cancer survivors and their parents. *Journal of Pediatrics, 114,* 488–493.

Hammond, G. D. (1986). Keynote address: The cure of childhood cancer. *Cancer, 58,* 407–413.

Hilgard, J. R., & LeBaron, S. (1982). Relief of anxiety and pain in children and adolescents with cancer: Quantitative measures and clinical observations. *International Journal of Clinical and Experimental Hypnosis, 30,* 417–442.

Holmes, H. A., & Holmes, F. F. (1975). After ten years, what are the handicaps and life styles of children treated for cancer? *Clinical Pediatrics, 14,* 819–823.

Jackson, R. H. (1983). Parenting: The child in the context of the family. In C. E. Walker & M. C. Roberts (Eds.), *Handbook of clinical child psychology* (pp. 905–936). New York: John Wiley & Sons.

Jay, S. M. (1988). Invasive medical procedures: Psychological intervention and assessment. In D. K. Routh (Ed.), *Handbook of pediatric psychology* (pp. 401–425). New York: The Guilford Press.

Jay, S. M., & Elliott, C. H. (1983). Psychological intervention for pain in pediatric cancer patients. In G. B. Humphrey, B. B. Grindey, L. Dehmer, R. T. Acton, & T. J. Pysher (Eds.), *Adrenal and endocrine tumors in children* (pp. 123–154). Boston: Martinus Nijhoff.

Jay, S. M., Elliott, C. H., Katz, E., & Siegel, S. (1987). Cognitive-behavioral and pharmacologic interventions for children's distress during painful medical procedures. *Journal of Consulting and Clinical Psychology, 55,* 860–865.

Jay, S. M., Elliott, C. H., Ozolins, M., Olson, R. A., & Pruitt, S. D. (1985). Behavioral management of children's distress during painful medical procedures. *Behaviour Research and Therapy, 34,* 513–520.

Jay, S. M., Elliott, C. H., & Varni, J. W. (1986). Acute and chronic pain in adults and children with cancer. *Journal of Consulting and Clinical Psychology, 54,* 601–607.

Katz, E. R., Kellerman, J., & Siegel, S. E. (1980). Behavioral distress in children with cancer undergoing medical procedures: Developmental considerations. *Journal of Consulting and Clinical Psychology, 48,* 356–365.

Katz, E. R., Sharp, B., Kellerman, J., Marsten, A. R., Hershman, J. M., & Siegel, S. E. (1982). B-Endorphin immunoreactivity and acute behavioral distress in children with leukemia. *Journal of Nervous and Mental Disease, 170,* 72–77.

Kazak, A. E., & Meadows, A. T. (1989). Families of young adolescents who have survived cancer: Social-emotional adjustment, adaptability, and social support. *Journal of Pediatric Psychology, 14,* 175–191.

Kellerman, J., Zeltzer, L., Ellenberg, L., & Dash, J. (1983). Adolescents with cancer: Hypnosis for the reduction of acute pain and anxiety associated with medical procedures. *Journal of Adolescent Health Care, 4,* 85–90.

Kolko, D. J., & Rickard-Figueroa, J. L. (1985). Effects of video games on the adverse corollaries of chemotherapy in pediatric oncology patients: A single-case analysis. *Journal of Consulting and Clinical Psychology, 53,* 223–228.

Koocher, G. P. (1986). Psychosocial issues during the acute treatment of pediatric cancer. *Cancer, 58,* 468–472.

Koocher, G. P., O'Malley, J. E., Gogan, J. L., & Foster, D. J. (1980). Psychological adjustment among pediatric cancer survivors. *Journal of Child Psychology and Psychiatry, 21,* 163–173.

Koocher, G. P. & O'Malley, J. E. (1981). *The Damocles syndrome: Psychosocial consequences of surviving childhood cancer.* New York: McGraw-Hill.

Kratochwill, T. R., Accardi, A. & Morris, R. J. (1988). Anxiety and phobias. In J. L. Matson (Ed.), *Handbook of treatment approaches in childhood psychopathology* (pp. 249–276). New York: Plenum Press.

Kun, L. E., Mulhern, R. K., & Crisco, J. J. (1983). Quality of life in children treated for brain tumors. *Journal of Neurosurgery, 58,* 1–6.

Kupst, M. J., & Schulman, J. L. (1988). Long-term coping with pediatric leukemia: A six-year follow-up study. *Journal of Pediatric Psychology, 13,* 7–22.

LeBaron, S., & Zeltzer, L. (1984a). Assessment of acute pain and anxiety in children and adolescents by self-reports, observer reports, and a behavior checklist. *Journal of Consulting and Clinical Psychology, 52,* 729–738.

LeBaron, S., & Zeltzer, L. (1984b). Behavioral intervention for reducing chemotherapy-related nausea and vomiting in adolescents with cancer. *Journal of Adolescent Health Care, 5,* 178–182.

LeRoy, S. S., Noll, R. B., & Mondoux, D. (1988, August). *Adjustments of families and children with cancer.* Paper presented at the 96th Annual Convention of the American Psychological Association, Atlanta, GA.

Li, F. P., & Stone, R. (1976). Survivors of cancer in childhood. *Annals of Internal Medicine, 84,* 551–553.

Meadows, A. T., & Hobbie, W. L. (1986). The medical consequences of cure. *Cancer, 58,* 524–528.

Michael, B. E., & Copeland, D. R. (1987). Psychosocial issues in childhood cancer: An ecological framework for research. *The American Journal of Pediatric Hematology/Oncology, 9,* 73–83.

Miser, A. W., Ayesh, D., Broda, E., McCalla, J., Steinberg, S., Wall, R., Jelenich, S., Lees, D. E., Wilkinson, T. K., & Miser, J. S. (1988). Use of a patient-controlled device for nitrous oxide administration to control procedure-related pain in children and young adults with cancer. *The Clinical Journal of Pain, 4,* 5–10.

Morrow, G. R., Carpenter, P. J., & Hoagland, A. C. (1984). The role of social support in parental adjustment to pediatric cancer. *Journal of Pediatric Psychology, 9,* 317.

Mulhern, R. K., Wasserman, A. L., Friedman, A. G., & Fairclough, D. (1989). Social competence and behavioral adjustment of children who are long-term survivors of cancer. *Pediatrics, 83,* 18–25.

Nannis, E. D., Susman, E. J., Strope, B. E., Woodruff, P. J., Hersh, S. P., Levine, A. S., & Pizzo, P. A. (1982). Correlates of control in pediatric cancer patients and their families. *Journal of Pediatric Psychology, 7,* 75–84.

Noll, R. B., LeRoy, S. S., Bukowski, W., Mondoux, D. A., Lindauer, H., & Rogosch, F. A. (1988, August). *Childhood cancer: The impact on children's friendships.* Paper presented at the 96th Annual Convention of the American Psychological Association, Atlanta, GA.

Olson, A. L., Boyle, W. E., & White, M. E. (1987). Functional health status of children cured of cancer. *American Journal of Diseases of Children, 141,* 372.

O'Malley, J. E., Foster, D., Koocher, G., & Slavin, L. (1980). Visible physical impairment and psychological adjustment among pediatric cancer survivors. *American Journal of Psychiatry, 137,* 94–96.

O'Malley, J. E., Koocher, G., Foster, D., & Slavin, L. (1979). Psychiatric sequelae of surviving childhood cancer. *American Journal of Orthopsychiatry, 49,* 608–616.

Russo, D. C., & Varni, J. W. (1982). Behavioral pediatrics. In D. C. Russo & J. W. Varni (Eds.), *Behavioral pediatrics: Research and practice* (pp. 3–24). New York: Plenum Press.

Sawyer, M., Crettenden, A., & Toogood, I. (1986). Psychological adjustment of families of children and adolescents treated for leukemia. *The American Journal of Pediatric Hematology/Oncology, 8,* 200–207.

Schuler, D., Bakos, M., Zsambor, C., Polcz, A., Koos, R., Kardos, G., & Revesz, T. (1985). Psychosocial problems in families of a child with cancer. *Medical and Pediatric Oncology, 13,* 173–179.

Skelton, J., & Pizzo, P. A. (1986). Problems of intensive therapy in childhood cancer. *Cancer, 58,* 488–503.

Smith, K. E., Gotlieb, S., Gurwitch, R. H., & Blotcky, A. D. (1987). Impact of a summer camp experience on daily activity and family interactions among children with cancer. *Journal of Pediatric Psychology, 12,* 533–541.

Spinetta, J. J., & Deasy-Spinetta, P. (1986). The patient's socialization in the community and school during therapy. *Cancer, 58,* 512–515.

Spirito, A., Hewett, C., Masek, B., & Berman, S. (1987, March). *Anticipatory nausea/vomiting patterns in pediatric cancer patients on chemotherapy protocols with moderate and severe emetic potential.* Paper presented at the annual meeting of the Society of Behavioral Medicine, Washington, DC.

Spirito, A., Stark, L. J., Cobiella, C., Drigan, R., Androkites, A., & Hewett, K. (1990). Social adjustment of children successfully treated for cancer. *Journal of Pediatric Psychology, 15,* 359–371.

Stehbens, J. A. (1988). Childhood cancer. In D. K. Routh (Ed.), *Handbook of pediatric psychology* (pp. 135–161). New York: The Guilford Press.

Sulzer-Azaroff, B., & Mayer, G. R. (1977). *Applying behavioral-analysis procedures with children and youth.* New York: Holt, Rinehart & Winston.

Tebbi, C. K., & Mallon, J. C. (1987). Long-term psychosocial outcome among cancer amputees in adolescence and early adulthood. *Journal of Psychosocial Oncology, 5,* 69–82.

Teta, M. J., Del Po, M. C., Stanislav, V. K., Meigs, J. W., Myers, M. H., & Mulvihill, J. J. (1986). Psychosocial consequences of childhood and adolescent cancer survival. *Journal of Chronic Disabilities, 39,* 751–759.

van Eys, J. (1987). Living beyond cure: Transcending survival. *The American Journal of Pediatric Hematology/Oncology, 9,* 114–118.

Wahler, R. G., & Hann, D. M. (1986). A behavioral systems perspective in childhood psychopathology: Expanding the three-term operant contingency. In N. A. Krasnegor, J. D. Arasteh, & M. F. Cataldo (Eds.), *Child health behavior: A behavioral pediatrics perspective* (pp. 147–167). New York: John Wiley & Sons.

Wells, K. C. (1988). Family therapy. In J. L. Matson (Ed.), *Handbook of treatment approaches in childhood psychopathology* (pp. 45–61). New York: Plenum.

Worchel, F. F., Copeland, D. R., & Barker, D. G. (1987). Control-related coping strategies in pediatric oncology patients. *Journal of Pediatric Psychology, 12,* 25–38.

Worchel, F. F., Nolan, B. F., Willson, V. L., Purser, J. S., Copeland, D. R., & Pfefferbaum, B. (1988). Assessment of depression in children with cancer. *Journal of Pediatric Psychology, 13,* 101–112.

Young, J. L., Ries, L. G., Silverberg, E., Horm, J. W., & Miller, R. W. (1986). Cancer incidence, survival, and mortality for children younger than age 15 years. *Cancer, 58,* 598–602.

Zeltzer, L., Kellerman, J., Ellenberg, L., Dash, J., & Rigler, D. (1980). Psychological effects of illness in adolescence: II. Impact of illness in adolescents—Crucial issues and coping styles. *Journal of Pediatrics, 101,* 1032–1035.

Zeltzer, L., & LeBaron, S. (1982). Hypnosis and nonhypnotic techniques for reduction of pain and anxiety during painful procedures in children and adolescents with cancer. *The Journal of Pediatrics, 101,* 1032–1035.

Zeltzer, L., LeBaron, S., & Zeltzer, P. M. (1984). The effectiveness of behavioral intervention for reduction of nausea and vomiting in children and adolescents receiving chemotherapy. *Journal of Clinical Oncology, 2,* 683–690.

11 Reducing Stress in Child and Psychiatric Patients by Relaxation Therapy and Massage

Tiffany M. Field
University of Miami Medical School

Stress and emotional disturbance are commonly accompanied by muscular tension. Massage and relaxation therapy are two currently popular procedures that are thought to reduce stress and stress-related muscular tension. Whereas massage involves the direct application of pressure and stroking motions on successive muscle groups, relaxation therapy or progressive muscle relaxation reduces stress most directly by instructing the patient to voluntarily relax each muscle group in succession.

Although very little research has been conducted on the effects of massage on stress, a number of studies have reported reductions in stress following relaxation therapy. Relaxation therapy is a catchall term that refers to procedures that are employed to reduce tension and anxiety by training individuals to relax their muscles. A variety of relaxation techniques have been investigated including progressive muscle relaxation and yoga exercises. For progressive muscle relaxation, patients are instructed to relax each of the body's muscles in succession until they achieve complete relaxation. After the subjects are relaxed, guided imagery can be used by suggesting that they imagine pleasant places/experiences that have been a source of enjoyment or that they visualize becoming healthier and stronger. Patients typically show a relaxation response including a decrease in muscle tension and heart rate. Imagery can enhance this relaxation response as is shown by a greater decrease in heart rate when it is combined with relaxation therapy (Jasnoski & Kugler, 1987).

Yoga stretching and breathing are other relaxation techniques used to reduce muscle tension. Although the exercise associated with yoga often leads to an increase in heart rate and cortisol levels, yoga sessions typically elicit a relaxation response (Funderbark, 1979). Yoga stretching prior to the progressive muscle relaxation may produce a more significant reduction in tension than relaxation alone.

The typical physiological effects of the relaxation include decreases in heart rate, blood pressure, and oxygen consumption (Davidson, Winchester, Taylor, Alderman, & Ingels, 1979). Generally, relaxation therapy is thought to induce a "wakeful hypometabolic state" whereby the patient is still awake but has a slowing down of physiological processes (Benson, Kotch, Crassweller & Greenwood, 1977). Whereas the magnitude of the reduced heart rate is typically only a few beats per minute, a reduction of heart rate is consistently reported (DeGood & Redgate, 1982; Hosmand, Helmes, Kazarian, & Tekatch, 1985). Unlike the consistently reported reduction in heart rate, however, the data on cortisol levels are mixed. Stressful experiences are usually accompanied by increases in cortisol, probably due to the activation of the hypo-thalamic-pituitary-adrenocortical system (McCabe & Schneiderman, 1985). At least one study (DeGood & Redgate, 1982) showed significant decreases in plasma cortisol paralleling decreases in heart rate following relaxation sessions. In contrast, no significant change was noted in cortisol levels following similar training by another group of investigators (Cooper, Joffe, Lamprey, Botha, Shires, Baker, & Seftel, 1985). This inconsistency may relate to the first group having assessed cortisol levels within subjects in a repeated measures design (DeGood & Redgate, 1981) whereas the latter investigators (Cooper et al., 1985) compared a group who received relaxation training with a group who simply relaxed for the same amount of time.

Self-reports of anxiety levels are used more frequently than physiological measurements. Relaxation therapy is usually noted to decrease self-report anxiety. Using the State-Trait Anxiety Scale (STAI; Spielberger, Gorsuch, & Lushene, 1970) a reduction in self-reported anxiety was noted in psychiatric patients following nine sessions of relaxation therapy (Hosmand et al., 1985). Similarly, on the Profile of Mood States (POMS; McNair, Lorr, & Droppleman, 1971), elevated mood was noted following a brief relaxation therapy session (Matthew & Gelder, 1969). Although several have suggested that self-report data should be confirmed by behavioral observations, for some unexplained reason behavioral observations are rarely used in relaxation therapy studies.

Very few studies on relaxation therapy (RT) have employed clinical samples. In at least one of these, relaxation therapy was an effective technique for symptom reduction in depression (Blaney, 1981). In another study on depressed adults, relaxation therapy was used as an attention control group. The results suggested that RT was as effective as psychotherapy and pharmacotherapy in reducing depression-related anxiety (McLean & Hakistian, 1979).

Only a few studies (see Richter, 1984, for a review) have been conducted on relaxation therapy with child and adolescent psychiatric patients. In a study on cognitive-behavioral treatment and relaxation therapy with depressed adolescents (Reynolds & Coats, 1986), significantly less anxiety was noted following RT, an effect that persisted after the end of 10 50-minute sessions. In another study, adolescent psychiatric patients showed less acting-out behavior following the use of relaxation techniques (Corder, Whiteside, & Haslip, 1986). As in many of the other studies, however, the self-report and behavioral measures were not standardized, making the results difficult to evaluate. Nonetheless, these studies suggest that depressed children and adolescents can be given relaxation therapy as an effective treatment for anxiety symptoms and depression.

Surprisingly, as has already been mentioned, there is virtually no literature on the use of massage for alleviating stress and anxiety in adults, let alone children and adolescents. We have, however, recently demonstrated a reduction of stress behaviors in neonatal intensive care unit preterm infants after a 10 day period of 45 minutes of massage per day (Field & Schanberg, 1990). We also noted a significant increase in weight gain and an increase in catecholamine activity including norepinephrine and epinephrine (Kuhn, Schanberg, Field, Symanski, Zimmerman, Scafidi, & Roberts, 1990).

In this chapter we review the findings of two recent studies we conducted on relaxation therapy and massage with child and adolescent psychiatric patients who were hospitalized for depression or adjustment disorder. These diagnostic groups were targeted because of their prevalence among hospitalized children and adolescents. We anticipated that these forms of stress reduction would produce the following effects: (a) that self-reported anxiety and depressed mood (on the STAI and the POMS) would decrease following the relaxation class or massage session; (b) that motor activity, anxious and fidgety behavior would also decrease, and that alertness, positive affect, and cooperation would increase following the relaxation therapy class or massage (as measured by behavior observation ratings); and (c) that heart rate and saliva cortisol levels taken after relaxation therapy or massage would be lower than baseline levels.

Study 1. Relaxation Therapy Reduces Anxiety in Child and Adolescent Psychiatry Patients.

METHOD

Subjects

The sample consisted of 40 children and adolescents who were hospitalized in a child and adolescent psychiatric unit. The subjects were randomly selected from all those patients who had been diagnosed as having depression or adjustment disorder. Twenty of the patients were diagnosed as depressed (14 females) and 20 were diagnosed as adjustment disorder (10 females). The subjects ranged in age from 8 to 18 years (mean = 13.9), with half the sample being adolescent.

The diagnoses were made based on a one-hour intake interview by a staff psychiatrist employing DSM III-R criteria. Approximately 25% of the patients had previous admissions to a psychiatric facility, and the average hospital stay for the sample at the time of the study was 7 days. The depressed and adjustment disorder patients did not differ in age, intelligence quotient, previous admissions, or duration of hospital stay. Ten of the subjects who participated in the relaxation therapy classes (five adjustment disorder and five depressed) were also observed during a television viewing control condition.

Procedures

Relaxation Therapy. One hour relaxation therapy classes were routinely offered (two times a week in the late afternoon) on the unit by a relaxation therapist. The data for this study were taken from the first session of relaxation therapy for each of the subjects. In a given class of approximately 8 to 10 children and adolescents, 1 to 3 of them were subjects in this study. The class included 30 minutes of yoga exercises followed by 30 minutes of progressive muscle relaxation followed by guided imagery interspersed with a brief massage. The subjects used exercise mats for the first 30 minutes of yoga stretching exercises and then rolled into a prone position for a brief back/shoulder massage (approximately 2 to 3 minutes). For the next 30 minutes a modified version of progressive muscle relaxation was administered by the relaxation therapist. The subjects were instructed to breathe deeply for several minutes, and then the therapist asked the subjects to relax and tense eight different muscle groups (in a feet-to-head progression). After the progressive muscle relaxation, the instructor introduced visual imagery to enhance the subjects' feelings of relaxation while they continued to breathe deeply.
subjects who had received relaxation therapy. They viewed television for a similar period of time in a common meeting room on a day either before or after their relaxation therapy and they were observed in the same way that they had been in relaxation therapy.

Assessments. Several assessments were made by the research assistants who were participant observers in the RT class. The assessments were made on the following schedule:

1. 30 minutes prior to the class the following baseline measures were taken: heart rate (pulse), a saliva sample for cortisol, the State Anxiety Inventory for Children (STAIC), and the POMS depression factor items. Actometer readings (activity level recorded on an activity watch) and behavior observation ratings were also made based on the 30-minute period prior to the class;

2. at the end of the yoga exercise portion of the class the following measures were taken: heart rate, saliva cortisol and actometer reading;

3. at the end of the class heart rate was measured, an actometer reading was taken, and behavior ratings were made based on behavior observed during the class; and

4. 30 minutes following the termination of the class baseline measures were repeated: heart rate, saliva cortisol, actometer reading, STAIC, POMS, and behavior observation ratings based on the 30-minute period following the class.

The STAIC is an adaptation of the State Anxiety Inventory specifically designed for the study of anxiety in school age children and adolescents who are below average in reading level (Spielberger et al., 1970). The inventory consists of 20 items, statements such as "I feel . . . very calm, calm, or not calm." The POMS is a 5-point adjective rating scale asking subjects to describe how well an adjective describes his/her feelings for the past two weeks (including today) on adjectives such as *happy* or *gloomy*. The behavior observation ratings included seven scales (state, affect, activity, anxiety, fidgeting, vocalization, and cooperation) rated on a 3-point continuum. The actometer (Timex) was used to measure these subjects' activity levels. The actometer is a watch that cumulatively reports movements in the horizontal and vertical plane. The subject wears it on his wrist like a normal watch and activity level is then calculated by subtracting the reading taken from the monitor at the beginning of the class from the monitor reading taken at the end of the class.

The physiological measures included heart rate and saliva cortisol. Heart rate was measured by taking the subject's radial pulse for 30 seconds one-half hour prior to the class, during the class (following the yoga exercise), at the end of class, and at the end of the 30-minute follow-up period. Saliva cortisol samples were collected one-half hour prior to the class, following the exercise portion of the class, and one-half hour after the class was finished. Due to the 20 minute lag in cortisol change, saliva samples reflect the cortisol levels at 50 minutes prior to the class, at the middle of the yoga exercise portion, and at the end of the relaxation portion. Saliva cortisol samples were obtained by having subjects place a cotton dental swab dipped in sugar-free lemonade crystals along the gumline for 30 seconds. The swab was then placed in a syringe and the plunger depressed to insert the saliva into a microcentrifuge tube. Saliva samples were frozen and subsequently assayed for cortisol levels at Duke University by Dr. Saul Schanberg's laboratory.

RESULTS

Because there were significantly more depressed female than depressed male patients, gender was entered as a covariate in the repeated measures analyses of variance. Data analyses suggested that significant decreases (4 points) occurred

TABLE 11.1

Mean Behavior Observation Scale Ratings for Baseline (A), Immediately Post Class (B), and 30 Minutes Post Class (C)
(S.D.'s are in Parentheses)

Behavior Ratings*	Groups						Effect
	Depressed			Adjustment Disorder			
State	A	B	C	A	B	C	
(.87)**	2.76 (.43)	2.88 (.48)	2.66 (.65)	2.36 (.65)	2.27 (.63)	2.50 (.59)	G^3

	Assessment Periods			
	A	B	C	Effect
Affect (.88)	1.95 (.6)$_a$	2.30 (.6)$_b$	2.25 (.7)$_b$	R^2
Activity (.80)	1.86 (.4)$_a$	2.12 (.5)$_b$	1.95 (.5)$_{ab}$	R^1
Anxiety (.93)	1.87 (.6)$_a$	1.47 (.6)$_b$	1.46 (.5)$_b$	R^4
Fidgeting (.86)	1.67 (.7)$_a$	1.35 (.4)$_b$	1.32 (.4)$_b$	R^3
Vocalization (.72)	1.75 (.5)$_a$	1.85 (.5)$_a$	1.92 (.5)$_a$	NS
Cooperation (.96)	2.33 (.6)$_a$	2.52 (.6)$_a$	2.70 (.5)$_a$	NS
Summary	14.82 (2.0)$_a$	16.85 (2.2)$_b$	17.22 (2.1)$_b$	R^4

*Different letter subscripts indicate significant Tukey post-hoc comparison effects ($p < .05$).
**Interoberver reliability coefficients are in parentheses.

1 = $p < .05$.   R = Repeated Measures Effect
2 = $p < .01$.   G = Group Effect
3 = $p < .005$.   NS = Not Significant
4 = $p < .001$.

224

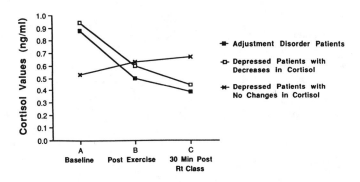

FIG. 11.1   Group by assessment period interaction for cortisol values.

for both self-report measures (the STAIC and the POMS) following the relaxation therapy session. The scores were also lower following RT than following the television viewing condition, even though the scores started out being the same. As can be seen in Table 11.1 on the Behavior Observation Scale Ratings, the subjects showed the following: (a) affect became more positive across the three assessment periods; (b) an increase occurred in activity level; (c) a decrease in anxiety ratings between the first and second and between the first and third assessment periods; (d) a decrease in fidgeting behavior between the first and second and between the first and third periods; and finally (e) an increase in summary scores, suggesting an overall improvement in behavior.

The subsample who participated in both relaxation therapy and television viewing showed lower anxiety ratings and higher summary scores following relaxation therapy than following television viewing. Heart rate and activity level were higher following the exercise portion of the class and were lower by the end of the RT class. They were also lower following RT as compared to following television viewing. Adjustment disorder patients showed a tendency for lower cortisol levels following the RT class whereas the depressed subjects showed a slight increase in cortisol levels following RT. Closer examination revealed that 62% of the depressed subjects had slightly higher than baseline cortisol levels, and 38% had lower cortisol levels following RT. Interestingly, the self-reported decrease in anxiety on the STAIC tended to parallel the decrease in cortisol in the "decreased cortisol" subjects. The cortisol levels were also lower following the RT class than following the television viewing condition (see Fig. 11.1).

DISCUSSION

The consistency of the self-report and behavior observation data support the use of this treatment approach for children and adolescents on psychiatric units (Reynolds & Coats, 1986). Not only did the patients' self-reported anxiety scores drop significantly, but the children and adolescents also showed less fidgeting and anxious behavior during and after the relaxation therapy class. In addition, their self-reported mood increased as did their observed positive affect, consistent with the literature suggesting alleviation of depressed mood (Bernstein & Borkevoc, 1973). These changes were also apparent when the values for the children receiving both relaxation therapy and the television viewing control condition were compared. The subsample of patients participating in both conditions showed a reduction in anxiety and fidgeting as well as reduced activity levels and diminished heart rate following their relaxation therapy. This is perhaps not surprising as diminished heart rate is a frequently reported component of the relaxation response (Benson et al., 1977).

Also, as would be expected, the cortisol values were lower during and after the relaxation session than during or after the television viewing session, indicating that the reductions were related to the intervention and not to diurnal changes in cortisol. However, only the adjustment disorder group and approximately one third of the depressed group showed reduced levels in cortisol. This raises the possibility that two types of depression are represented in this group, one having a stronger anxiety component than the other. The anxious-depressed subjects may have shown the expected decrease in cortisol levels due to an apparent decrease in behavioral anxiety whereas those who showed an increase or no change in cortisol values may have an endogenous depression (Van Zerssen, Berger, & Doerr, 1984). Alternatively, the small subsample of depressed patients ("decreasing") may have been misdiagnosed or they may have experienced co-morbidity (i.e., depression and adjustment disorder).

Despite the positive effects of RT on behavior and physiology, it is not clear what the effective treatment component was in this study (yoga exercise, massage, progressive muscle relaxation, or visual imagery). It would be important to compare the individual components of relaxation therapy to determine their differential effects. Although RT clearly reduces stress and anxiety at least in the short term, this study highlighted the need to examine the individual relaxation therapy components and the longer-term effects. The subsequent study was designed to examine the independent effects of massage as well as its short and longer-term effects.

Study 2. Massage Reduces Anxiety in Child and Adolescent Psychiatry Patients.

METHOD

Sample

The sample was comprised of 52 children and adolescents (30 boys, 22 girls). The subjects ranged in age from 7 to 18 years (mean = 13). The subjects were diagnosed as having adjustment disorder problems (including conduct disorder and oppositional disorder) (N = 32) or having depression (or dysthymic disorder) (N = 20). The subjects were hospitalized for a mean of 21 days (R = 4 to 64 days). The subjects came from lower socioeconomic backgrounds, and the ethnic distribution was approximately 40% Caucasian, 40% Latin, and 20% black.

Procedures

Massage Therapy.   The subjects received 30 minutes of Swedish massage per day for 5 days. The massage consisted of carefully timed stroking movements for 5-minute periods in each of three regions: up and down the neck, from the neck across the shoulders and back to the neck, and from the neck to the waist and back to the neck along the vertebral column. The 15-minute sequence was comprised of 30 back and forth strokes per region at 10 seconds each. This same 15-minute sequence was repeated in its entirety for a total of 30 minutes. Massage was administered by a psychology student trained in the standard massage procedure.

Assessments.   The assessments of the effects of the massage therapy included the same assessments that were made in Study 1. These included self-reports of anxiety (State/Trait Anxiety Inventory for Children (STAIC; Spielberger et al., 1970) and the Profile of Mood States (POMS; McNair et al., 1971); behavior ratings by an independent examiner on the seven behavior rating scales already described in the previous study (state, affect, activity level, anxiety level, fidgeting/nervous behavior, vocalization, and cooperation); activity monitoring by an actometer or "activity watch" worn on the wrist; pulse rate; saliva samples of cortisol; time-lapse videotaping of nighttime sleep; and urine samples for cortisol and catecholamines including norepinephrine, epinephrine, and dopamine. On the first and last days of the treatment period the baseline, session, and follow-up assessment measures were collected according to the following schedule: (a) 30 minutes prior to the massage: STAIC and POMS; (b) immediately prior to the massage: saliva samples, activity level, pulse rate, and behavior observation ratings based on the previous 30 minutes of subjects' behavior; (c) immediately after the session: activity level, pulse rate, behavior ratings based on behavior noted during the session, and self-report measures; and (d) 30 minutes following the session: saliva samples, activity level, pulse rate, and behavior ratings based on the previous 30 minutes of behavior. Finally, on the first and last treatment days, nighttime sleep was videotaped using a time lapse video projector, and subjects were asked to collect a 24-hour urine sample to be assayed for urine cortisol and catecholamines (norepinephrine, epinephrine, and dopamine). To ensure subject compliance, the children/adolescents were given a game or an audiotape of their choice. The videotapes were subsequently coded using a time lapse video system enabling 8 hours of videotape to be coded in 2 hours time. They were coded for quiet sleep (no body movement), active sleep (body movement), awake and lying quietly, and awake and active. The urine and saliva samples were frozen and later sent to Saul Schanberg's laboratory at Duke University for analysis.

RESULTS

Repeated measures by group (adjustment disorder/depression) analyses of variance were conducted to determine the immediate and the longer-term effects of the massage therapy period. These analyses were first made between pre- and post-session data for the first day of treatment to determine the immediate effects of the massage sessions. These were followed by repeated measures comparing the baseline values (or presession values) on Day 1 and Day 5 of this study to determine longer-term effects. Finally, repeated measures analyses of variance were conducted on the subsample of subjects who received both massage therapy and the television viewing control condition.

First, the adjustment disorder patients, as compared to the depressed patients, were generally more active and showed more positive affect (as might be expected). However, they were also less cooperative. As can be seen in Table 11.2, a number of short-term changes occurred (changes between baseline and postmassage session values). They were as follows:

1. On self-report measures the subjects showed lower levels of state anxiety (STAIC) and depression (POMS) following the massage session;

2. On the behavior observations the state and affect ratings increased following the massage, and activity, anxiety and fidgeting decreased. Vocalization and cooperation ratings remained the same;

3. Like the behavior observation ratings on activity, the actometer readings decreased following the massage;

4. Pulse rates paralleled the decreases in activity level; and

5. Saliva cortisol levels were lower following the massage.

Similarly, as can be seen in Table 11.3, a number of longer-term changes occurred between the baseline observations on Day 1 and the baseline observations on Day 5 of the 5-day massage period. They were as follows:

1. State anxiety (STAIC) and depression (POMS) both decreased between Days 1 and 5 of the massage;

2. On the behavior observation ratings, the state and affect ratings increased, the anxiety and fidgeting ratings decreased, and the activity, vocalization, and cooperation ratings remained the same;

3. Activity level as measured by the actometer and pulse rates remained the same as did the activity behavior ratings;

TABLE 11.2
Means for Measures Pre- and Post-Massage, Day 1 (N = 46)

	Pre	Post	p Value
Self-report			
State anxiety (STAIC)	37.4	27.2	.000
Depression (POMS)	19.7	16.5	.03
Behavior observation ratings			
State	1.5	2.6	.01
Affect	1.8	2.3	.000
Activity	1.7	1.2	.04
Anxiety	1.6	1.2	.003
Fidgeting	1.8	1.2	.04
Vocalization	1.9	2.0	NS
Cooperation	2.8	2.8	NS
Activity level (Actometer)	6.1	2.3	.01
Pulse (BPM)	87.8	82.4	.01
Saliva cortisol (ng/ml)	1.9	1.3	.02

TABLE 11.3
Means for Measures at Baseline, Days 1 and 5
(N = 46)

	Day 1	Day 5	p Value
Self-report			
State anxiety (STAIC)	37.4	30.2	.02
Depression (POMS)	19.7	16.0	.05
Behavior Observation Ratings			
State	1.5	2.5	.01
Affect	1.8	2.4	.02
Activity	1.7	1.8	NS
Anxiety	1.6	1.2	.04
Fidgeting	1.8	1.2	.04
Vocalization	1.9	1.8	NS
Cooperation	2.8	2.6	NS
Activity Level (Actometer)	6.1	5.7	NS
Pulse (BPM)	87.8	83.8	NS
Saliva cortisol (ng/ml)	1.9	1.5	.04
Urine cortisol (ng/ml)	133.9	114.8	.05
Sleep Recordings			
% Time asleep (States 1 & 2)	81.3	92.9	.05
% Time awake (States 3 & 4)	11.5	2.1	.05

4. Saliva cortisol levels decreased between Days 1 and 5 of the massage period, as did urine cortisol levels; and

5. the percent of bedtime that sleep occurred increased over the 5-day period and the percent time that wakefulness occurred correspondingly decreased over the same period.

DISCUSSION

Child and adolescent psychiatric units in the United States have a no-touch policy, corresponding to strong taboos on touching psychiatric patients. Thus, psychiatric patients are frequently hospitalized for months at a time without physical contact. These data suggest that the immediate and the short-term (1 week) effects of a daily massage are beneficial in increasing positive affect (both self-report and behavioral) and decreasing anxiety (self-report, behavioral, and physiological). Although this is the first study in the literature on massaging child and adolescent psychiatry patients, the data are consistent with the literature on relaxation therapy that suggests decreases in anxiety and depression following treatment sessions (McGrady, Younker, Tan, Fine, & Woerner, 1981; Reynolds & Coats, 1986; Richter, 1984). Patients' self-reported scores of anxiety and depression decreased significantly, their activity levels decreased, and they exhibited less anxious behavior following the massage sessions. The consistency of the self-report, the behavior observation, and the physiological (heart rate and cortisol) data support the use of this treatment for children and adolescents in psychiatric units.

Although the longer-term data did not exactly parallel the short-term data, they basically supported the reduction of anxiety and depression. Like the pre-post massage comparison, the self-reports on anxiety and depression decreased as did the behavioral ratings of anxiety and fidgeting. However, the activity ratings were very similar on Days 1 and 5, as were the actometer readings of activity level and the parallel pulse rate recordings. Nonetheless, urine cortisols suggested a reduction in anxiety, and sleep pattern changes also suggested a reduction in anxiety. Namely, the amount of sleep time increased and the amount of awake time decreased, suggesting that sleep was becoming more organized over the massage period. It is, however, unclear whether these effects can be entirely attributed to the massage treatment. Other treatments were occurring at the same time, and general clinical progress would be expected over a 1-week period.

It is also not clear whether the specific treatment effect noted in our previous relaxation therapy study (Study 1) was related to the massage per se because we have not yet compared the massage treatment with the other components of relaxation therapy, including yoga exercise, progressive muscle relaxation, and visual imagery. Nonetheless, until such comparisons are made, these data suggest that massage treatment may be effective for hospitalized child and adolescent psychiatric patients.

ACKNOWLEDGMENTS

This research was supported by NIMH Research Scientist Award #MH00331 to Tiffany Field and an NIMH research grant #MH40779. The author would like to thank Adele Platania-Solazzo, Sandra Larson, June Blank, Fred Seligman, Cynthia Kuhn, Saul Schanberg, Connie Morrow, Jackie Roberts, Sheri Goldstein, Tom Flaa, and Chad Valdeon for their collaboration on this study.

REFERENCES

Benson, H., Kotch, J. B., Crassweller, R. D., & Greenwood, M. M. (1977). Historical and clinical considerations of the relaxation response. *American Scientist, 65,* 441–445.

Bernstein, R., & Borkevoc, R. (1973). *Progressive muscle relaxation training: A manual for the helping profession.* Champaign, IL: Research Press.

Blaney, P. H. (1981). The effectiveness of cognitive and behavior therapies. In L. P. Rehm (Ed.), *Behavioral therapy for depression: Present status and future directions* (pp. 1–32). New York: Academic Press.

Cooper, R., Joffe, B. I., Lamprey, J. M., Botha, A., Shires, R., Baker, S. G., & Seftel, H. C. (1985). Hormonal and biochemical responses to transcendental meditation. *Postgraduate Medical Journal, 61,* 301–304.

Corder, B., Whiteside, R., & Haslip, T. (1986). Biofeedback, cognitive training and relaxation technique as a model adjunct therapy for hospital aides: A pilot study. *Adolescence, 21,* 339–346.

Davidson, D., Winchester, T., Taylor, B., Alderman, E., & Ingels, W. (1979). Effects of relaxation therapy on cardiac performance and sympathetic activity in patients with organic heart disease. *Psychosomatic Medicine, 41,* 303–308.

DeGood, D. E., & Redgate, E. S. (1982). Interrelationship of plasma cortisol and other activation indices during EMG biofeedback training. *Journal of Behavioral Medicine, 5,* 213–223.

Field, T., & Schanberg, S. (1990). Massage enhances growth in preterm neonates. In T. Field & T. B. Brazelton (Eds.), *Advances in touch.* Skillman, NJ: Johnson & Johnson.

Funderbark, J. (1979). Science studies—Yoga: A review of physiological data. *Yoga Life,* pp. 3–11.

Hosmand, L., Helmes, E., Kazarian, S., & Tekatch, G. (1985). Evaluation of a relaxation training program under medical and nonmedical conditions. *Journal of Clinical Psychology, 41,* 23–29.

Jasnoski, M. L., & Kugler, J. (1987). Relaxation, imagery and neuroimmodalities. *Annals of New York Academy of Sciences, 496,* 722–730.

Kuhn, C. M., Schanberg, S. M., Field, T. M., Symanski, R., Zimmerman, E., Scafidi, F., & Roberts, J. (1990). Tactile/kinesthetic stimulation effects on sympathetic and adreno-cortical functions in preterm infants. In review.

Matthew, A. M., & Gelder, M. G. (1969). Psychophysiological investigations of brief relaxation training. *Journal of Psychosomatic Medicine, 13,* 1–12.

McCabe, P., & Schneiderman, N. (1985). Psychophysiological reactions to stress. In N. Schneiderman & J. Tapp (Eds.), *Behavioral medicine. The biopsychosocial approach* (pp. 220–238). Hillsdale, NJ: Lawrence Erlbaum Associates.

McGrady, A., Younker, R., Tan, S., Fine, T., & Woerner, M. (1981). The effect of biofeedback assisted relaxation training. *Biofeedback & Self-Regulation, 6,* 343–353.

McLean, P. D., & Hakistian, R. (1979). Clinical depression: Comparative efficacy of outpatient treatments. *Journal of Clinical and Consulting Psychology, 47,* 818–836.

McNair, D., Lorr, M., & Droppleman, L. (1971). *Profile of mood states manual.* San Diego, CA: Educational & Industrial Testing Services.

Reynolds, W., & Coats, K. (1986). A comparison of cognitive-behavioral therapy and relaxation training for treatment of depression in adolescents. *Journal of Consulting and Clinical Psychology, 54,* 653–660.

Richter, N. C. (1984). The efficacy of relaxation therapy with children. *Journal of Abnormal Child Psychology, 12,* 319–344.

Spielberger, C. D., Gorsuch, R. L., & Lushene, R. E. (1970). *The state-trait anxiety inventory.* Palo Alto, CA: Consulting Psychologists Press.

Van Zerssen, D., Berger, M., & Doerr, P. (1984). Neuroendocrine dysfunction in subtypes of depression. In D. Shah (Ed.), *Psycho-neuroendocrine dysfunction* (pp. 131–143). New York: Plenum Press.

Author Index

Subject Index